FANTASIES OF IDEN

Cultural Front

GENERAL EDITOR
Michael Bérubé

Manifesto of a Tenured Radical
Cary Nelson

Bad Subjects: Political Education for Everyday Life
Edited by the Bad Subjects Production Team

Claiming Disability: Knowledge and Identity
Simi Linton

The Employment of English: Theory, Jobs, and the Future of Literary Studies
Michael Bérubé

Feeling Global: Internationalism in Distress
Bruce Robbins

Doing Time: Feminist Theory and Postmodern Culture
Rita Felski

Modernism, Inc.: Body, Memory, Capital
Edited by Jani Scandura and Michael Thurston

Bending Over Backwards: Disability, Dismodernism, and Other Difficult Positions
Lennard J. Davis

After Whiteness: Unmaking an American Majority
Mike Hill

Critics at Work: Interviews 1993–2003
Edited by Jeffrey J. Williams

Crip Theory: Cultural Signs of Queerness and Disability
Robert McRuer

How the University Works: Higher Education and the Low-Wage Nation
Marc Bousquet
Foreword by Cary Nelson

Deaf Subjects: Between Identities and Places
Brenda Jo Brueggemann

The Left at War
Michael Bérubé

No University Is an Island: Saving Academic Freedom
Cary Nelson

Fantasies of Identification: Disability, Gender, Race
Ellen Samuels

FANTASIES OF IDENTIFICATION

Disability, Gender, Race

ELLEN SAMUELS

New York University Press

NEW YORK AND LONDON

NEW YORK UNIVERSITY PRESS
New York and London
www.nyupress.org

LIBRARY OF CONGRESS CATALOGING-IN-PUBLICATION DATA

Samuels, Ellen Jean.
Fantasies of identification : disability, gender, race / Ellen Samuels.
pages   cm. — (Cultural front)
Includes bibliographical references and index.
ISBN 978-1-4798-1298-1 (cloth : alk. paper)
ISBN 978-1-4798-5949-8 (pbk. : alk. paper)
1. Identification—Social aspects. 2. Group identity. 3. Identity (Psychology)
4. Disabilities. I. Title.
HM753.S26 2014
305.9'08—dc23

2013042415

References to Internet websites (URLs) were accurate at the time of writing
Neither the author nor New York University Press is responsible for URLs that
may have expired or changed since the manuscript was prepared.

New York University Press books are printed on acid-free paper, and their
binding materials are chosen for strength and durability. We strive to use
environmentally responsible suppliers and materials to the greatest extent
possible in publishing our books.

Manufactured in the United States of America

10 9 8 7 6 5 4 3 2 1

Also available as an ebook

THE
AMERICAN
LITERATURES
INITIATIVE

A book in the American Literatures Initiative (ALI), a collaborative
publishing project of NYU Press, Fordham University Press, Rutgers
University Press, Temple University Press, and the University of Virginia
Press. The Initiative is supported by The Andrew W. Mellon Foundation.
For more information, please visit www.americanliteratures.org.

Contents

ACKNOWLEDGMENTS

A room of her own is a marvelous sanctuary for a writer, but even more necessary is the companionship and solidarity of other people. So many friends and colleagues have supported me through the many years of completing this project that no words I can write here can fully recognize the crucial role they have played. Every word in this book is a testimony to exquisite interdependence, and I am grateful to every person whose presence in my life enriched this work.

At Oberlin College, Carol Lasser, Yopie Prins, Wendy Hesford, and Sandy Zagarell taught me how to write, read, and exist as a feminist scholar. More than anyone else, Barbara Helfgott Hyett helped me to find my poetic voice. At Cornell University, A. R. Ammons, Ken McLane, Robert Morgan, and Debra Fried taught me fine-tuning, while Nina Revoyr, Angela Bommarito, Nancy Kok, Jennifer Gilmore, Bethany Schneider, Katie-Louise Thomas, and Dana Luciano helped me survive Ithaca winters. Lisa Diamond and Judi Hilman became family in the best sense of the word, and Sarah McKibben brought the deliciousness of salads and the vigor of scholarship back into my life. Meanwhile Andi Gladstone, Anne McLaughlin, and the other women of the Ithaca Breast Cancer Alliance reminded me of the inseparability of activism, research, and writing and taught me not to fear my future.

I had the tremendous good fortune to arrive at the University of California, Berkeley at the inception of its disability studies program, and over the next eight years I flourished in the company of brilliant and outrageous crip scholar-artist-activists like Georgina Kleege, Marsha Saxton, Devva Kasnitz, Neil Marcus, Anne Finger, Cathy Kudlick, Corbett O'Toole, the late Paul Longmore, and many others. I owe more than I can say to Sue Schweik for guiding me through those years and beyond as the most generous mentor and friend anyone could hope for. Sam Otter opened my eyes to the rigorous joys of nineteenth-century American literature, while Ula Taylor kept me honest and attentive to the many intersecting meanings of race and disability. In seminars and exams and in the hallways of the department, Celeste Langan, James Turner, Cathy Gallagher, Colleen Lye, Hertha D. Sweet Wong, Bryan Wagner, and Patricia Penn Hilden taught me to be a thorough and irreverent researcher and writer, while Len von Morzé, Gretchen Case, Marja Mogk, and Anna Mollow helped keep the ground level under our collective feet.

Since coming to the University of Wisconsin, I have discovered the joys of belonging to two academic departments in which respect is combined with incisive thinking and a good dose of humor. In the Department of Gender and Women's Studies, I am grateful for the support and mentorship of Judith Leavitt, Janet Hyde, Frieda High Tesfagorgis, Lynet Uttal, Nancy Kaiser, Aili Tripp, Jane Schulenberg, Marianne Whatley, Nancy Worcester, Jill Casid, and especially Christina Ewig, Judy Houck, Finn Enke, Cyrena Pondrom, Julie D'Acci, and Jane Collins. My compatriots and companions in this journey, Pernille Ipsen, Keisha Lindsay, Jenny Higgins, and Chris Garlough, are the wisest and most generous colleagues anyone could wish for, and throw a mean dance party to boot.

In the English Department, I rely upon Russ Castronovo, David Zimmerman, and Jeff Steele to keep me current with the tides of American literary studies, and Christa Olson, Jordan Zweck, Colin Gillis, Aida Hussen, Lisa Cooper, Timothy Yu, and Robin Valenza to bring happiness at the appropriate hours. Susan Stanford Friedman told me hard and necessary truths about writing a book, and this project is immeasurably better for her guidance. Elizabeth Bearden arrived just in time to teach me everything I needed to know about tenure dossiers, swordcraft, and graceful recoveries. My senior colleagues Lynn Keller, Susan Bernstein, Sara Guyer, Leslie Bow, Anja Wanner, Rob Nixon, Anne McClintock, and Karen Britland have been generous with their time, support, and words of wisdom. At UW, I have also been lucky in the friendship and intellectual companionship of Linn Posey-Maddox, Christie Clark-Pujara, Steve Kantrowitz, Nan Enstad, and Karma Chávez. Tom Jones contributed his art, his insight, and his sympathetic ear at a crucial stage in this project, for which I am deeply grateful.

It has been my tremendous luck to participate in the UW Disability Studies Initiative with Walt Schalick and Teryl Dobbs as colleagues, and Steve Stern and Cathy Trueba as our guardian angels. I am grateful also for the support of Alta Charo, Linda Hogel, Morton Ann Gernsbacher, and Rob Asen. Eunjung Kim and Jenell Johnson are the glue that holds it all together and two of the smartest and kindest people I have ever known.

I could never have made it without my brilliant and fierce community of disability scholars and activists. Love always to Alison Kafer, whom I met at my very first disability conference and who remains my intellectual muse and dearest conference companion. Cindy Wu and Robert McRuer read drafts, offered advice, and provided moral support at the most crucial stages. Gratitude and appreciation beyond words to Petra Kuppers, Mike Gill, Kim Q. Hall, Susan Burch, David Serlin, Mel Chen, Jennifer James, Martha Stoddard Holmes, Simi Linton, Rosemarie Garland Thomson, David Mitchell, Lenny Davis, Bethany Stevens, Therí Pickens, Anita Mannur, Eli Clare, Samuel Lurie, Robin Stephens, Margaret Price, Carrie Sandahl, Jim Ferris, Alice Sheppard, Kristen Lindgren, Ann Fox, Sunny Taylor, Sami Schalk, Riva Lehrer, Nirmala Erevelles, Kim Nielsen, Jeff Brune, Jenifer Barclay, the late and sorely missed Laura Hershey, and many others whom my crip brain may not recall but my crip heart assuredly holds dear.

My friends within and beyond academia have been my strength and sustenance through the decade of writing that produced this book. Rob Henn has been family for twenty years and my most faithful Boston spouse since my arrival in Madison (and his name means "chicken"). Laura Linton is the sister of my heart and my rock in every storm. Ilene Sperling and Joy Goldsmith are there in thick and thin, even (and especially) when we're getting into trouble, and Emily Bender and Hannah Doress nourish body, spirit, and *Star Trek* soul. Thank goodness for Kathryn "Busfriend" Herzog, Noelle Howey, Chris Healy, Jay Williams, Timnah Steinman, Anoosh Jorjorian, Kevin Miller, Saraswati Bryer-Bass, Amy Morrissey, Margaret Carne, Sara Greavu, Rebecca Targ, Sarah Stickle, and Joanne Chao. Jonathan Zarov arrived at the end, and also the beginning.

Charlie Samser has not read a word of this book, but he is the living heart of it nonetheless. Jordan Samuels, together with Carol Madey, Maddie, and Ben, can always be counted on to support, succor, and entertain, while Joan Mohr Samuels inspires me equally with her dedication to the environment, her kindness, and her apple pie. Eric Riutort, Kevin Riutort, and Helen Madorma know me in a way no else can, and Gail Bearden is my second mother and culinary hero.

My father, Stephen Mitchell Samuels, was never prouder of me than when he admitted he couldn't understand a word of my manuscript. My mother, Myra Lee Samuels, earned her Ph.D. at the University of California at Berkeley forty years before I did, when women faculty were few and far between, especially in the mathematical sciences. The two of them raised me with an equal passion for social justice, written words, and intellectual vigor, and this book is dedicated to their memory.

Finally, I must thank the many disability aides without whose assistance this book could literally never have been written: Katie Ramos, Paul Hurh, Len von Morzé, Caroline Roberts, Max Camp, Stephanie Rytilahti, and Anna Vitale. Ari Eisenberg also provided invaluable research assistance. Thank you for your hands, your eyes, your legwork, your brilliant minds, and most of all for your patience and dedication.

For early sponsorship of this project, I am grateful for a Chancellor's Opportunity Fellowship at the University of California, the Phi Beta Kappa of Northern California Graduate Fellowship, and the Andrew Vincent White and Florence Wales White Scholarship of the University of California Humanities Research Institute. For crucial support to complete this book, I thank the American Association of University Women, the Graduate School of the University of Wisconsin at Madison, and the Vilas Life Cycle Professorship at the University of Wisconsin.

An earlier version of chapter 1 first appeared in *MELUS: Journal of the Society for the Study of Multi-Ethnic Literature of the United States* 31.3 (2006) and is reprinted by permission of the journal.

Portions of chapters 2 and 3 first appeared in *Leviathan: A Journal of Melville Studies* 8.1 (2006) and are reprinted by permission of the journal.

Portions of chapter 5 first appeared in the *Oxford Handbook of Nineteenth Century American Literature* (2012) and are reprinted by permission of Oxford University Press.

Introduction: The Crisis of Identification

In the mid-nineteenth century a crisis began to emerge within modern nations regarding the identifiability and governability of the individual bodies making up their bodies politic. This crisis of identification was driven by a multiplicity of factors, including greater geographic and class mobility; urbanization, colonialism, and expansion; the beginnings of the welfare state; and challenges to racial and gendered hierarchies. Intersecting with these material developments, and no less essential to the making of the crisis, were ontological concerns about the naming and classifying of persons as they moved within and across categories of meaning. The shift in European countries from social worlds based upon local and personal affiliations to those that Michael Ignatieff has called "societies of strangers" (87) was even more dramatic and problematic in the United States, with its tremendous geographic breadth, racial and class diversity, federalist political structure, and uneasy allegiance to ideals of equality and democracy predicated upon the exclusion of certain kinds of persons. Cultural texts from the United States during this period reveal a landscape of intensifying anxieties regarding embodied social identities, particularly those that differed from the recognizable subject of democracy: women, disabled people, and racial others.

A number of events at the century's midpoint signal both the accelerating crisis and its attendant cultural responses. The American Medical Association was founded in 1845, the same year as the publication of the phenomenally popular *Narrative* of Frederick Douglass and the intensification of abolitionist movements. Three years later feminist activists met at Seneca Falls to issue a declaration of hypocrisy against American democracy, setting the stage for six decades of agitation to achieve the vote for women. Meanwhile the word *normal* in its modern sense of "constituting or conforming to a type or standard; regular, usual, typical" entered the English language around 1840, signaling a new social investment in regularizing objects and people.[1] The particular race and disability inflections of this regularization can be read through the evolution of the national census, which began to count deaf and blind persons in 1830, people labeled "idiotic" and "insane" in 1840, and "mulattoes" and physically disabled people in 1850.[2] In 1842 a defining legal decision addressed the increasing rates of physical disability due to industrial accidents by making it more difficult for injured workers to sue for compensation, thus consigning increasing numbers of disabled men and women to poverty and street begging (Braddock and Parish 35), a shift that not only heightened anxieties regarding real and fake disabilities but also challenged ideologies of self-reliance emerging from the American renaissance: "That a man might be a virtuous worker one day and an indolent pauper the next doubtless raised uneasy questions about an individual's capacity for unlimited self-determinism" (Garland Thomson, *Extraordinary Bodies* 48). These ideological and material shifts resulted in a proliferation of charities and institutions established between 1840 and 1900, as well as the rise of eugenic practices and immigration restrictions, both responding and contributing to "the idea that a tide of disability from without and within threatened to swamp the nation" (Welke 119).[3] Finally, rapid expansion and urbanization taking place in the country during this period produced unprecedented anxieties regarding the knowability of identity, while the increasing numbers of light-skinned African Americans and racially mixed American Indians meant that "the nineteenth century was a period of exhaustive and—as it turned out—futile search for criteria to define and describe race differences" (Gossett 69).[4]

In this book I argue that, in response to this modern crisis of identification, a range of fantastical solutions began to circulate in midcentury, eventually becoming solidified into our twenty-first-century discourses about bodies and identities. These *fantasies of identification* seek to definitively identify bodies, to place them in categories delineated by race, gender, or ability status, and then to validate that placement through a verifiable, biological mark of identity. Fantasies of identification share certain signifying features: they claim a scientific, often medical framework and function to consolidate the authority of medicine yet in practice often exceed or contradict any actual scientific basis. Nor do they confine themselves to the scientific realm but invariably penetrate into the wider culture, influencing law, policy, and representation. Once embedded in the cultural realm, fantasies of identification stubbornly persist, despite being disproved, undermined, or contradicted, and this persistence provokes resistance and disidentifications from subjects attempting to escape the fantasy's totalizing imposition of identity. Fantasies of identification operate on the level of the "obvious," the "commonsense," yet simultaneously claim that only the expert can fully discern their meanings. And because they are fantasies, they merge imagination and the real through desire, a desire that manifests in material effects on actual people's bodies and lives. Finally, fantasies of identification are haunted by disability even when disabled bodies are not their immediate focus, for disability functions as the trope and embodiment of true physical difference.

In Benedict Anderson's conception of imagined communities, a narrative of national coherence emerges through the "forgetting" of historical disruption and violence (205). However, the fantastic narratives discussed in this book not only serve to cover over the incoherence of the past but must be continuously circulated to reassemble a coherent present, without which the nation ceases to function. Such continuous forgettings are then best described in the language of fantasy, distinguished from mere imagination by the element of persistent and willed desire, what Lauren Berlant calls the linking of "regulation and desire" (5). Yet while Berlant is concerned with how texts doing the work of national fantasy realize or "stage" the nation through forms, I trace a dialectic between text, body, and nation that is at once mutually constitutive and highly unstable. Fantasy forms the bridge between the social and the textual, the material body and the discourses that constrain and enable that body's intelligibility. These fantasies jarringly combine a certain wistful desire to know and understand certain identities with a persistent and often violent imposition of identity upon people whose subjectivity is overruled by a homogenizing, bureaucratic imperative. Indeed fantasies of identification are driven by a desire for incontrovertible physical identification so intense that it produces its own realization at the same time that it reinterprets that realization as natural and inevitable. And while certain discrete fantasies may be discarded, the master fantasy circulates flexibly, attaching to different types of embodied social identities according to historical, economic, and political circumstance.

Fantasizing Fingerprints

Like all good fantasies, this one begins with a story. In 1903 an African American man named Will West was convicted and sent to the U.S. penitentiary at Leavenworth, Kansas, where he was photographed and measured according to the Bertillon anthropometric method in wide use at the time. The clerk, thinking West looked familiar, checked his records and found that a William West was already on record with the same picture and measurements. Yet West denied having been in Leavenworth before, and as it turned out, the other William West was already in custody. The two men were brought together and observed to be identical in all respects, until their fingerprints were taken and compared, proving both their unique identities and the superiority of fingerprinting to all other methods of identification known at the time.

This founding story of modern fingerprinting, famously recorded in Charles Edward Chapel's 1941 forensic guide *Fingerprinting: A Manual of Identification* and told in dramatic detail in the Federal Bureau of Investigation's 1991 official pamphlet, *Fingerprint Identification*, is indeed a dramatic example of the power of modern identification (Fig. I.1).[5] As the FBI pamphlet declares, "It would be hard to conceive a more nearly perfect case for refuting the claims of rival systems of identification" (7). For many years visitors to FBI headquarters could even view a wall-sized version of the story, which is retold in many histories and forensic textbooks.[6]

There is just one problem with the story of Will West: It isn't true. Kansas fingerprint examiner and historian Robert D. Olsen has conclusively demonstrated that, while the two Wests did exist, the scene described above simply did not take place. The Wests were never incarcerated at the same time and place, and there is no record of their fingerprints being taken and compared. In fact Leavenworth did not even begin recording prisoners' fingerprints until 1904. Olsen concludes that it "makes a nice case to tell over port and cigars, but there is evidence it never happened" (3). Yet "over the years, popular true crime authors and professional scholars alike have repeated the Will West story as if it really happened" (S. Cole 146). The FBI pamphlet was published in 1991, four years after Olsen publicly appealed to forensic professionals to abandon the West story, declaring that "it is not necessary to use a fable to illustrate the value of the fingerprint system" (3). A decade later one could still find intellectually rigorous

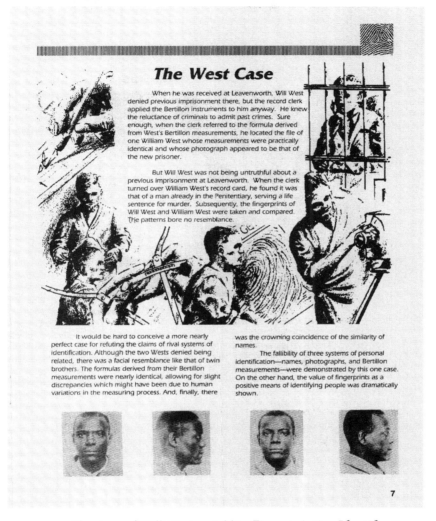

The West Case

When he was received at Leavenworth, Will West denied previous imprisonment there, but the record clerk applied the Bertillon instruments to him anyway. He knew the reluctance of criminals to admit past crimes. Sure enough, when the clerk referred to the formula derived from West's Bertillon measurements, he located the file of one William West whose measurements were practically identical and whose photograph appeared to be that of the new prisoner.

But Will West was not being untruthful about a previous imprisonment at Leavenworth. When the clerk turned over William West's record card, he found it was that of a man already in the Penitentiary, serving a life sentence for murder. Subsequently, the fingerprints of Will West and William West were taken and compared. The patterns bore no resemblance.

It would be hard to conceive a more nearly perfect case for refuting the claims of rival systems of identification. Although the two Wests denied being related, there was a facial resemblance like that of twin brothers. The formulas derived from their Bertillon measurements were nearly identical, allowing for slight discrepancies which might have been due to human variations in the measuring process. And, finally, there was the crowning coincidence of the similarity of names.

The fallibility of three systems of personal identification—names, photographs, and Bertillon measurements—were demonstrated by this one case. On the other hand, the value of fingerprints as a positive means of identifying people was dramatically shown.

7

FIGURE I.1. The story of Will West, as told in *Fingerprinting Identification* (1991). (Federal Bureau of Investigation, U.S. Department of Justice)

scholars citing the official version of the Will West incident (Joseph 170; Rowe 163). And still a decade after that, at the time of this writing, a simple Internet search yields numerous sites by popular and professional devotees of fingerprinting, including law enforcement officials and forensic science instructors, which repeat the legend as fact.[7]

This adherence to the Will West story in defiance of historical contradiction establishes it as not simply myth or fable but fantasy: a thing we not only imagine but desire to be true. The fantasy of the two Will Wests is also an inextricably racialized fantasy; it is no coincidence that the two Wests were African American.[8] Nineteenth-century interest in fingerprinting was originally driven by colonialist imperatives and figured as a means to distinguish between racially homogeneous "others"—in the British context, Indian natives, and in the United States, Chinese immigrants.[9] Sir Francis Galton, the figure most notably associated with introducing fingerprinting to a wide audience, was also the acknowledged "father" of modern eugenics and was deeply invested in his ultimately unrealized goal of using fingerprints in the service of racialist science.[10]

In the West story, and in many other examples discussed in this book, the fantasy of identification merges notions of individual and group identity: West is at once himself, a criminal, and a black man, and the supposed power of fingerprinting is to fix and merge these identities into a single knowable subject. Indeed the remarkable success of fingerprinting over the past century stems from its real and imagined ability to encompass and link different realms of identity. As Max Horkheimer and Theodor W. Adorno observe, the paradoxical individuality of modern culture is represented by "fingerprints on identity cards which are otherwise exactly the same, and into which the lives and faces of every single person are transformed by the power of the generality" (154). The power of fingerprints to stabilize personal identity is accomplished only through the existence of a state apparatus to organize and frame that identity, and, as historian Simon Cole convincingly argues, the primary challenge for nineteenth-century fingerprinting researchers was to develop a working system for the organization and retrieval of fingerprint data, "a link between an individual body and a paper record held by the state" (4). The centrality of this link between body, text, and state underscores the crucial difference of modern identificatory practice, what Foucault describes as "cellular power," in which individuality is legible only in relation to a homogeneous, regularized grouping (*Discipline and Punish* 149). The fantasy of identification, then, is always far less concerned with individual identity than with placing that individual within a legible group.

Among the "elementary signs of modern identity . . . the name, the portrait, and the fingerprint," only fingerprints provide a sign of identity rooted firmly in the physical body (Caplan 52).[11] While portraits (and photographs) provide a textually mimetic reflection of personal identity,

and names formalize identity into language, for many years only fingerprints—what Mark Twain famously called our "natal autographs"—
combined the textual, linguistic, and physical into a master signifier, "a
kind of serial number written on the body" (L. Davis, *Enforcing Normalcy* 32). While Simon Cole claims that "fingerprinting . . . embedded
firmly within our culture the notion that personhood is biological" (5),
I suggest the reverse is true, that prior notions of biological personhood
influenced the selection of fingerprinting as the preferred means of
identification in the modern era (since the existence of fingerprints was
known cross-culturally for many centuries before its modern European
and American implementation in the late 1800s). Lennard J. Davis connects this development to the emergence of normative bodily models, as
"the notion of fingerprinting pushes forward the idea that the human
body is standardized" (*Enforcing Normalcy* 32). The normalizing power
of the fingerprint provides an apparent resolution to the dilemma of
identification outlined at the start of this introduction—the paradox of
reconciling unique individuality with democratic social equality—as
every individual's fingerprints are "qualitatively unique, yet capable of
being enrolled in a numerical series for the purposes of classification,
retrieval, and communication" (Caplan 53). To this extent, fingerprints
function as a perfectly Foucauldian mechanism that disciplines individuals into objects of state control while maintaining the illusion of
individual autonomy.

However, the fissures in this totalizing view of fingerprints provide
glimpses of the ambiguity, tension, and subversion that lurk within. In
nineteenth-century America, with its intense "desire for coherent and
legible identities" (Chinn 47), the discovery of the fingerprint signified
less an advance in material technology than the power of a fantasy of
identification to produce and naturalize its own systematic realization.
This dynamic becomes dramatically clear when we discover that fingerprinting was deployed fictionally before it was ever used in legal or forensic settings; in fact this fantastical power of fiction may even have enabled
the eventual implementation of this form of identification. Twain's 1898
novella, *Pudd'nhead Wilson*, discussed at length in chapter 5, famously
introduced fingerprinting to the wider cultural discourse, touting its
unparalleled ability not only to distinguish between unique individuals
but also to delineate the different identities of racially ambiguous subjects. This solution to the crisis of identification so deeply satisfied the
nation's fantastic desires that, startlingly, Twain's fictional statements
on the accuracy of fingerprints were repeatedly cited in actual criminal

trials of the early twentieth century to produce convictions—both literally and in the sense of a powerful state of belief. Indeed Twain's protagonist's famous speech on the power of this "physiological autograph" is still cited and repeated in forensic textbooks, granting the power of the expert to a character who exists as pure invention.[12] Thus we see that the blurring of truth, imagination, and desire in the West story is not an aberration in the story of modern identification but rather its defining feature.

Time Travels: Staging, Penetrance, Institutionalization

In Raymond Williams's description of dominant and residual cultures, the residual comprises those "experiences, meanings and values, which cannot be verified or cannot be expressed in terms of the dominant culture, [but] are nevertheless lived and practiced on the basis of the residue—cultural as well as social—of some previous social formation" (159). In the case of fantasies of identification, representation is both residual and prescient, both preceding and emerging from social formations. The narrated fingerprinting of the two Will Wests takes place a full year before fingerprinting technology is introduced at Leavenworth. Twain employs fingerprinting in a fictional trial, and only decades later is it used in actual courtrooms. This paradoxical dynamic becomes even more complicated when we move to the current day, as modern science is increasingly evoked to support fantastic claims of identification, most notably in the area of DNA testing. As I demonstrate in chapter 9, both representations and implementations of genetic forms of identification tend to precede—and yet also skip past—the necessary scientific knowledge regarding the meaning and reliability of these identifications, and the material effects of this process are considerable.

For this reason I argue that to fully understand the persistence of fantasies of identification it is necessary always to consider not only their visible material effects but also their circulation within multiple cultural spheres. In this book the literary, filmic, and artistic texts I discuss reveal a much more complex, ambivalent, and subversive view of identification than do the corresponding legal, historical, and medical documents against which they are read.[13] The tensions revealed by these texts are crucial because of the deeply imbricated and mutually entangled relation of this literature to the material reality represented by the legal, medical, and historical texts, demonstrating "a powerful and effective oscillation between the establishment of distinct discursive domains and the collapse of those domains into one another," one element of which is the attempt to isolate "fantasies in a private, apolitical realm" (Greenblatt 7–8).[14] I foreground the public nature of fantasy in shaping racial, gendered, and dis/abled identification, as fantasy functions both to forecast and to reinforce the supposedly concrete and fixed matter of identification that takes place daily in courtrooms, medical offices, border checkpoints, and countless other realms of the "real."

In the nearly two centuries covered in this study, we will see how the fantasy evolves from its nineteenth-century incarnation as an imagined or staged relation conveyed most tellingly in the representative sphere to its current, twenty-first-century realization as a highly institutionalized regulatory structure most visible in the workings of state bureaucracy and the law. The argument and structure of this book follow this development. In the first part I examine how versions of the fantasy emerged in literature and film in relation to social anxieties about bodily identification, with these representational fantasies often exceeding or even compensating for their relatively incomplete penetration into other spheres. In part II I bring works of literature into conversation with medicolegal discourses to demonstrate the growing penetrance of fantasies in these realms, often through an illogical reversal of the usual relationship between social "realities" and their representations. Part III brings us firmly into the present, in which the fantasy of identification has been fully institutionalized through the process I call *biocertification*. This neologism describes the massive proliferation of state-issued documents purporting to authenticate a person's biological membership in a regulated group. I demonstrate how biocertification began to take hold at the turn of the century and has become ever more powerfully instituted into the present.

My focus in part III on the millennial period between 1980 and 2012 is shaped by a notable clustering of texts and events during this period, much like that of the mid-nineteenth century, and similarly provoked by a rapidly changing social world. A century after the events described in the opening of this introduction, we find a markedly similar acceleration of anxieties about identity, also spurred by rapidly increasing social and geographic mobility, now in the form of globalization; a tremendous expansion of and corresponding backlash against the welfare state; and technological innovations, such as DNA and the Internet, that render bodily identities more anonymous and unknowable while paradoxically promising to confirm bodily truths with more certainty than ever before. The parallel between the mid- to late nineteenth-century crisis of identification and that of the mid- to late twentieth century is also forecast in part I through analysis of films about disability fakery that notably proliferated during these two periods.

The civil rights movements that took place between these two clusters of events and texts, overturning long-entrenched racial, gendered, disabled, and sexualized hierarchies of power, are a powerful background to this study, and indeed created the conditions of its very existence. Yet, ironically, such movements have not functioned, either historically or in their current incarnations, to significantly disrupt or dilute the influence of fantasies of identification in American or global power structures. These fantasies have not only persisted largely unchanged despite the radical cultural shifts produced by social justice movements but have often integrated the language and goals of those movements into their discursive structures and power regimes. So, for example, a new cultural valuation of American Indian identity, which grew out of the American Indian Movement of the late 1960s and 1970s in resistance to assimilation and relocation, provided a broader stage and greater perceived stakes for the updated fantasy of blood quantum as a measure of "Indianness," as discussed in chapters 7 and 8. Similarly the civil and material gains of the disability rights movement, most notably the passing of the Americans with Disabilities Act in 1990, produced a resurgence of cultural suspicions of disabled people and a proliferation of required "proofs" of disabled status.

Yet it is also crucial to note that the social movements of the late twentieth century enabled greater and more diverse forms of resistance to the institutionalized fantasy of identification. This resistant turn is signaled not only historically but also generically in this study. In the nineteenth- and early twentieth-century texts discussed in parts I and II, we find emergent fantasies of identification staged primarily through imaginative works that only gradually and incompletely affect social power structures. In contrast, in the recent period covered by part III, such fantasies have become firmly institutionalized and can be read through legal and bureaucratic documents, with works of literature, film, and visual art now functioning primarily as sites of resistant counterdiscourses to the fantasy. Thus while part I primarily focuses on traditional representational works, the part II brings such works into conversation with texts from legal and bureaucratic spheres, and part III then reads legal and bureaucratic texts *as* works of representation whose language is similarly revealing of deeply invested cultural assumptions.

Fantasy Bodies: Disability, Gender, Race

At the core of the fantasy of identification lies the assumption that embodied social identities such as race, gender, and disability are fixed, legible, and categorizable. This assumption, by now deeply naturalized in our social and ontological structures, in fact required elaborate construction and ongoing policing throughout the nineteenth century and early twentieth. In their twenty-first-century institutional forms, these governing assumptions continually fracture under the weight of their own unverifiability and thus must ever more insistently invoke the supposed empiricism of science as their bedrock truth. This process is starkly visible in the practice of genetic sex testing, which, as discussed in chapter 9, spent over four decades invoking reductive "science" to regulate identity despite the concerted opposition of the scientists themselves. This example drives home the fact that, as in the example of fingerprinting addressed earlier, our modern practices of identification are not simply mapped onto given bodily characteristics. Rather medical, legal, and political authorities have anxiously scanned our bodies in search of such characteristics—without which the increasingly unwieldy social apparatus of normalization and difference would collapse—and then made strident retrospective claims as to their obvious and natural existence: "This signification produces as an *effect* of its own procedure the very body that it nevertheless and simultaneously claims to discover as that which *precedes* its own action" (Butler, *Bodies That Matter* 30). This process can be observed to accelerate in the mid-nineteenth century with regard to many subjugated groups of people, most notably those marked as racial others or as mentally or physically disabled, and to achieve full institutional power by the middle of the twentieth century with the advent of modern genetics.

Medicine has played a central role in shaping this process. While today we are more likely to associate medical identification with disabled bodies, medicine in mid-nineteenth-century America was centrally focused on questions of race, and racialist medicine served both to buttress the institution of slavery and to consolidate medical authority during its period of professionalization. Prominent physicians such as Samuel A. Cartwright, Josiah C. Nott, and John Van Evrie argued for the biological inferiority of African Americans and American Indians and explicitly supported slavery and settler colonialism as the natural system resulting from the superiority of the white race.[15] In 1851 Cartwright famously outlined "the anatomical and physiological differences between the negro and the white man," which he claimed were "more deep, durable, and indelible . . . than that of mere color" (qtd. in Martin 54), and Nott contended three years later that "to one who has lived among American Indians, it is in vain to talk of civilizing them. You might as well attempt to change the nature of the buffalo" (Nott and Gliddon 69). These doctors and their associates peeled back layers of black skin, dissected the bodies of dead slaves, and measured hundreds of Indian skulls in their fruitless search for those "deep, durable, and indelible" differences between the races (Martin 54; D. Thomas 40). This search became ever more determined as the "visible, progressive 'whitening' of the slave body throughout the century," accelerated by the banning of the slave trade in 1807, undermined the reliability of skin color as racial marker (Wiegman 47). Legal developments mirrored these medical trends, for "even though American slave codes had always articulated racial difference, in the 1830s legal formulations of slave status became increasingly dependent on the identification of 'black' bodies" (Keetley 4). By the antebellum period law and medicine intersected, as "doctors presented themselves to courts as experts on racial identity, claiming a monopoly on scientific racial knowledge" (Gross 10).[16]

Many scholars pinpoint the beginning of "classifying *according to* somatic/morphological criteria" in the eighteenth century, arguing that during this period "skin color [became] visible as a basis for determining the order of identities and differences and subsequently penetrate[d] the body to become the truth of the self" (Guillaumin 32; Kawash 130).[17] By the mid-nineteenth century, however, the "truth of the self" was not so clearly apparent in skin color, and so, as discussed in chapter 4, questions of racial identity were increasingly determined based upon hair, nose, feet, and other anatomical features that supposedly signaled race. In courtroom settings such features were mentioned arbitrarily and inconsistently, and no clear policy of racial identification could be formed from the competing claims regarding the true "Negro foot" or "Indian hair" (Gross 9). Thus I suggest that these claims testify not to the presence of a true fantasy of identification but rather to the dominant power structure's deep and abiding desire for such a fantastical solution.

The modern conundrum of individual identity that is legible only in its regularized group context took on a new valence when combined with the paradox of a system that must at once recognize and deny the individuality—the very humanity—of the people it enslaves. The answer offered by racialist medicine was to naturalize racial difference, thus placing it outside the realm of human control and therefore of human culpability: "Only a theory rooted in nature could systematically explain the anomaly of slavery existing in a republic founded on a radical commitment to liberty, equality, and natural rights" (Roberts 186).[18] This solution became a crucial ingredient in the emergence of fantasies of identification that also naturalize identity and root it firmly in the physical body. The association of racial difference with physical immutability is a complex and deeply historicized cultural dynamic, which one contemporary African American writer describes as "the experience of black people of being reduced to their bodies . . . [with] one's claim to individuality . . . constantly vulnerable to being erased" (Espinoza and Harris 442). Lindon Barrett similarly observes "the manner in which African American bodies are taken as signs of nothing beyond themselves—signs of the very failure of meaning—for these bodies are able to signify, in their obdurate physicality, only a state of obdurate physicality" (322).

Thus when we turn to disability, the social identity most closely associated with the immutability of the physical body, we find that it plays a dual role in these fantasies, as both the *object* of identification and the symbolic *anchor* that enables its function. As object, the disabled body presents a unique challenge to an identificatory system based upon classification, since its nonnormativity manifests itself through a vast diversity of form and function: "The concept of disability unites a highly marked, heterogeneous group whose only commonality is being considered abnormal. . . . Disability confounds any notion of a generalizable, stable physical subject" (Garland Thomson, *Extraordinary Bodies* 24). On the one hand, then, disability resists identification through classification because of its instability and particularity. We can see this tension at work in histories of disability policy, such as Deborah Stone's *The Disabled State*, which investigate the process by which "originally distinct classes" of "the aged and infirm . . . lunatics and defectives, invalids and the lying-in, able-bodied and impotent beggars, and orphans" came with modernity to be "lumped together in one unified category . . . with enough shared cultural meaning to serve as a defining characteristic for public welfare programs" (26). Stone shows the extent to which this process of categorization was not only arbitrary and incomplete, but also profoundly influenced by cultural differences. As a result we now find ourselves living within another identificatory paradox, in which "the category 'disability' begins to break down when one scrutinizes who make up the disabled" (L. Davis, *Enforcing Normalcy* xv), yet individuals with disabilities must nevertheless navigate social and governmental classifications of disability to obtain resources necessary for daily existence.

This paradox, with its concomitant rituals of identity testing and perpetual suspicion, can be traced in Stone's analysis back to the inherent uncertainty of the disability category. She argues that "because no single condition of 'disability' is universally recognized, and because physical and mental incapacity are conditions that can be feigned . . . the concept of disability has always been based on the perceived need to detect deception" and thus "the very category of disability was developed to incorporate a mechanism for distinguishing the genuine from the artificial" (24, 32). Stone's argument certainly holds true with regard to the examples of disability identity testing discussed in this book, such as cultural depictions of fake disabled beggars and rituals of surveillance of disabled parking permit holders. However, one may also extend her argument into the representational realm to investigate the other side of disability's confounding of classificatory systems. The extraordinary and unique quality of the disabled body, I argue, can be seen not only as resisting identification but also, and conversely, as providing a symbolic and actual basis on which to structure a system of identification that seeks to fix individual bodily identity. As the imperative to define a coherent category of disability increasingly relied upon its supposedly solid physicality, its location in "the immutability of the flesh" (Garland Thomson, *Extraordinary Bodies* 25), contemporaneous efforts at identification evoked disability in their emphasis upon fixed and legible bodily truths. Even mental or intellectual disability, subsumed at this time under the category of "feeblemindedness," was characterized as both physical and unchanging (Marks 82; Trent 88).

This dynamic returns us to the relationship of race, gender, and modern identification, a relation I contend is mediated by the symbolic function of disability as the trope of physicality, the body that is "somehow *too much* a body, *too real*, too corporeal" (J. Porter xiii). The increasing drive throughout the nineteenth century to define "race as an unchanging, biological feature" and "an inherent and incontrovertible difference" in order to give "white supremacy . . . a logic lodged fully in the body" (Wiegman 31), drew both explicitly and implicitly on disability's symbolic power. Douglas Baynton has demonstrated the proliferation of disability imagery in debates over slavery and the postbellum status of African Americans as well as women's education and suffrage (37–39). I argue that the significance of disability extends beyond these explicit references to pervade racial and gendered debates centering upon the concepts of the "natural" and the "normal," two ontological categories historically defined in opposition to disability.[19]

In fact it was virtually impossible to separate race from disability in nineteenth-century discourses of normalcy: "Just as medical textbook illustrations compared the normal body with the abnormal, so social science textbooks illustrated the normal race and the abnormal ones" (Baynton 39). Van Evrie's 1854 racialist treatise *Negroes and Negro "Slavery": The First an Inferior Race: The Latter its Normal Condition* insists upon the biological "fact" of racial difference as "original, invariable, and everlasting" and "fixed by the Creator himself" (132–133). Van Evrie soon afterward articulated the disability subtext of his book, claiming in the 1860s that the education of African Americans resulted in bodies "dwarfed or destroyed": "an 'educated negro,' like a 'free negro,' is a social monstrosity, even more unnatural and repulsive than the latter" (qtd. in Baynton 38).[20] This explicit evocation of disability in relation to arguments about natural or normal racial difference contextualizes the frequent deployment of those terms in nineteenth- and twentieth-century racial discourse. Colette Guillaumin describes modern conceptions of race as "a natural closed category . . . that is first of all fixed and secondly hereditary" (27). Teresa Zackodnik has documented the persistence of this concept in nineteenth-century legal cases related to racial identity, which "appealed to a notion of race as naturalized by invoking bodily differences like complexion and fractional quantities of black 'blood' and thereby reading the biological as 'fact'" (425). The natural and normal often merged in these discourses, signaling a paradoxical embrace of modernity's normative classifications coupled with a reluctance to abandon the moral certainty granted by notions of race determined by God and nature.[21]

Henry Louis Gates Jr. has suggested that "the biological criteria used to determine 'difference' in sex simply do not hold when applied to 'race.' Yet we carelessly use language in such a way as to *will* this sense of *natural* difference into our formulations" (5). What Gates describes as a *willing* of racial difference, Guillaumin identifies as the "fantastic and legalized affirmations" of racial boundaries as "immutable," "obvious," and "commonsense" (27). In this book I adopt Guillaumin's language of fantasy over Gates's "will" to emphasize the crucial role of the cultural imaginary in displacing a sense of bodily difference from the body into language.

In contrast to Gates, I also investigate how increasingly unstable the idea of biological criteria for sex has become, such that, while female bodies were repeatedly deployed in the nineteenth and early twentieth centuries as the representational grounds on which to contest racial and disability identities, by the late twentieth century "femaleness" itself became a contested category to be stabilized through biologizing fantasies. Indeed while my discussion thus far has focused primarily on the crisis of identification in relation to race and disability, sex has been hauntingly present as a "natural" bodily difference historically invoked to provide, through contrast, a sense of the comparatively artificial nature of race as social construction. Such invocations are similar to the strategy Mitchell and Snyder describe as "methodological distancing," in which, as areas of study based on certain embodied social identities have "sought to unmoor their identities from debilitating physical and cognitive associations, they inevitably positioned disability as the 'real' limitation from which they must escape" (*Narrative Prosthesis* 2). Throughout this book I note instances of methodological distancing—from sex, from race, and, as Mitchell and Snyder attest, most often from disability, which I argue frequently functions in a supplementary fashion to enable fantasies of racial and sexual identification, as well as their resistance. Indeed historically "both abolitionist and feminist discourses countered the inscription of the black and the female body as an incontrovertible signifier of otherness and inferiority by attempting to define selfhood as a product of something other than physical being" (Klages 5), and in so doing often explicitly defined their movements in opposition to disability (Baynton 34). In recent years much scholarship has addressed the intersection of gender and disability, producing crucial works on disability's relationship to women, feminism, and queer identity, while a smaller but significant body of work has appeared addressing the intersections of disability with race.[22] In the context just outlined, however, we can see the urgent need for a new kind of intersectional analysis to address how these categories have often formed mutually constitutive frameworks in support of—or in resistance to—dominant social, political, and economic structures of power.[23]

The mutually entangled and constitutive dynamic of disability, gender, and race in modern fantasies of identification determines the shape and trajectory of this book. If, at times, one of these embodied social identities comes to the foreground, such that parts of the book address disability or race or gender more centrally, the overarching argument remains structured around the inseparability of their meanings. In particular I highlight the supplementary role of disability in precisely those cases that may seem to be "just" about race or gender. In each case, identity is structured by intersecting vectors of power: not only disability, race, and gender, but also economic status, geopolitical location, sexuality, medicalization, and enslavement. Thus at no point do I centralize a single identification to the exclusion of others. Rather I seek to expose the mutual constitution that allows fantasies of identification to persist as powerful and flexible mechanisms of social discipline in relation to a wide variety of bodies and categories.

Visualizing the Body of Fantasy

The fantasy of identification, like many features of modernity, is predicated on an epistemology of visibility, in which identity can be easily read upon the body. Yet as the nineteenth century increasingly produced ambiguous and illegible bodies, the fantasy also began to look inside those bodies, invoking the "simultaneous strengthening of the corporeal as the bearer of . . . meaning *and* a deepening of that meaning as ultimately lodged beyond the assessing gaze of the unaided eye" (Wiegman 23). Modern systems of identification rely upon the authority of the expert whose authoritative gaze trumps not only an individual's appearance but, more disturbingly, her own narrative of bodily and social identity. Yet, paradoxically, these systems also depend upon the easy recognizability of bodies, the "commonsense" ability to discern identity visually through markers as historically charged as skin color and as deeply naturalized as biological sex and physical disability.[24] Language becomes the means by which fantasy attempts to close this gap even as language also functions to signify the multiplicity of cultural responses to its existence: this is the paradox at the heart of biocertification.

The fantasies I discuss exist in a state of perpetual tension between physical and linguistic means of identification—a tension figured by race, mediated through disability, and often inscribed onto contested female bodies. This tension is crucially shaped by the simultaneous reliance upon and undermining of the visual knowability of bodily identity, the haunting "possibility that the body, which is meant to reflect transparently its inner truth, may in fact be a misrepresentation" (Kawash 132). Such mis/representations then evoke fantasies of bodily identification authorized in the medico-administrative sphere by the "assumption that . . . the body is a surface that is written on and read out of and that the information one can read on a body can provide essential and reliable information" (Chinn 25). This assumption links body and text in a scheme of biocertificative legibility in which identity is at once marked upon the body and buried within it, requiring expert scrutiny to be revealed.

Fantasies of identification are then predicated upon the rejection of individual identity claims, as Garland Thomson argues in the case of disability: "Medical validation of physical incapacity solved the problem of malingering by circumventing the testimony of the individual. Under this confirmation scheme, the doctor sought direct communication with the body regarding its condition, eliminating the patient's ability for self-disclosure and, ultimately, for self-determination" (*Extraordinary Bodies* 50). The same dynamic operates with regard to race from the nineteenth century onward and with regard to sex and gender in the late twentieth and twenty-first centuries. The physician-detective scrutinizes the body for clues that will support or disprove the individual's claims about that body's status, and then issues or denies biocertification according to his (or occasionally her) findings.[25] This privileging of medical authority in validating identity reflects the modern turn toward visualizing bodies such that "the 'glance' has simply to exercise its right of origin over truth" (Foucault, *The Birth of the Clinic* 4).

In part I, "Fantasies of Fakery," I explore early negotiations of the crisis of identification during the late nineteenth century and the resonances of these negotiations through the present day. In these chapters the fantasies at work are not yet fully realized structures of identification but circulate as anxious dreams, occupied with the looming possibility that unknowable bodies in a newly mobile world provide unprecedented possibilities for deception. These fantasies of fakery demonstrate the reversal of cause and effect, proceeding from the possibility of imposture to the assumption that imposters are everywhere. The dramatic emergence of cultural fantasies about fake disabled bodies in this period intersects with and sustains concerns about other forms of identity imposture based on gender, race, and class. This enmeshed anxiety emerges vividly in my analysis of representations of Ellen Craft, a light-skinned African American woman whose escape from slavery was enabled by her disguise as a white, wealthy, disabled man. Craft's successful manipulation of ideas about race, gender, class, and disability demonstrates that the instability of these identifications could be a source of resistant mobility. Yet later retellings of her story in the twentieth century are marked by the consolidation and immobilization of her identity, in particular through the erasure of the disability component of her disguise. This dynamic, I argue, must be understood in the context of a profound anxiety regarding disability imposture—what I call the *disability con*—which emerged powerfully in late nineteenth-century American culture and again in the late twentieth century through the present, in both cases in response to new extensions of social benefits to disabled people and others understood as the "worthy" poor. In chapter 2, then, I turn to an early representation of the disability con in Herman Melville's 1857 novel *The Confidence Man: His Masquerade*, exploring its complex negotiations between body and text, appearance and essence, to show the unfixability of identity. In chapter 3 I extend this discussion to examine how the new medium of cinema adopted the disability con as a central trope, finally realizing it as a fantasy of identification in which false disability could be identified and unmasked—and yet how the instability of categories of "real" and "fake" bodies continues to haunt these filmic representations.

In part II, "Fantasies of Marking," the penetrance of the fantasy into areas of policy and law can be read in its dramatic courtroom appearances, both real and representational. Birthmarks and fingerprints appeared in mid- to late nineteenth-century legal and cultural realms as possible solutions to problems of identification, often merging questions of individual and racial identification through the figure of a suspect on trial. In chapter 4 I examine the 1845 suit for freedom by Salomé Müller, an enslaved woman in New Orleans who claimed to be a white German immigrant kidnapped in childhood. Müller won her freedom largely due to the evidence of her birthmarks, yet this apparently physical and incontrovertible evidence, I argue, is ultimately verified discursively through verbal testimony. This dynamic is even more apparent in the case of fingerprinting, which I explore in chapter 5 through further discussion of Twain's 1894 novel and story, *Pudd'nhead Wilson* and "Those Extraordinary Twins." Twain's literary representation of racial misidentification resolved through fingerprints has been extensively discussed; I draw upon and also complicate these critical conversations by pointing out how the novel represents a negotiation of a fantasy of identification, as the haunting remains of its excised disability components underpin a powerful semantic link between fingerprinting, identification, race, and disability.

I then explore the practical deployment of the fantasy's conflation of body and text in part III, "Fantasies of Measurement," through historical and current institutions of biocertification. I first demonstrate that, even in the area of physical disability, the identity category most presumptively defined by the authority of biomedical science, biocertification functions through highly contingent, contested, and paradoxical constructions of bodily meaning. In chapter 6, through close readings of the bureaucratic and cultural discourses shaping the system of disabled parking in the United States, we see that the link between body, text, and social power structures must be endlessly and proliferatively policed even in the most local and limited of examples. I then move in chapter 7 to a less obviously "physical" arena of biocertification, exploring the history and current controversies surrounding the use of blood quantum requirements for American Indian and other Native peoples of North America and Hawai'i. Here I also consider Native writers' and artists' reimaginations of identity that both reject and refigure tropes of blood in an ongoing process of negotiation and resistance. In chapter 8 I bring together these two local examples through the shared and mutually constitutive history of biocertification for Native and disabled people in the United States, through historicolegal connections drawn between blood quantum, mental disability, competence, and rehabilitation in the nineteenth and early twentieth centuries. In all of these cases I demonstrate the power of the fantasy of biocertification to both evoke and exceed science through claims that identity is fixed, measurable, and intrinsically connected to social worth and citizenship.

This sets the stage for chapter 9, in which I explore how the comparatively solid scientific basis of modern genetics does not signal either an end or an answer to fantasies of identification but instead has been quickly subsumed into potent new versions of the fantasy previously attached to pseudo- or nonscience. I first look at the burgeoning industry of home DNA tests, particularly those that claim to be able to measure Native identity. I then turn to the example of sex testing in sports, focusing on the 2009 controversy surrounding the South African runner Caster Semenya. I show that when a fantasy of sex/ gender identification finally does become realized, beginning in the late twentieth century, it closely resembles the historical and ongoing fantasies about race and disability identification discussed throughout this book, demonstrating the flexibility and persistence of these fantasies from modernity into postmodernity.

Notes on Terms and Methods

I define disability quite broadly to include a range of physical and mental differences that in the 1800s were beginning to coalesce under the modern signifier of disability: differences including not only paralysis, missing limbs, blindness, and deafness but also more vaguely delineated figures such as "the invalid," "the idiot," and "the Siamese twins." Here I follow the work of disability historians who recognize that "disability has never been a monolithic grouping" but has described "people with a variety of conditions, despite considerable differences in etiology, [who] confront a common set of stigmatizing social values and debilitating socially constructed hazards" (Longmore and Umansky 4, 12). The social model of disability, in which disability is understood as located not primarily in the individual but in "the set of social, historical, economic, and cultural processes that regulate and control the way we think about and think through the body" (L. Davis, *Enforcing Normalcy* 2–3), allows us to consider how physical and mental variation serves to reveal cultural anxieties about and investments in bodies understood as "ordinary" or "normal." A profoundly influential concept since its inception in the 1980s, the social model of disability separates impairment, as physical or mental difference, from disability, the social effects of that difference. While the social model has been critiqued and expanded on many levels, it remains a useful construct with which to examine many historical and current practices of disability categorization and regulation.[26] In this study I keep the social construction of disability firmly in mind while remaining critically aware of its inescapable connection to actual bodies and minds whose differences often result in social and material disempowerment.

Similarly I follow the work of critical race theorists in examining race as a social construction that nevertheless has material consequences. As Ian Haney López explains, "The absence of any physical basis to race does not entail the conclusion that race is wholly hallucination. Race has its genesis and maintains its vigorous strength in the realm of social beliefs. Nevertheless, race is not an inescapable physical fact. Rather, it is a social construction that, however perilously, remains subject to contestation at the hands of individuals and communities alike" ("Social Construction" 172). Thus analysis of racial fantasies of identification must at once recognize the lack of a biological basis for race and contend with the persistence of social, linguistic, and representational associations of race with biological difference. As I discuss in chapter 9, this is a particularly vexed and persistent issue in the current genetic age, when new scientific discoveries continue to be used to reinscribe old ways of understanding and classifying human difference. The persistence of claims for a physiological basis for racial divisions illustrates the fantasy's compulsion to invoke the authority of science while ignoring its complexity; thus the ongoing "discovery" of new genetic markers for race, despite the widely accepted finding that there is more genetic variation within a given racial group than between them: "We may know that race is a fiction. . . . This knowledge, however, does not launch us into a new orbit of experience. Rather, this knowledge names and marks the historical, epistemological, and philosophical limit of modernity, a limit at which we continually find ourselves" (Kawash 21).[27] One of these limits, it seems, is the refusal to give up on the fantasy of identification's promise to locate identity firmly and measurably in the body.

Indeed rather than scientific developments undermining the power of the fantasy, they have served to offer it new realms of deployment. Thus in the nineteenth and early twentieth centuries, while ambiguously sexed bodies posed a challenge to emerging systems of classification, physicians were unable to locate sex definitively in the body, beyond the commonsense solution of genital inspection (which failed in the case of ambiguous or changing genitalia).[28] However, the discovery of sex-linked chromosomes in 1955, much like the development of fingerprint technology in the 1890s, provided the scientific underpinning for a fantasy of identification that had been increasingly searching for a home.

How to name that fantasy has been a challenge throughout this book: while the general scholarly tendency would be to speak of "gender" rather than "sex," the fantasy's insistent location of this identity in the body places it in the biological realm traditionally ascribed to sex in contrast to the socially constructed category of gender. Yet in the examples of sex testing discussed in chapter 9, referred to by authorities as "gender verification" tests, we find the division between the biological and the social deeply muddled, in ways that are both frustrating and potentially productive. While many have understandably criticized the inaccuracy of the term *gender verification* for biological sex tests, this apparent slippage coincides with a recent trend in feminist and queer theories of gender toward a denaturalization of the category of sex and a blurring of the traditional opposition between sex/biology and gender/culture. Judith Butler, the most influential proponent of this view, has rejected the idea that "sex" is "a simple fact or static condition of the body," instead describing it as "an ideal construct which is forcibly materialized through time" (*Bodies That Matter* 1–2). Critical work by intersex activists and scholars has concretized this claim, responding to the prevalence of medical interventions on ambiguously sexed infants that tend to prioritize normative appearance over sexual function and bodily integrity. As Morgan Holmes observes, "Physicians produce gender because society demands that they do so, and in the process of production, through assurances that every individual has but one true sex, the demand is hidden" (*Intersex* 69). Here we decidedly see the presence of a fantasy of identification, which retroactively naturalizes its determinative effects. We also see a refusal to separate gender from sex, as the act of producing gender as a legible social category is impossible without the literal construction of the body's sex, and thus gender is here biologically constructed while sex is determined according to social demands. This interrogation of the social management of inter-sexuality nuances Butler's claim that "if gender is the social construction of sex, and if there is not access to this 'sex' except through gender, then it appears not only that sex is absorbed by gender, but that 'sex' becomes something like a fiction, perhaps a fantasy" (*Bodies That Matter* 5).[29] Butler raises this notion in part to reject it, or at least to confirm that "if 'sex' is a fiction, is it one within whose necessities we live, without which life itself would be unthinkable" (6). However, I find the notion of biological "sex" as fantasy deeply relevant to the project at hand, as acknowledging the fictionality of determinable sex may allow us to find new grounds for contesting oppressive practices proceeding from the fantasy of its reality. Therefore, throughout this book I speak of gender *and* sex as both socially and biologically constructed categories and sometimes merge them as *sex/gender* to emphasize their inseparability as targets and modes of fantastical identifications.

As this discussion indicates, the history of identification explored in this book is not merely a matter of the state imposing control over docile subjects nor of historical evolution producing a totalizing and inevitable system, but also crucially involves the threads of resistance, subversion, and uncertainty that accompany all cultural transformations. As fantasies of identification were beginning to take nascent shape during the second half of the nineteenth century, we can see not only their deep-rooted power investments but also their vulnerability to manipulation by wily historical subjects such as Ellen Craft and Salomé Müller and slippery characters like Melville's Thomas Fry and Twain's Roxy. In the twentieth and twenty-first centuries we find new versions of the fantasy transformed through counter- and disidentifications in the works of writers, performers, and visual artists drawing upon indigenous and crip cultural traditions. We also see the potential of organized resistance to change policies based on the fantasy's distorted understanding of identity, such as the abandonment of genetic sex testing in international sports just as the writing of this book was coming to a close. Thus even as this book demonstrates the power of the fantasy of identification, it also insists we remember that this power is not, and never has been, irresistible.

PART I

FANTASIES OF FAKERY

1 /   Ellen Craft's Masquerade

The crisis of identification that emerged in the mid-nineteenth century United States was fundamentally driven by the anxieties of "a culture that worried that a full knowledge of a person's racial origins could become obscured" (Otten 231). In the antebellum period these anxieties emerged in increasingly desperate attempts to codify racial difference as biological and therefore inescapable. The ability of fugitive slaves to subvert, manipulate, and defy these attempts through their successful escapes both challenged and accelerated southern white efforts to define race as physically fixed. Additionally, by midcentury the increased public role taken by women in the abolition and suffrage movements and accompanying challenges to raced and classed notions of masculinity and femininity created new fears over the "natural" roles and attributes of the sexes.[1] The many historical and literary studies of these related dynamics, however, have rarely addressed the contemporaneously emerging anxiety regarding the knowability of the disabled body. Yet this too is a fundamental and inextricable element of the identificatory crisis, and figures of feigned or suspected disability began to emerge prominently to represent this deepening fear.

In one such figure, the fugitive slave and author Ellen Craft, we find all three forms of embodied social identity unmoored from physical and representational certainty, and so her story represents a touchstone for the eventual emergence of fantasies of identification surrounding disability, race, and gender. By examining a series of representations of

Craft, including critical and creative responses by African American and feminist writers, we see not only the inextricability of these identities but also the crucial role played by disability in enabling flexible understandings of other supposedly biological identities.

A Complication of Complaints

In 1845 Ellen Craft and her husband, William, escaped from slavery in Georgia by traveling disguised as a "white invalid gentlemen" and his valet. After a four-day journey they arrived on free soil in Philadelphia and soon became prominent in the Boston-based abolitionist movement, telling their story to large audiences and swiftly gaining fame that eventually led to pursuit by southern agents seeking to reenslave them. The Crafts escaped once again, this time to England, where they later authored a narrative of their escape, *Running a Thousand Miles for Freedom*, published in 1860 by London's William Tweedie.[2] The Crafts' narrative has received a significant amount of critical attention, much of which has focused on the racial and gender passing perpetrated by Ellen, while a secondary concern has been the prominence of the Crafts on the abolition circuit before the Civil War.[3] However, no historian or literary critic has yet grappled with the presence of disability in the narrative; while the fact that Ellen pretended to be disabled is often mentioned in the course of other concerns, disability has not been addressed as a social identity that can be manipulated or interpreted, as can race and gender. Yet disability, and in particular the feigning of disability—what I call the "disability con"—plays an essential function in both the Crafts' narrative and the social context in which it appeared.[4]

Indeed the disability con is an important element for many fugitive slave narrators, such as James Pennington, who pretended to have smallpox, and Lewis Clarke, who employed disguises very similar to those of Ellen Craft, including green spectacles and handkerchiefs tied around his forehead and chin (Pennington 565; Clarke and Clarke 139, 147). A number of historians have briefly noted the use of feigned illness and disability among slaves as a means of resistance, as well as the related cultural dynamics of suspicion and surveillance, yet this context is not generally invoked in discussions of Ellen Craft, unlike examples of gender or race-based masquerades.[5] My consideration of disability in the Crafts' narrative is not to negate other critics' arguments but rather to enhance and complete them, particularly those that argue for the narrative's portrayal of a mutually constitutive relationship between race, gender, and class. In these many insightful analyses of Ellen Craft's "tripartite disguise" (Browder 121), the *fourth* crucial element of that disguise is rendered invisible and haunting.[6]

Yet a close reading of the narrative evolution of Ellen Craft's disguise clearly demonstrates the intimate and constitutive relationship of race, gender, class, and disability. In William's narration, he and Ellen first think of racial masquerade, suggested by Ellen's white skin. Next they decide upon gender-crossing, due to the perceived impropriety of a white woman traveling with a black man. But the class status of the white male persona adopted then presents the new obstacle of literacy:

> When the thought flashed across my wife's mind, that it was customary for travelers to register their names in the visitors' book at hotels, as well as in the clearance or Custom-house book at Charleston, South Carolina—it made our spirits droop within us. So, while sitting in our little room upon the verge of despair, all at once my wife raised her head, and with a smile upon her face, which was a moment before bathed in tears, said, "I think I have it!" I asked what it was. She said, "I think I can make a poultice and bind up my right hand in a sling, and with propriety ask the officers to register my name for me." (Craft and Craft 23–24)

At this point the concept of the invalid—of passing as disabled—enters the disguise and soon becomes its central enabling device. The crucial function of disability for the disguise is emphasized by its remarkable proliferation throughout the narrative, which begins immediately after the conversation just quoted. Ellen fears that "the smoothness of her face might betray her; so she decided to make another poultice, and put it in a white handkerchief to be worn under the chin, up the cheeks, and to tie over the head" (24). Then, nervous about traveling in the "company of gentlemen," Ellen sends William to buy "a pair of green spectacles [tinted glasses]" to hide her eyes (24). We immediately discover the efficacy of these stratagems, as William observes that, during the escape, "my wife's being muffled in the poultices, &c., furnished a plausible excuse for avoiding general conversation" (24). At the time of the disguise's inception, no specific illness or condition is referenced, although later in their journey, Ellen will claim to have "inflammatory rheumatism" (38).

In fact during the Crafts' four-day journey, Ellen acquires new impairments whenever discovery is threatened: when spoken to by an acquaintance who might recognize her voice, she "feigns deafness" (Craft and Craft 29); when other passengers are inclined to become too social, she goes to bed, citing her rheumatism (30); and when two young white ladies appear overly interested in the dapper gentleman, Ellen quickly becomes faint and must lie down quietly (39). As "problems of possible recognition, of hotel registration, and of reading are all solved by more and more complete adoption of the role of invalid master" (Byerman 74), we see that the validity of Ellen's racial, gender, and class passing hinges upon the *invalidity* of her body.

Yet that invalidity has been naturalized or ignored by critical readings of the Crafts' narrative, discussed as a purely material and expedient factor rather than a social identity requiring analysis. For instance, it is only after the Crafts' narrative has explained the elements of the invalid disguise that we reach that favorite moment of critics, the transformation of Ellen into a "most respectable-looking gentleman" through cross-dressing and a haircut (Craft and Craft 24). The transgression of this gender, race, and class masquerade is so interesting that critics and historians alike tend to disregard the fact that Ellen does not actually travel as this "respectable-looking gentleman" but *as his invalid double*, bandaged and poulticed and spectacled in the extreme. Clearly, passing as white, male, and even wealthy is not enough to effect the Crafts' escape. In fact none of these acts of passing could have succeeded, apparently, without the necessary component of passing as disabled.

This complex interdependency of identities, signified in the text when William tells an inquiring traveler that his master suffers from "a complication of complaints," presents a troubling challenge to scholars of African American history. Both abolitionists and freedmen of the Crafts' time and African Americanist scholars and critics today appear deeply invested in the recuperation of the black body from a pathologizing and dehumanizing racism that often justified enslavement with arguments that people of African descent were inherently unable to take care of themselves—in other words, disabled.[7] Thus we find throughout nineteenth- and twentieth-century narratives and scholarship an emphasis on wholeness, uprightness, good health, and independence—all representational categories that the Crafts paradoxically needed to subvert in order to attain actual freedom.[8] As Jennifer James observes, "In post–Civil War African American literature particularly, it was imperative that the black body and the black 'mind' be portrayed as uninjured by the injuring institution of slavery in order to disprove one of the main antiblack arguments that surfaced after emancipation—that slavery had made blacks 'unfit' for citizenship, 'unfit' carrying a dual physical and psychological meaning" (15). With this awareness of the complicated and important history behind representations of disability in the African American context, it is never-theless important to elucidate the presence of disability in the Crafts' nar-rative to understand how the entwined fantasies of racial, gender, and dis-ability identification functioned both to enable their escape and to shape its subsequent interpretations.

Lindon Barrett, for example, argues that "the central act of the Crafts' escape is the removal of what is designated as an African American body from [a] position of meaninglessness to the condition of meaning and signification" (323). By claiming that the bodies of African Americans have been "taken as signs of nothing beyond themselves," Barrett recasts the function of whiteness in the Crafts' escape as providing not only lit-eral freedom but ontological existence. In contrast, Dawn Keetley sug-gests that Ellen's passing as a white man functions as "a concealment of any distinguishing features, rather than as a positive accrual of 'white' and 'male' features" (14). Thus Ellen's disguise—or at least the descrip-tions of her disguise in the narrative—"highlight what she is *not*" (14). Both of these analyses draw upon deconstructive theory to read race as a matter of a paradoxically absent presence or present absence. This analy-sis relies on Derrida's concept of the supplement, as that which is added to an apparently complete text but is actually necessary to its meaning, "the not-seen that opens and limits visibility" (163).

I suggest that not only is the supplement a useful concept for exam-ining the function of disability in the Crafts' narrative but that many critical analyses of the narrative also unconsciously rely upon disabil-ity as supplement. Sterling Lecater Bland, for example, discusses Ellen's mobility and agency without referencing her invalid disguise, instead emphasizing "Ellen's remarkable *ability* to challenge a series of raced, classed, and gendered associations" (*Voices* 148, my emphasis). Such a dynamic is also particularly noticeable in Barrett's repeated referrals to Ellen's bandaged hand in a paragraph ostensibly devoted to analysis of her racialized body:

Like the bandaged hand, the inscription of the white male figure on the black female body of Ellen is an essential element of the Crafts' escape. . . . *Like the bandaging of her hand*, Ellen's regender-ing refigures advantageously "the absence of a presence, and always already absent present" on which signification depends. . . . What is more, the transfiguring of Ellen's body, *like the bandaging of her hand*, divides her body. The new status of this body within the con-dition of meaning necessitates that it be divisible. *The bandaging*

of her hand and cropping of her hair redirect and redistribute the
interpretive gaze aimed at her. (331, my emphasis)

The mantra-like repetition of "the bandaged hand" in this paragraph
repeatedly evokes but endlessly defers the presence of disability as fundamental to Ellen's disguise—and thus to her racial meaning. In this
sense disability appears to function for Barrett, much as it functions
within the narrative, as the necessary "bridge" that enables racial and
gender mobility while itself remaining fixed and apparently immobile.
This dynamic can also be understood through Butler's concept of the
constitutive outside, "the excluded and illegible domain that haunts the
former domain as the spectre of its impossibility, the very limit to intelligibility" (*Bodies that Matter* xi). The pertinence of Butler's analysis to
this particular example is highlighted in her further clarification of the
constitutive outside as "a domain of unthinkable, abject, unlivable bodies" (xi). The extent to which the body marked by disability is unthinkable and even frightening for contemporary critics studying the Crafts'
narrative is captured in Barbara McCaskill's description of Ellen's bandaged face as a "facial monstrosity" ("Yours" 520).

McCaskill is referring to Ellen's "likeness," the engraved portrait
that was sold to raise money for the abolitionist cause even before the
publication of the Crafts' narrative, and which has accompanied every
published edition of the narrative (Fig. 1.1). The engraving shows the
head and upper body of what appears to be a smooth-faced young white
gentleman with curly dark hair escaping a top hat to cover his ears. He
is dressed in a black suit and stiff white collar, with a light-colored tartan plaid sash crisscrossing his front. His face is not bandaged, and the
"green spectacles" used during the escape appear to have been replaced
by a pair with clear lenses. The only remaining element of the invalid
disguise is the white sling, which no longer supports the figure's arm
but simply hangs around his neck, slightly tucked between elbow and
body. In this hanging position, parallel to the tartan sash, the sling looks
like another sash or scarf, its disability function obscured to the point of
invisibility.

The fact that this engraving purports to represent Ellen in her disguise
yet actually represents an adapted version of the disguise with all signs
of disability removed or obscured, has confounded many critics. Bland,
referring to William/the narrator's observation that "the poultice is left
off in the engraving, because the likeness could not have been taken
well with it on" (Craft and Craft 24), remarks, "What is unclear is whose

FIGURE 1.1. Ellen Craft in her adapted disguise. From Craft and Craft, *Running a Thousand Miles for Freedom*.

likeness would be obscured by the poultice. Is the engraving intended to represent Ellen, William's wife? Or is the engraving intended to show Ellen in the disguise she used to pass as a white gentleman traveling with his black slave? The engraving fully succeeds at neither, thus forcing the reader to ponder the reason for the apparent deviation" (Bland, *Voices* 150). While Bland does not offer an answer to this question, Ellen Weinauer concludes that the removal of the poultice suggests that "it would appear that the purpose of the engraving is to represent not 'Mr. Johnson,' but Ellen herself" (50). But if the purpose was to represent Ellen, why is she still dressed in her male costume? As Keetley observes, the picture does not show one "discernible race or gender," instead portraying "a permanent state of racial and gender ambiguity" (14).

I contend that the purpose of the portrait is to represent the "most respectable-looking gentleman" so beloved of critics—that is, to represent the aspects of Ellen's disguise that subvert nineteenth-century assumptions regarding the immutability of race and gender, while removing those aspects that even by implication show the African American body as unhealthy, dependent, and disabled. Thus McCaskill's characterization of a couple of bandages as a "monstrosity" is clarified by her claim that "[with] her bandaged maladies a mere and known pretense, Ellen's frontispiece portrait articulates the death of herself as a captive commodity and her resurrection as a wily, liberated subject" ("Yours" 516). Here McCaskill clearly applauds the removal of signs of disability and reads their removal metonymically as an indicator of freedom and autonomy.

The irony of obscuring or removing signs of disability from representations of Ellen is that disability, like race, has historically been viewed as a fixed bodily condition; it is not so easily removed as a bandage. Yet in the case of Ellen Craft, it appears at first that the performative, constructed nature of both disability and gender contrast with the seeming inherency of race. For Ellen must don bandages and spectacles to pass as disabled and must cut her hair and wear a suit to pass as a man, but apparently she need *do* nothing at all in order to pass as white. For she *is* white, if whiteness is defined purely by the color of her skin and texture of her hair.[9] An 1849 article in the Wisconsin *Free Democrat* insisted, "Let it not be understood that she is a Negro. Ellen Crafts [*sic*], though a slave, is white" (Keetley 18n17). By 1852 the abolitionist Rev. Frances Bishop could emphasize another slave woman's fairness, not with the common comparison to a British or southern white woman but simply by describing her as "quite as white as Ellen Craft," a sign of Ellen's resignification into a pure and reified whiteness (Armistead,

LAS 44).[10] Josephine Brown, daughter of the prominent abolitionist William Wells Brown, writes that "Ellen was as white as most persons of the clear Anglo-Saxon origin. Her features were prominent, hair straight, eyes of a light hazel color, and no one on first seeing the white slave would suppose that a drop of African blood coursed through her veins" (76).[11]

When Josephine Brown calls Ellen "the white slave," she is clearly not suggesting that Ellen is a European kidnapped into slavery but rather is making the common abolitionist point that racial justifications of slavery were becoming increasingly more difficult to support, due to the "visible, progressive 'whitening' of the slave body throughout the century" (Wiegman 47). For the idea of race as inherent and fixed was exactly contradictory to the aims of the Crafts' narrative and the abolitionist movement, both of which sought to display racial ambiguity precisely to "deauthorize racial categories" and thus counter a racially based system of slavery (Keetley 14; Bland, *Voices* 145). Instead representations of Ellen Craft function according to Marjorie Garber's claim for the transvestite (285), demonstrating how social anxiety regarding the idea of inherent bodily identity is displaced from race onto gender and class and finally—and most fundamentally—onto disability.

Representations of Ellen's whiteness in the abolitionist press were almost always accompanied by references to gender and class, as when William Wells Brown described an encounter between Ellen and Lady Byron in which the British noblewoman found that Ellen "was so white, and had so much the appearance of a well-bred and educated lady, that she could scarcely realize that she was in the presence of an American slave" (J. Brown 80–81). The invocation of Ellen as a genteel lady was echoed by Samuel May, general agent of the Anti-Slavery Society, when he wrote that Ellen appeared to be "a Southern-born white woman" and expressed extreme horror at the thought "of such a woman being held as a piece of property, subject to be traded off to the highest bidder" (Sterling 23–24). In this case, idealized (white) womanhood functions as supplement, a placeholder for social distinctions based on physical difference, so that racial difference may be shown to be an arbitrary legal construction. Weinauer makes this point forcefully in her critique of the Crafts' narrative, arguing that William Craft as narrator "insists, finally, on the natural status of gendered categories, writing Ellen into her proper place within them. Unlike the meanings assigned to race and class memberships, meanings that Craft presents as discursive, interested constructions, 'woman' is assigned a meaning that is fixed, immutable, and presumably disinterested" (38).

The role played here by gender in supplementing race is undeniable. Yet I suggest that the meanings ascribed to disability are even more "fixed and immutable" and that disability functions as the invisible, submerged supplement to the bodily realities of both gender and race—even, or perhaps especially, when disability is represented through the disability con. This entanglement of meanings emerges from both nineteenth-century and contemporary efforts to negotiate the paradox of the racial body: the dilemma of arguing that race is a social, constructed identity even while confronted with the reality of racially marked bodies.[12] In the case of Ellen Craft, race is at once shown to be arbitrary and constructed, since she is defined as black yet appears white, and physically inherent, since her body itself is all the disguise she needs to appear white. Here disability comes into play, as the social identity most strongly identified with physical difference and the body, to function as the necessary supplement that allows the bodily nature of race to be obscured. This shadow function of disability is to hold the fact of physicality, unmoored from social or representational meanings; its effect is to produce arguments that define race and disability as separate and virtually incompatible entities, when in fact they are deeply connected and mutually constitutive.

Consider the topic of literacy, a central theme of African American literature from its inception, and certainly a key factor in the Crafts' narrative. Discussions of literacy and illiteracy are by definition discussions of ability and disability—the ability to read and write, or its lack. The disability of illiteracy profoundly impacted the lives of formerly enslaved authors like the Crafts and Frederick Douglass; the acquisition of literacy is a material and symbolic triumph that resounds from Douglass's *Narrative* to Richard Wright's *Black Boy* and beyond. Yet to discuss illiteracy as disability resonates with centuries of characterizations of African Americans as flawed or defective, incapable of acquiring the ability that has come to equal personhood in post-Enlightenment Western culture.[13] Such characterizations came as much from white proponents of slave rights as from slave owners, as in the quotation from *The New England Anti-Slavery Almanac for 1841* that Charles T. Davis and Henry Louis Gates Jr. use as the epigraph to their landmark study *The Slave's Narrative*:

"Things for the Abolitionist to Do"

1. Speak for the Slave, . . .
2. Write for the Slave, . . .
"They can't take care of themselves." (4)

In his extended discussion of literacy in the Crafts' narrative, Barrett argues that literacy is a more powerful sign of whiteness than the white body itself, that "light or racially ambiguous skin is ultimately insufficient as an 'ontological' marker of whiteness" (324). Thus he complicates the claim that Ellen need "do" nothing to appear white, when whiteness is understood as a social identity predicated upon literacy. Here Barrett teeters on the edge of an analysis of the mutually constitutive nature of race and disability, noting that the bandaging of Ellen's hand "is the indispensable correlate to Ellen's racially ambiguous skin. In this context it is the ultimate sign of whiteness" (326–327). But to Barrett, the social meanings mobilized by Ellen's bandaged hand are stable and fixed: it will be "read not as a sign of illiteracy but as a sign of illness that will earn her credibility and sympathy" (325). The deflection of possible intellectual disability onto physical disability is, for Barrett, inescapably tied to the fact of whiteness. He essentially equates the bandaged hand, a physical sign of the inability to write, with the visible fact of black skin, also at that time assumed to signify the inability to write. Such an equation at once hints at the importance of examining intersections of race and disability and excludes such an examination.

For Ellen Craft, displacing the disability of illiteracy onto a physical impairment enables her escape from slavery by allowing her to travel as a white man: it allows her to function as a mobile subject. The complex relation of literacy and mobility, and its necessary connection to disability, is apparent in the contrasting circumstance of Harriet Jacobs in her well-known 1861 narrative, *Incidents in the Life of a Slave Girl*. Even while confined to a tiny crawlspace, Jacobs was able to employ her literacy to manipulate her former owner and obtain her children's freedom by writing false notes to be mailed from various locations. Both women brilliantly played upon assumptions about their abilities to achieve freedom; Jacobs, however, suffered long-term physical effects from her long confinement, while Ellen Craft was able to learn to read and write and thus shed the disability of illiteracy. So disability in each case was neither fixed nor immutable but existed as a shifting, contingent identity. And in each case, disability surfaced in relation to race through the issues of literacy and mobility.

Multiple Identities, Multiple Representations

We can see this dynamic, as well as the continued entanglement of gender, race, and disability, in the numerous "retellings" and adaptations of the Crafts' escape. Not only did the Crafts tell their story on the abolitionist stage countless times during the nearly twelve years before publication of their narrative, but a number of authors retold or adapted their tale in the cause of abolition, and, later, racial pride and historical memory. Probably the first of these "retellings" was Williams Wells Brown's letter to the abolitionist newspaper the *Liberator* on January 12, 1849, about two weeks after the Crafts arrived in Boston (Craft and Craft 76). Brown describes the disguise in an order reflecting his own probable assumptions about the importance of social identities: first, he tells us that "Ellen is so nearly white, that she can pass without suspicion for a white woman." Then he informs us that "Ellen dressed in men's clothing," and finally, about halfway through his letter, Brown mentions that Ellen "tied her right hand up as though it was lame." Even this brief allusion to disability appears to require immediate recuperation, as Brown immediately adds, "which proved to be of service to her, as she was called upon several times at hotels to 'register' her name," thus foregrounding the substitution of one ability for another—the ability to pass for the ability to read and write. Brown's account reflects simultaneously a heightened consciousness of race and gender passing and a submerged anxiety regarding disability passing, especially by an enslaved African American.

When Brown later adapted the Crafts' story for his 1853 novel *Clotel; or, The President's Daughter*, he similarly downplayed the element of disability and, to a certain extent, gender in the disguise. His character, Clotel, has lived a privileged existence as a white man's mistress before being enslaved, so she is presumably literate and thus need not bind up her arm. Probably to accord with his characterization of Clotel as a highly refined, sentimental, and modest Victorian heroine, Brown also downplays her choice of man's clothing for the disguise, portraying this element as largely a product of Clotel's cruel and jealous mistress having forced her to cut her hair short. Interestingly, though, Brown's Clotel also expresses a sentiment entirely absent in the Crafts' own account, as the character of William (in this version only an acquaintance) tells her, "You look a good deal like a man with your short hair." Clotel responds, "I have often been told that I would make a better looking man than a woman. If I had the money I would bid farewell to this place" (141).

The first half of this response expresses a rather radical notion of gender crossing for our Victorian heroine, while the second half strangely equates male appearance with the ability to escape, as if Brown had never heard of the countless women who escaped from slavery.[14] This is a rare moment when Brown's sentimental, abolitionist authorial mask slips to offer tantalizing glimpses of a more individual view that both expands and forecloses the possibilities of gender. It is not surprising that, immediately following this comment, Brown tells us that Clotel "feared that she had said too much" (141).

Clotel also uses the same alias as Ellen Craft, "Mr. Johnson," and Brown actually reproduces a newspaper correspondent's eyewitness account of Ellen's disguise as if it referred to his fictional heroine (*Clotel* 145–146).[15] And like Ellen, Clotel travels as an invalid, wearing green glasses, tying a white silk handkerchief around her head, and pretending "to be very ill" (143). Yet without the bandaged hand necessitated by illiteracy, Brown's heroine does not need to perform disability in the repeated and proliferative manner of Ellen Craft; she does not pretend to faint, feign deafness, limp, or stagger around dramatically as in the Crafts' narrative. Brown's downplaying of disability here is probably motivated by his dislike for portraying his slave heroes as weak or damaged, an interpretation that is strengthened by the revisions he made when he republished his novel in 1864. In this version Brown greatly shortened his account of the escape and removed disability completely from the disguise, omitting the bandages and including the green glasses as part of his heroine's "gentlemanly appearance" rather than as a sign of invalidism (*Clotelle* 47).[16] (Although the heroine keeps to her stateroom "under a plea of illness," the idea that she is actually playing the role of an invalid is never mentioned in this version.) These changes suggest a retreat from the disability aspects of the Crafts' story prompted by the postbellum need to present the newly emancipated African American subject as healthy, independent, and worthy of freedom, in opposition to proslavery claims that freedom was unhealthy and even disabling for African Americans, producing, in one southern physician's words, "a beautiful harvest of mental and physical degradation" (Baynton 39). Without the necessary factor of illiteracy, other devices of disability such as the bandaged hand, limp, and feigned deafness are easily sloughed off from Brown's conception of the necessary and acceptable components of a slave's triumphant escape. (I would argue that, then as now, signs of disability are viewed as acceptable *only* when necessary.)

This dynamic is taken even further in another adaptation of the Crafts' story in the 1858 play *The Stars and Stripes: A Melo-drama* by the white abolitionist and feminist Lydia Maria Child. Like Brown, Child chooses to make the Crafts literate, and thus erases the element of disability from their disguise. In fact Child aggressively foregrounds her characters' literacy, portraying William reading aloud about freedom from the newspaper and Ellen writing a pass for another slave to use for his escape (141, 147). This characterization is of a piece with Child's choice to make *both* of the Crafts light-skinned, clearly seeking to portray them to a white audience as "refined" in every aspect. As a northern abolitionist character says to Ellen, "No one would believe that you were not a white woman," and William is described in the stage directions as a "genteel-looking light mulatto" (165, 123).

There is no mention of disability or illness in Child's portrayal of the Crafts' escape, but illness enters her play in another fashion, when her comic white proslavery characters speak of "drapetomania" as the reason that William and Ellen ran away:

MASTERS: The fact is, sir, the niggers are a very singular race. They have several diseases, peculiar to themselves. The one which prevails most *generally*, is called by our doctors, drapetomania; and the only way I can account for this strange affair, is by supposing that Bill and Nellie had an attack of that *disease*.

NORTH: Pray what sort of disease may that be, sir?

MASTERS: It means a mania for running away. . . . The learned Dr. Cartwright, of Louisiana University, has written a celebrated book about nigger diseases. He advises that the whip should be freely applied for the first symptoms of drapetomania. He calls it "whipping the devil out of 'em." But the fact is, I never perceived any symptoms of it in Bill. He always seemed healthy. It is a very singular disease, that drapetomania! There's no telling who may be seized by it. Some of the planters think it is becoming epidemic.   (173–174)[17]

Child reverses the actual circumstances of the Crafts' escape: rather than portraying healthy slaves *pretending* to be ill, she portrays healthy slaves being *labeled* as ill by their white oppressors. Since we are clearly meant to mock and disbelieve the white proslavery characters, their very insistence on William and Ellen as "diseased" (the word *disease* appears seven times during the full exchange) is meant to convey the fugitives' supreme healthiness—and by extension, the healthy and natural character of freedom itself. Showing Ellen as a bandaged and hobbling invalid would severely undercut this message, and so Child foregoes the tremendous dramatic potential of the disguise in favor of conventional didacticism.

Child instead invents various disguises and other tricks to liven up the escape. Most notably she creates a third character, Jim, who escapes from slavery at the same time as the Crafts. Jim is everything that Child's William and Ellen are not: they are light-skinned, and he is dark; they speak in standard, genteel English, and he speaks in comic dialect; they deliver earnest, sentimental speeches, and he sings humorous ditties and capers in stereotypical "darky" fashion. Child is clearly catering to her northern audience's expectations. It is as if she is trapped by competing stereotypes: heroes must be sympathetic, so they must be light-skinned, but a play about "Negroes" must include "darky humor," so Jim enters to mimic the Crafts like a doppelganger formed from the dark pigment that has been literally excised from William's skin. Such "mimicry is also the sign of the inappropriate . . . a difference or recalcitrance which coheres the dominant strategic function of colonial power, intensifies surveillance, and poses an immanent threat to both 'normalized' knowledges and disciplinary powers" (Bhabha 86).

This intensive surveillance is apparent in a scene in which Jim appears to "shadow" the Crafts during their escape, at a point when William and Ellen are hiding in the woods and singing a sentimental verse:

[While they are singing, a black face peeps out from between the boards, and watches them curiously for a minute, and is then lighted up with a broad smile. The head is withdrawn behind the boards, and presently, when all is still, a voice is heard singing:]

"Jim crack corn—don't care!
Ole massa's gone away!"

[William and Ellen start, and look behind them.]

WILLIAM: I could almost swear that was Jim's voice.
ELLEN: You know *all* the slaves sing that. It can't be that Jim is
   here.   (158–159)

Jim appears here as the dark other that haunts the Crafts, the anonymous "black face" that substitutes for personhood in nineteenth-century white conceptions of African Americans. He is further associated with an anonymous dark-skinned mass in Ellen's claim that *"all* the slaves sing" the song Jim is using to signal them, and William and Ellen's singularity is emphasized by the fact that they are *not* singing that traditional song. In the absence of disability, Jim seems to represent racial bodily difference in an exaggerated extreme, so that the Crafts may remain heroically "white."

However, the racial erasure and rematerialization produced in the play appears to collapse back upon itself when the three fugitives must escape into Canada, pursued, like the real Crafts, by their former owners under the Fugitive Slave Act. In Child's version, William and Ellen must be "stained black" to escape recognition. Meanwhile Jim must vanish altogether, since he "can't be stained any blacker" (176). The fugitives join a group of mourners, and Jim is actually carried inside a coffin—a trick possibly inspired by the notorious 1849 escape of Henry Box Brown who shipped himself to freedom in a wooden crate. Jim also hides under an icehouse while Ellen and William picnic with abolitionists above, her identity hidden by a veil and his by a "brown wig" (163–165). Again Child invents disguises and subterfuges to replace those actually used by the Crafts and in doing so splits them in two and buries the darker half in a cellar, a move strangely reminiscent of Charlotte Brontë's madwoman in the attic, and liable to similar interpretations as those of feminists who see the lunatic, mixed-race Bertha as personifying the exiled rage and sexuality of the pallid Victorian heroine Jane Eyre.[18] Yet, by the play's closing scenes, William and Ellen are not only stained black but "locked up in a tomb" along with Jim, to escape with him into Canada the next day. Without disability to function as bodily supplement, the play finally constructs race as an inescapable and confining fact, the "drop of black blood" in William and Ellen's veins binding them inexorably to racial otherness.

We may contrast this portrayal with that of Georgia Douglas Johnson's *William and Ellen Craft: A Play in One Act*, published in 1935. Johnson portrays the Crafts speaking in dialect, reflecting a newfound valuation of African American cultural specificity and language traditions (McCaskill in Craft and Craft 106). And while it seems at first that Johnson's retelling will also omit disability from the disguise, since William initially describes the plan as involving only gender crossing, this does not prove to be the case:

ELLEN (*going up to William trembling*): You sho you kin get us through, William?

WILLIAM: Sho honey; ain't I been on the train time and time again wid young Marse, an' can't I read and write?

ELLEN: But how kin I be like young Marse? I'm all a shakin' now.

WILLIAM (*soothing her*): All you got to do is walk. You don't have to talk,

you don't have to do a thing but just walk along bigity like a white
man. See here. (*Shows her how to walk.*) Try it.

ELLEN (*tries to walk like him*): Dis way?

WILLIAM: You doin fine! You see now you is supposed to be sick, you
got a toothache, you goin' to a doctor in Philadelphia, you is nearly deaf, an' yo' nigger slave is taking you—understand? (Johnson
173–174)

Johnson depicts William as hyper-able: able to conceive of the plan, able
to read and write, able to show Ellen how to walk like a white man and
to bolster her failing spirits. The sudden proliferation of impairments in
the end of this conversation appears seemingly from nowhere—neither
Ellen's illiteracy nor its arm-sling solution are even mentioned—but is
symbolically produced as the feminized abject other to William's hyper-
able masculinity. Disability and stereotyped femininity are both stabilized here to supplement the racial pride and empowerment that appear
as Johnson's primary theme and motivation for her play.

Like Johnson's, most narratives of the Crafts' escape portray William as the primary devisor and motivator of the disguise and Ellen as
requiring persuasion and assistance. This is certainly true of the Crafts'
own narrative, in which William tells us, "After I thought of the plan,
I suggested it to my wife, but at first she shrank from the idea" (Craft
and Craft 21). In contrast, Josephine Brown's account of the escape in
her 1856 biography of her father, William Wells Brown, emphatically
reverses these roles:

"Now, William," said the wife, "listen to me, and take my advice,
and we shall be free in less than a month."

"Let me hear your plans, then," said William.

"Take part of your money and purchase me a good suit of gentleman's apparel. . . . I am white enough to go as a master, and you can
pass as my servant."

"But you are not tall enough for a man," said the husband.

"Get me a pair of very high-heeled boots, and they will bring
me up more than an inch, and get me a very high hat, then I'll do,"
rejoined the wife.

"But then, my dear you would make a very boyish looking man,
with no whiskers or mustache," remarked William.

"I could bind up my face in a handkerchief," said Ellen, "as if I
was suffering dreadfully from the toothache, and no one would discover the want of beard."

"What if you were called upon to write your name in the books at hotels, as I saw my master do when traveling, or were asked to receipt for any thing?"

"I would also bind up my right hand and put it in a sling. . . . "

"I fear you cannot carry out the deception for so long a time, for it must be several hundred miles to the free States," said William, as he seemed to despair of escaping from slavery by following his wife's plan.

"Come, William," entreated his wife, "don't be a coward!"

(76–77)

I have reproduced this account at length since it provides such a dramatically contrasting view, not only to the Crafts' narrative—which, after all, was published four years later than this account and thus can achieve only a tenuous status as the "original"—but to William Wells Brown's own account discussed earlier.[19] While William L. Andrews, in his introduction to Josephine Brown's *Biography of an American Bondsman*, characterizes the work as "primarily a digest of her father's autobiographical writings . . . [offering] little information about her subject that was genuinely new," her chapter devoted to the Crafts certainly presents a far different account from that given by her father in his letter to the *Liberator* (Andrews, introduction xxxiii). One can only speculate as to the source of Josephine Brown's unorthodox version of the Crafts' story. Certainly she must have heard their story told many times in the seven years intervening between her father's letter and her book's publication, since the Crafts were touring with her father on the abolitionist circuit. However, accounts of the Crafts' appearances, both in the United States and England, concur that William was always the spokesman and Ellen spoke only when entreated by the audience.[20] Without further historical evidence, it is impossible to know whether Brown's account was based on private conversations with Ellen or whether its peculiar nature stemmed from her own stymied feminist sensibility, straining at the confines of "acceptable" black female writing of her time, and particularly frustrated with confining her writing to memorializing her famous father. In either case it is clear that Josephine Brown's account should lead us to view with healthy skepticism portrayals of Ellen Craft as passive and meek and William as active and strong.[21]

Looking closely at Josephine Brown's account, we may discover evidence for her impatience with gender inequities.[22] She adds a problem and a solution never mentioned in the Crafts' or other accounts, when William objects that Ellen is "not tall enough for a man" and Ellen responds by demanding "high-heeled boots" and "a very high hat." Being "not tall enough for a man" appears, to Brown's William, a more immediate objection than clothing, hair, smooth cheeks, or even illiteracy—all the elements that contribute to the disguise in the Crafts' account. Symbolically being "not tall enough for a man" suggests the devaluing and underestimating of Ellen's authority; practically it presents a problem of normalization that demands prosthetic adjustment. Significantly disability appears here not as a mask or bandage placed upon the body but as a condition inherent in the body that must be "fixed" to meet social expectations.

Many historians have noted that constructions of femininity in the nineteenth century and beyond characterized the female body as inherently deficient, unhealthy, and abnormal.[23] Additionally, in the nineteenth century there was a proliferation of medical claims that women would become disabled by education or political participation, as in claims that overeducated women's "reproductive organs are dwarfed, deformed, weakened, and diseased" and that "enfranchising women would result in a twenty-five percent increase in insanity among them" (Baynton 42). These arguments often pointed to reading and writing as activities that would exacerbate women's inherent frailty and tendency toward disease (Herndl 78). As a black woman claiming authorship, Josephine Brown contended not only with the oppressive relationship of femininity and disability but with parallel claims regarding the very humanity of African Americans. It is not surprising, then, that while she was engaged in so radical (for her time) a project as authoring a biography, questions of power and authority subtly emerged between the lines of her "purely factual" account.[24]

Enclosing the Invalid

To further explore these mutual interweavings of race, gender, and disability through issues of authority and power, I will close with an examination of the racial dimensions of the particular disability con performed by the Crafts. It is clear that William's presence as the servant of "Mr. Johnson" is as fundamental to Ellen's successful performance of invalidism as are the sling, poultice, and green spectacles she wears. For instance, one of Ellen's proliferating impairments is a difficulty in walking, apparently produced not by logistical necessity (like the bandaged hand or face) but simply because such infirmity is part of the expected invalid role. This disability is primarily performed by William, who ostentatiously assists Ellen when entering and leaving buildings and train carriages (Craft and Craft 34, 36, 48). This performance shores up the image of Ellen as a feeble invalid and thus ironically reinforces her male persona; since conventionally women would be assisted in this fashion, William's chivalry would undermine Ellen's male disguise were the gesture not naturalized by her adoption of the feminized invalid persona (and by the racial assumption that white women did not lean upon black men). By appearing to assist Ellen in walking, William functions as a sign of her impaired legs, much as the bandage on her hand signifies its impairment. This apparent interchangeability of William with nonverbal signs such as a cane, crutch, or invalid (wheeled) chair at once objectifies him and undermines that objectification through the reader's knowledge that he is in fact a speaking subject engaged in a daring rebellion.[25]

William's agency is more apparent when he performs Ellen's disability in her absence. On the steamer from Savannah to Charleston, when his "master" turns in early, William explains that "as the captain and some of the passengers seemed to think this strange and also questioned me respecting him, my master thought I had better get out the flannels and opodeldoc which we had prepared for the rheumatism, warm them quickly by the stove in the gentleman's saloon, and bring them to his berth" (Craft and Craft 30). Clearly the performance of disability falls as much to William as to his "master"; when William responds to the passengers' questions with a public display of his role as caretaker to a white invalid, he reenacts Ellen's feigned deafness of the previous scene. In both cases the Crafts deflect attention by mobilizing white assumptions regarding the validity and presumptive innocence of illness. At the hotel in Charleston, William again makes a public display of heating the bandages, ensuring that Ellen receives the best service and sympathy of the proprietors, even as William himself is treated with the usual disdain (34). Afterward, on the train to Richmond, a white passenger questions William before joining Ellen in her carriage: "He wished to know what was the matter with [my master], where he was from, and where he was going" (38). In a reversal of the usual nineteenth-century white assumptions about white and black reliability, the passenger appears to seek validation from William before speaking to his "master" directly. This reversal appears in another white passenger's first-person account, in which he privileges William's information about "Mr. Johnson's" condition over his own observation that the invalid "walked rather too gingerly for a person afflicted with so many ailments" (Sterling 15).[26] In this instance William's role as servant is more crucial to the deception than Ellen's apparently imperfect acting of her part.

Once the Crafts reach freedom, however, the caretaking relationship between subordinate servant and invalid master must be restored to its "natural" form of husband caring for (subordinate) wife. Weinauer comments on the necessity of representing Ellen as an ideal Victorian woman to compensate for the dangerous gender transgression of the preceding narrative in which Ellen not only dresses as a man but is referred to as "he" and "my master" (Weinauer 38–48). To accomplish this task, ironically Ellen is narratively transformed into the very white invalid she was pretending to be: highly sentimentalized, weak, genteel, and sensitive.[27] Even as their train approaches Philadelphia, Ellen begins to take on this role. During a brief stop, she is filled with "terror and trembling" because William is not there to help her from the carriage (Craft and Craft 48).

Once the Crafts arrive on free soil, Ellen, now "wife" again in William's narration, "burst into tears, leant upon me, and wept like a child . . . [She was] so weak and faint that she could scarcely stand alone" (Craft and Craft 50). She is subsequently described in the narrative as "nervous and timid" (52), having "unstrung nerves" (53), and "unwell" (66). Biographer Dorothy Sterling amplifies this account: "The next days were a blur to Ellen. She had moments of exhilaration, when, once more in women's clothing, she tossed the bits and pieces of her disguise around the room. Then reaction set in, and the sleepless nights and anxious days took their toll. Exhausted physically and emotionally, she rested in her room at the boarding house, while news of the Crafts' escape spread to antislavery circles in the city" (19). In Sterling's description, Ellen is confined like an invalid woman to her bedroom, discursively and physically isolated as "the news" spreads without her. This immobility is emphasized on the next page of Sterling's biography, when the Crafts are urged to leave Philadelphia for Boston, but Ellen is "physically very much prostrated" and needs to rest before making another move (20).

During the Crafts' subsequent voyage to England, William tells us that Ellen "was very poorly, and was also so ill on the voyage that I did not believe she could live to see Liverpool. However," he adds, "after laying up at Liverpool very ill over two or three weeks, [she] gradually recovered" (Craft and Craft 66). Sterling again amplifies this account with imagery of motion and confinement: "Ellen spent the crossing in a dark, crowded cabin in the hold of the ship, seasick and feverish, while William paced the deck, wondering if she would survive" (37). Like the character of Jim trapped in the coffin in Child's play, Ellen becomes narratively consigned to immobility and darkness, despite having just pulled off one of the lengthiest and most daring escapes in fugitive slave history. And, as in Child's play, this symbolic confinement resonates with the struggle to reconcile race as free signifier with race as bodily fact, and disability emerges as the product and anchor of that struggle.

There appears to be no question that Ellen experienced bouts of physical illness during her life after slavery. However, the ways she is described not only in her narrative but by biographers and abolitionists seem significant beyond their basis in her physical experience. For example, "in letters to a member of the Boston Female Anti-Slavery Society, Mary Estlin . . . said of Ellen 'I think Ellen's health has never sufficiently recovered the shock of their cruel persecution in Boston to make her equal to all the tossing about she has since had to encounter and I'm never so happy as when she is under our immediate protection'" (Sterling 41). An abolitionist wrote of the attempt to kidnap William and Ellen under the Fugitive Slave Act in Boston in 1850, "Somebody took care of Ellen Craft. William less needed help; he armed himself with pistols . . . and walked in the streets in the face of the sun" (qtd. in Craft and Craft 100). Ellen needs "protection"; she needs to be taken "care" of. Certainly these descriptions are inflected by gender and race, by assumptions about frail females and dependent slaves. But those inflections intersect with statements about Ellen's health to portray her in reality as the invalid we previously knew as a fraudulent construction.[28] Thus at the very moment of the successful manipulation of fantasies of identification to achieve freedom, those fantasies emerge ironically with the apparent power to redefine the resistant subject into her immobilized double.

The centrality of the disability con to Ellen Craft's masquerade demonstrates how disability, race, and gender became mutually entangled in the production of both crises of identification and their fantastic solutions. Before turning to other examples of that entanglement in parts II and III, however, extended discussion of the disability con is warranted. Such discussion is crucial for two reasons: first, as indicated in this chapter, analyses of race and gender in American culture have rarely integrated disability as an equally constructed and significant social category, and thus focused attention to disability is needed to set the stage for discussions of how these identities combine into modern fantasies of identification. Second, as in the preceding discussion of Ellen

Craft's disguise, I will continue to highlight the supplementary dynamic in which disability is not merely another factor entwined with race and gender but often functions in a supplementary role to anchor physical difference. Thus I argue that racial and gendered difference is repeatedly found to be identifiable only through and against the disabled body, and further consideration of the complex constitution of that body is a vital first step.

2 / Confidence in the Nineteenth Century

From the entanglements and potent implications of Ellen Craft's masquerade, we now move to consideration of the disability con writ large, in its peculiarly prominent cultural emergence in the middle of the nineteenth century. Just four years after the Crafts' escape, on July 8, 1849, an article appeared in the *New York Herald* describing the crimes of one William Thompson, better known as the "Confidence Man."[1] While Thompson himself quickly faded from historical record, the moniker of confidence (or con) man persists to this day, describing a type of wily swindler whose success derives from his manipulation of others' perceptions. Yet the central significance of disability in portrayals of the con man has rarely been noted or integrated into the many cogent analyses of how this figure emerged in the mid-nineteenth-century United States as a symbol of growing social anxieties driven by rapid changes in personal and geographic mobility, urbanization, and the breakdown of class- and appearance-based systems of knowledge.[2] These intersecting anxieties, which I have described as the crisis of identification, included deep fears about the deceptive potentials of disabled bodies, and thus cultural portrayals of con men have included the disability con as a central and recurring element.[3] By examining one key literary portrayal of the disability con man, in Melville's 1857 novel, *The Confidence Man: His Masquerade*, this chapter introduces some of the key tensions integral to fantasies of identification: tensions between body and text, truth and appearance, science and social relationships.

The Confidence Man is notable for a proliferation of characters with real and assumed physical disabilities, which has only recently garnered critical attention.[4] Attention to the disability con in the novel thus is an ideal window into the relationship of disability to the social crisis of mobility and belief that produced the figure of the con man.[5] Melville's manipulation of disability in his novel points to the inherence of bodily identity in the growing problem of how to manage social relations between individuals no longer clearly regulated into economic and physical spheres, and thus no longer easily identifiable. Like Samuel Otter, I read Melville's novel "as a revealing structure that shows how nineteenth-century Americans articulated their world" (*Melville's Anatomies* 3); however, I argue that the disabled body is as crucial to such analysis as the raced and classed body, and that in fact these bodily formations are intimately and inseparably enmeshed. As Lennard J. Davis observes, "disability, as we know the concept, is really a socially driven relation to the body that became relatively organized in the eighteenth and nineteenth centuries" (*Enforcing Normalcy* 3). Published in 1857, *The Confidence Man* testifies to a country and culture not only verging on massive racial and economic disruption but also navigating a fundamental transformation of perceptions and attitudes toward disability that eventually produced our modern systems of rehabilitation and social entitlements.[6] This transformation, predicated on the fantasy of easily identifiable and governable disabled bodies, notably coincided with the emergence of the confidence man as an influential cultural figure.

As Deborah Stone notes, the codification of "disability" as a coherent social category was integrally tied to notions of deception (23). Stone observes that the need to regulate both disability and vagrancy—two historically entwined concepts—emerged during the transition to modern capitalism as a response to greater social and physical mobility. She makes this point particularly with regard to begging: "Given its connection to deception, at least in the common understanding, the phenomenon of begging must have been a threat to the social order in another very profound way. It challenged people's *confidence* that they could know the truth" (33, my emphasis). Stone's conclusions indicate the importance of disability for understanding the confidence man as a figure for cultural anxieties over issues of identity, truth, and community (Halttunen 1–7; Lenz 22; Lindberg 5).

The remarkable correspondence between the history of disability and that of the confidence man suggests that the presence of characters with disabilities in Melville's novel is crucial to his exploration of "American social activity [as] a confidence game" (Lindberg 45). In fact I argue that the trope of disability functions centrally in Melville's exploration of the real and the fake, body and text, truth and language. By portraying his characters' physical disabilities as uncertain, contested, and linguistically constructed, he interpellates the reader into a system of confidence in which identity and truth are integrally linked to bodily form. And by connecting those figures to the central character of the confidence man, a wily and articulate antihero, Melville both enacts and undermines the historical linkage between disability and victimhood, embodied in the figure of the pathetic disabled beggar.

Thus the novel not only portrays the new American figure of the con man but provides a new version of a historically persistent character: the fake-disabled swindler. As Stone's observations suggest, this character has been most persistently associated with begging. We can read the long European history of the fake-disabled beggar in *The Prince and the Pauper*'s sixteenth-century characters, "the Bat and Dick Dot-and-go-One," and find evidence of these figures' nineteenth-century import by their appearance in Twain's 1881 novel. And in the world of *The Confidence Man* we can see considerable social tension around the issue of fraudulent beggars, such as the character Mark Winsome's response to a Poe-like beggar, whom he calls "a cunning vagabond, who picks up a vagabond living by adroitly playing the madman" (168).

Yet the version of the fake-disabled swindler that emerges through the figure of the con man is significantly different from the previous stereotype of the fake-disabled beggar. In both Stone's historical survey and Twain's fictional presentation, the fake-disabled beggar appears as a shifty vagrant who, having already occupied or been consigned to the social role of beggar, then seeks to increase his or her profits by playing on public sympathy for the disabled. The disability con man, by contrast, refuses to occupy any stable social role: he plays on social categories of identity through manipulation and masquerade, thus destabilizing fixed notions of ability/disability, rich/poor, and hero/villain. He refuses the victimhood traditionally associated with beggars and instead positions himself as mocking social critic.

I am speaking here primarily of the disability con man as he appears in American literature and culture, as a symbolic actor and literary convention that has both reflected and shaped our social conceptions in the past two centuries. Yet we can see the intersection of this shadowy cultural figure with the material, everyday world, from Hollywood films to television news exposés to Social Security benefits hearings. The distinction I have suggested between the age-old figure of the beggar and the relatively new figure of the disability con man is mirrored in contemporary law enforcement, as in the title of a 1993 article from *Police Chief* magazine, "The Street Beggar: Victim or Con Artist?" (Luckenbach 126).

As I discuss in chapter 3, the power of this new figure is such that, by the late twentieth century, the disability con man had become so ubiquitous (and popular) a figure in contemporary film and television that one can hardly find a visual narrative about the confidence game that does not incorporate some element of the disability con. It seems that one trope simply cannot appear without the other, so entwined have they become in our cultural imagination. Furthermore this entwinement implies the reversal of its terms: if con men almost always pretend to be disabled, maybe disabled people are especially prone to con games. Such representational logic both reflects and shores up the "guilty until proven innocent" attitude that frames much modern discourse about physical ability: one is often assumed to be faking a disability unless and until it has been proved by either medical certification or obvious physical signs. Both means of proof are manipulated and challenged in *The Confidence Man*, and this novel offers a rich ground for an exploration of the origins and symbolic frameworks of the disability con.

Seeing the Disability Con

A number of disabled or fake-disabled figures appear in *The Confidence Man*, several of whom are generally interpreted as various guises or avatars of the confidence man himself. I will focus primarily on three characters, the mute, Black Guinea, and Thomas Fry (the "soldier of fortune"), introducing other characters as they relate to or illuminate these central figures. By analyzing these characters in the framework of cultural attitudes toward disability, I am departing from the general practice of Melville critics (and most literary critics to date) of treating disabilities as metaphors for other aspects of character—such as race, class, or political affiliation—rather than as being about disability itself.[7] In doing so, I am not denying the force of such metaphors or Melville's undeniable use of them; rather I am suggesting that such analyses are necessarily incomplete without a consideration of why and how various disabilities have come to signify certain symbolic properties—a consideration that necessitates analysis of the creation and mediation of the category of disability itself. This becomes an even more complex undertaking when the category under discussion is that of fake disability.

Helen Trimpi, for instance, offers a compelling interpretation of both "crippled" Black Guinea and the "man with the wooden leg" as figures for political campaigners. She cites the 1860 cartoon reproduced in Figure 2.1 to demonstrate that "it is fairly common in political cartoons of this period to represent a candidate for office as crippled in one or both legs—*i.e.*, having to 'stump it'" (Trimpi 51, plate 24).

Yet a closer examination of the cartoon shows that the figure apparently using a wooden leg (Stephen Douglas) has two intact legs of his own and is merely kneeling upon the wooden leg. Similarly his opponent Breckenridge (though depicted leaning upon a cane, with a bandaged foot) also has intact legs, even as he is handed a wooden leg and told that "as Dug has taken the stump you must stump it too." Thus these figures are not actually figures of disability, but of *the disability con*, meaning that the symbolic meaning they convey is twofold: the surface suggestion of "crippledom" carries associations of weakness, dependency, and victimhood, while the underlying message of "conning" voters implies deceit, fraud, and cunning. The conflation of these two symbolic meanings, which is evident in both the original cartoon and Trimpi's interpretation, demonstrates the potency and persistence of the cultural confusion between "real" and "fake" disabilities. At no point in Trimpi's otherwise excellent analysis does she mention the fact that *no one in the cartoon is actually missing a leg.* Nor does she distinguish in her analysis of the novel's characters between Black Guinea's apparently fake stumps and the man with the wooden leg's apparently real one.

Apparently is a key term here, of course. It is difficult, if not impossible, to pin down any reality in Melville's novel: "Interpretation is a labyrinthine entanglement that yields no firm or definite result" (Bellis 166). Yet if we continue to keep the word "real" in quotation marks, we may attempt to distinguish between various layers of reality within the novel's complex and shifting narrative. For example, it seems extremely likely that Black Guinea is an avatar of the confidence man; therefore neither his disability nor his blackness are "real." Similarly it appears very likely that the soldier of fortune's disability is "real," due both to the appearance of his "interwoven paralyzed legs, stiff as icicles," and to his narrative presentation, which lacks the irony accompanying descriptions of such characters as Black Guinea and the mute (*The Confidence Man* 79).

The mute, who appears in the opening sentence of the novel, remains a somewhat more ambiguous figure than either Black Guinea or the soldier of fortune. While a majority of critics consider the mute to be the

FIGURE 2.1. "'Taking the Stump' or Stephen in Search of His Mother."
Reproduced by permission of the Huntington Library, San Marino, California.

first avatar of the confidence man, there is certainly no consensus. The significance of the mute remains a subject of speculation and disagreement among Melville critics today, much as it is to the "miscellaneous company" in the novel who gather around his sleeping figure in chapter 2; however, all agree that the mute "means something" (*The Confidence Man* 4).[8] I would like to suggest that the mute functions as a portent of the novel's ongoing concern with issues of physical ability and bodily integrity—a concern that, intertwined with racial, gendered, and economic factors, was at the core of the national struggle to define an American self in Melville's time.

Although the title of the opening chapter, "A mute goes aboard a boat on the Mississippi," prepares the reader to immediately encounter a character who cannot speak, the mute's muteness goes unsignified until he produces his slate in the fifth paragraph. In contrast, the mute is at once marked racially as white by the insistent repetition of light colors: he wears "cream-colors," his cheek is "fair," his hair "flaxen," and his hat is made of "white" fur (*The Confidence Man* 1). In addition, the mute is marked as a vagrant, that is, one who lacks the elements of ownership and independence that define the American bourgeois citizen and who is therefore set apart from society: "He had neither trunk, valise, carpet bag, nor parcel. No porter followed him. He was unaccompanied by friends. . . . It was plain that he was, in the extremist sense of the word, a stranger" (1). Thus by the time the mute encounters the placard offering a reward for the apprehension of the confidence man in the third paragraph, he has already been marked as both an economic outsider and a racial insider—a crucial combination that, I would argue, defines the ideal recipient of charity emerging from nineteenth-century American ambivalence over the proper liberal response to the disabled.[9] Yet at the time of the novel's setting, this projected ideal had yet to take root in the cultural consciousness, and the passengers' responses to the mute, while ranging from relatively benign to openly hostile, never take the form of actual donations. Rather the passengers find him "harmless enough, would he keep to himself, but not wholly unobnoxious as an intruder," and he is also described as "simple," "innocent," "humble," "gentle," "lamb-like," "inarticulate," and "pathetic" (2-4). Thus Melville portrays the mute in terms that correspond to the stereotype of the pathetic disabled beggar.[10]

In the passengers' comments on the mute while he is asleep, however, we see a tripartite mixture of responses, ranging from the sympathetic ("Poor fellow," "Singular innocence," "Piteous") to the suspicious ("Humbug," "Trying to enlist interest," "Beware of him," "Escaped convict, worn out with dodging") and the mythic, natural, and supernatural ("Casper Hauser," "Green prophet from Utah," "Spirit-rapper," "Kind of daylight Endymion," "Jacob dreaming at Luz") (*The Confidence Man* 4). These "epitaphic comments" illustrate the historical circumstances described by Rosemarie Garland Thomson:

> Secular thinking and a more accurate scientific understanding of physiology and disease prevented nineteenth-century Americans from interpreting disability as the divine punishment it had been labeled in earlier epochs. . . . The social category "disabled" is a grudging admission of human vulnerability in a world no longer seen as divinely determined, a world where self-government and individual progress purportedly prevail. Such a classification elicits much ambivalence from a national consciousness committed to equating virtue with independent industry. (*Extraordinary Bodies* 47–48)

Thus the three categories of the passengers' comments—sympathetic, suspicious, and mythic—correspond to the three primary social responses to disability at that time. Most scholars agree that the mythic or divine interpretation of the disabled figure was on the decline by the

1850s, eventually to be replaced by the uneasy alliance of sympathy (compassion, charity) and suspicion (resentment, stigma).[11] In order to reconcile these contradictory responses, nineteenth-century social structures began to employ "rigorous, sometimes exclusionary supervision of people obliged to join the ranks of the 'disabled' . . . in an effort to distinguish between genuine 'cripples' and malingerers" (48–49). By the turn of the century these categories will have become highly regularized to clearly distinguish the "real" disabled, for whom one must show charity, from the "fake" disabled, against whom one can freely vent all one's resentment for their nonproductivity, compounded by righteous anger over their deception.

Yet at the time of Melville's writing these distinctions were not yet clear. Nor was the mute's aspect of the correct type to elicit contributions from his audience. (Disabled veterans were the most likely to inspire generosity, as shown later in the story of the soldier of fortune.) The mute is notably noninteractive with the other passengers (in contrast with Black Guinea's begging displays and impassioned speeches of self-defense), but when he does attempt communication, he is greeted with "stares and jeers" (*The Confidence Man* 3). Furthermore the mute uses his slate to produce only snippets of charitable cliché: "Charity thinketh no evil," and so on (2-3). Thus, in marked contrast to the confidence man's other personae, the mute never becomes a speaking subject but is instead a mouthpiece of cant, a figure of pure textuality. The mute thus becomes a key figure for understanding the use of language by Melville's disabled and fake-disabled characters, to whom we will return in more detail later.

The next figure of the disability con, Black Guinea, is much more successful at eliciting alms from the steamboat passengers. The flip side of this success, however, is that suspicions arise about the "realness" of Black Guinea's disability—a point that never arose with regard to the mute since he does not seem to profit from his disability. The passengers' suspicions of Black Guinea appear to arise quite abruptly, following an extended period of interaction during which they accept his role as a dehumanized object of charity. (He is described most often as a dog but also as a steer, a sheep, and an elephant; *The Confidence Man* 7-9) Once another character, the man with the wooden leg, makes his accusation, however, the passengers quickly begin to suspect that Guinea may be a "white operator, betwisted and painted up," for the words of accusation serve to release the passengers' latent anxiety regarding both racial and bodily masquerade (10).

In this context, the fear that the extension of social support to those with disabilities would encourage fraud was amplified by many centuries of symbolic association of physical disabilities with evil portent, moral failing, and sexual transgression.[12] While it may seem illogical that the association of "real" disability with evil would lead to a suspicion that certain disabled persons were *faking* their conditions, this metaphorical tangle has emerged necessarily from the strenuous efforts to define the boundaries between real and fake disabilities. The extremely contingent nature of disability itself means that any such boundaries are hopelessly fluid, allowing symbolic and actual meanings to bleed freely across them—a process that continues to this day.[13] In addition, and through a further tortured logic, the symbolic association of disability with immorality, dishonesty, and laziness is reflected and produced by racist ideologies that associate these characteristics with nonwhite peoples, ideologies voiced in Melville's novel through such characters as the Indian-hater: "Indian lying, Indian theft, Indian double dealing, Indian fraud and perfidy" (*The Confidence Man* 126) and descriptions of the evil Goneril, who is repeatedly compared to an "Indian" or "squaw" (50-53). Thus, just as the very fact of Guinea's disability symbolically suggests he is faking it, so paradoxically the fact of his blackness may symbolically suggest that he must be faking that as well.

In all these cases the tension produced is between inner and outer states of being, a tension that pervades the novel and surfaces in many instances, such as the Philosophical Intelligence Officer's analogical defense of boys, in which he proceeds "by analogy from the physical to the moral" (*The Confidence Man* 104), Mark Winsome's metaphor of the snake's rattle as a warning "label" (163), and the barber's disquisition on the false nature of man as seen through the use of wigs, fake mustaches, and hair dyes (199). Mitchell and Snyder thus read Melville's novel as a critique of the "sciences of the surface," which dominated both medical and social understandings of the relationship between bodily surfaces and inner essences during the nineteenth century (*Cultural Locations* 37–39).[14] Phrenology, physiognomy, craniometry, and palmistry all claimed to give essential information about a person's moral character and abilities by examining external features such as head shape and hand contours. Indeed much of *The Confidence Man* lends itself to such a critique; yet the fact that Mitchell and Snyder do not distinguish between real and fake disabilities in their analysis means that its full implications are not yet realized. This becomes an even more urgent issue when we consider how race and disability function in mutually constitutive ways to further undercut the assumptions of surface identifications, not only within the novel but in contemporary critics' interpretations of its meanings.

Consider the shifting status of Black Guinea, whose performance of disability is portrayed as at once incontrovertible and easily exposed. When we initially encounter Black Guinea, both race and disability operate to dehumanize him in the eyes of the passengers and are essentially inseparable factors in how he is perceived. As Peter J. Bellis observes, Black Guinea is "at first described in purely physical terms: 'a grotesque negro cripple,'" the combination of terms rendering it impossible to determine which is the source of the grotesque (167). Ultimately it is the suggestion that Black Guinea may be white and nondisabled that humanizes him in the passengers' eyes; from the moment the suddenly suspicious onlookers begin to "scrutinize" Black Guinea, all narrative descriptions of him as a dog or other animal cease, and he is referred to in human terms (*The Confidence Man* 9). In this way the narrator interpellates the reader into the passengers' ontological shift, thus naturalizing their suspicions and preparing us to accept Black Guinea as fraud and avatar of the confidence man—a perception apparently confirmed at the end of the chapter, when Guinea surreptitiously covers the business card of the merchant whom the confidence man will approach next (14). This merging of the reader with Black Guinea's audience takes on another valence in Dale Jones's analysis of the scene: "Again our reaction is an ambiguous one, for *not only are we simultaneously amused and disgusted by the Black Guinea's dog-like appearance and behavior*, but we are also repulsed by the crowd's *inhuman* treatment of him. This scene is abnormal and grotesque; it affronts any belief the reader may have held concerning the dignity and innate rationality of the *human* species and, coming as it does in an early chapter, it establishes the book's satiric and mordantly comic tone" (203, my emphasis). While the narrative shift interpellates the reader into a system of suspicion that will permeate the remainder of the novel, Jones's analysis assumes that the reader is a member of the "normal," "human" community who naturally responds to both Black Guinea and the crowd's behavior with amusement, disgust, and repulsion. In both cases, narrative functions to manipulate the reader much as the con man's tales and tactics manipulate his intended marks.

The novel functions both to encompass and to exceed the sciences of the surface, which purported to read a person's character from its external signs. In *The Confidence Man* this process is framed as a question of how to discern not merely the good or evil of a person but his very humanity, for "you can conclude nothing absolute from the human form" (193). Thus Black Guinea, *while perceived as black*, is described in racially charged animal-like terms, and the contemporary critic Hershel Parker opines that the Indian-hater story is "another reminder that the human form may be occupied by sub-human or extra-human creatures."[15] Similarly Gustaav Van Cromphout suggests that the figure of the mute "represents a category of being whose otherness is such that the passengers are unable to recognize it as fully human" (40). I contend that this category is that of the physically disabled, who are perceived as "solely bodies, without the humanity social structures confer upon more ordinary people" (Garland Thomson, *Extraordinary Bodies* 57). This notion of disability's pure and grotesque physicality, emerging in the late eighteenth and early nineteenth century, removed disability from the range of human variation while simultaneously defining the human as its opposite: as the confidence man exhorts the "ogre"-like soldier of fortune, the most visibly "real" disabled character in the novel, "Be human, my friend. Don't make that face; it distresses me" (*The Confidence Man* 80).

Yet the repulsion felt both by Melville's character and Jones's presumed normal reader is not necessarily an integral part of the human condition but must be situated both historically and culturally. In the United States physical disability has been traditionally associated with a fracturing of the ideal American self, characterized by independence, honesty, fairness, and self-control and carefully distinguished from the "blind," the "halt" and the "invalids" (Garland Thomson, *Extraordinary Bodies* 42).[16] The dependency and lack of self-control seen as inherent in physical disability is thus extended to include a lack of morality and, by further extension, a tendency toward fraud and deception—which then leads to a suspicion and condemnation of all disabled people. As Martin Norden observes of American society in the 1890s, "To some people of the day, beggars with feigned disabilities weren't that different from those with real ones" (16).[17]

We may further tease out the ongoing association between deception and disability that pervades the novel by examining the figure of the soldier of fortune, who appears in chapter 19. Other than the brief appearance of the wooden-legged man, Thomas Fry is apparently the only "cripple" in *The Confidence Man* who is not suspected of faking his disability, even though he freely admits that he lies about the origin of his paralysis since "hardly anybody" believes his story of becoming disabled while locked up in prison as a witness, and people are more likely to give alms if he pretends "to have been crippled at glorious Contreras" (83). For this reason, Kenneth Pimple asserts that, assuming we believe Fry's story and "if we give the [other] characters the benefit of the doubt, the only clear-cut fabrication [in the novel] is perpetrated by the soldier of fortune" (47). Thus in one reading, this character stands as one of the few solid points of "reality" in the story even as he admits that he routinely lies. The assumption anchoring this apparently contradictory interpretation is the bodily "truth" of Fry's disability; if his legs are truly paralyzed rather than simply bound together or concealed to imitate stumps, then it doesn't really matter what narrative he chooses to tell about it, as Pimple obligingly notes: "I for one find it easy to forgive that pathetic cripple his alms-begging ploy" (47). The confidence man himself, in his guise as the "herb-doctor," defends Fry from the "prim stranger" who wishes to expose the deception: "The vice of this unfortunate is pardonable" (*The Confidence Man* 83). While a nondisabled con man faking disability is seen as deplorable, a disabled con man impersonating a war veteran is acceptable, since he already qualifies as an object of charity.

Bellis notes that "a true story is not enough to authenticate [Fry's] disability, but a fiction does the trick. As narratives and texts displace bodies as evidence of identity, rhetorical effectiveness . . . comes to replace truth" in the novel (168). I suggest that the issue is not so much "authenticating" Fry's disability—which is verified by his bodily testimony—as interpellating it into the social schemes of rehabilitation and support that I have discussed. The reason the herb-doctor and other listeners refuse to believe the true story is that it negates the emerging belief that a democratic society does not allow its members to suffer so unjustly or refuse to compensate them afterward. (Having committed no crime, Fry is held in prison as a material witness until he loses the use of his legs and is then sent away with "five silver dollars, and these crutches"; *The Confidence Man* 83). Fry himself rails against "free Ameriky" and blames the government for his disability and poverty (84). The herb-doctor responds indignantly and insists that Fry's story, considered "in the light of a commentary on what I believe to be the system of things . . . so jars with all, is so incompatible with all" that it simply cannot be believed (83). Thus both he and the general public find it necessary to recast Fry's disability into a model that can be socially recognized and compensated: that of the wounded war veteran. Even though this deception is generally interpreted, by both characters and critics, as the forced choice of a pathetic victim rather than the devious ploy of a con man, it nevertheless continues the semantic association and symbolic blurring of disability and deception.

In addition, "from the outset of *The Confidence Man*, physical appearance and textual evidence are played off against each other as a basis for identifying the self," as in the case of the suspicious crowd's demand that Black Guinea produce "documentary proof," a "plain paper . . . attesting that his case was not a spurious one" (Bellis 167; *The Confidence Man* 10). Later the man with the weed apostrophizes Guinea in terms that conflate body and text: "you upon whom nature has placarded evidence of your claims" (*The Confidence Man* 24). This comment is of course deeply ironic, since both the (white) man with the weed and Black Guinea appear to be avatars of the confidence man, and thus it is impossible that either Guinea's race or disability—two supposedly fixed bodily markers—were "placarded" upon him. The equation of body with text and the demand for empirical proof of disability also underpin modern systems of biocertification; for example, as is discussed at length in chapter 6, one must provide a doctor's certificate to be issued a disabled parking placard in the state of California, *unless one is missing one or both legs and appears at the registry in person*, in which case the permit is simply handed over. Thus the authority of the doctor and the authority of the visibly disabled body are constructed to be equivalent and interchangeable.

The Quack Remedy of Language

The ability of language to connect the physical body and the written text then becomes crucial to the discussion of real and fake disability. While the soldier of fortune, the mute, and Black Guinea are the three most obvious examples of physically disabled characters in Melville's novel, several other characters are relevant for understanding his employment of narrative prosthesis, the mediating function of disability in furthering narratives that bridge "the realm of the literary and the realm of the body" (Mitchell and Snyder, *Narrative Prosthesis* 7). Within this second group I include the "sick man" in chapter 16 and the "invalid Titan" in chapter 17. Notably both of these characters appear during the confidence man's masquerade as the herb-doctor, the same avatar who interacts with the pivotal figure of Thomas Fry, the soldier of fortune. The extended appearance of the herb-doctor allows Melville to explore questions of truth and the efficacy of language within the socially relevant context of the increasingly medicalized understanding of bodies.

Language emerges as crucial to each of these characters' interactions with the herb-doctor and provides a necessary symbolic and semiotic link to the earlier characters of the mute, Black Guinea, and the soldier of fortune.

The interaction between the sick man and the herb-doctor tellingly corresponds to Mitchell and Snyder's observation that, in *Moby-Dick*, the first-person narration of Ishmael requires Melville to shift between "recording the truth of Ahab's identity in his spoken monologues and sculpting a bodily surface that mirrors an internal state of mind" (*Narrative Prosthesis* 130). The herb-doctor speaks in glib, extended paragraphs, interspersed with the sick man's mute responses. Yet neither Melville nor the herb-doctor will allow the sick man to remain mute; each persistently forces language upon him, the herb-doctor by continuing to question him, and Melville's narrator by translating his physical appearance into words: "The sick man replied not by voice or by gesture; but, with feeble dumb-show of his face, seemed to be saying, 'Pray believe me; who was ever cured by talk?'" (*The Confidence Man* 65). The "dumb-show look" is repeated twice more, as well as a "long glance," and each silence is smoothly translated into imagined dialogue (66-67). Thus the sick man appears as a recasting of the character of the mute writing on his slate. In this case, however, it is Melville's narrator who inscribes on the blank text of the sick man's face and body, and the reader who functions as the audience. The sick man's challenge to language—"Who was ever cured by talk?"—is overcome by the herb-doctor/confidence man/narrator's persistent linguistic power, and he eventually agrees to purchase several packages of the herb-doctor's quack remedy. One is left to wonder if perhaps language itself is meant to be a sort of "quack remedy" pressed upon the reader by the author himself. In support of this suspicion, we find the herb-doctor attempting to assuage the sick man's lingering doubts by textual means: "Take the wrapper from any of my vials and hold it to the light, you will see water-marked in capitals the word '*confidence*,' which is the countersign of the medicine, as I wish it was of the world. The wrapper bears that mark or else the medicine is counterfeit" (70). Like the sick man, we are expected to locate the authenticity of language inside the text, which is itself a linguistic construct. The sick man refuses to trust the watermark in the "absence" of the herb-doctor himself— in the absence of the physical body that provides a supposed material accountability (71). But the reader knows that that accountability itself is false and that the physical appearance, identity, and even existence of the confidence man is both shifting and unstable.

The sick-man episode suggests that linguistic exchange is necessary for the confidence man's schemes to succeed. This idea is reinforced in the next chapter, as the invalid Titan resists the herb-doctor's advances and refuses his interpretations, largely by manipulating the uneasy tension between body and text which pervades the novel, particularly in these chapters. When the herb-doctor, seeing the Titan's walking stick, asks if he is lame, the Titan replies, "Never was lame in my life," thus resisting the herb-doctor's attempts to interpret his bodily appearance as text (*The Confidence Man* 73). It would seem that the invalid Titan represents the ultimate contradiction of the disability con. Instead of masquerading as disabled, he refuses even that identity which is clearly marked upon him. Yet the Titan's later ability to disrupt the herb-doctor's success with other passengers relies precisely upon that negated bodily appearance. He challenges the herb-doctor for claiming to relieve pain without producing insensibility, and the sight of his "invalid" body apparently validates his statement and supersedes the herb-doctor's written affidavits: "Beyond this the dusk giant said nothing; neither, for impairing the other's market, did there appear much need to. After eyeing the rude speaker a moment with an expression of mingled admiration and consternation . . . those who had purchased looked sheepish or ashamed" (75). When the herb-doctor persists in reading aloud a "printed voucher," the Titan silences him with pure physicality, "a sudden side-blow" that almost knocks him down (75). This exchange foreshadows the upcoming dilemma of the confidence man when he is apparently moved to compassion and near-honesty by the soldier of fortune, the "real" disabled figure who destabilizes, *by fixing*, the confidence man's shifting narratives of body and truth.

One may certainly question whether the herb-doctor's sympathy for the soldier of fortune is sincere or simply an extension of his scheming manipulations, but his defense of Fry appears to have no particular advantage for his gains and thus may be argued to be "genuine." Also, while the herb-doctor eventually accepts payment for his remedy from the soldier of fortune, he twice attempts to give it to Fry for free. This may be a tactical move, but unlike the confidence man's other schemes, it could easily have resulted in a loss. Is the soldier of fortune, because of his "real" disability, somehow able to stabilize the confidence man into the compassionate, empathetic "human" figure imagined by Jones? If so, this stabilization is fleeting, and the herb-doctor proceeds in the next chapter to fleece the "old miser" with no apparent compunction.

The Confidence Man ends without closure or moral, with a final sentence that is both abrupt and enticing: "Something further may follow of this Masquerade" (217). Unlike the twist ending of the classic con man movie, there is no revelation that makes sense of the preceding narrative. Yet like the twist ending, the novel leaves the reader in the position of the mark, the object of the confidence man/author's narrative scheme. It seems absurd to end a novel that has virtually no plot progression (as generally understood) with a suggestion of suspense, yet perhaps the ending makes more sense if the "Masquerade" itself is understood as the linguistic project in which we and Melville have been engaged.

Such an understanding also sheds light on Melville's depiction of disability and the disability con in his novel. While the novel repeatedly deploys the trope of the disability con, it is not a simple or straightforward portrayal. The fantasy of disability fakery operates reductively, attempting to resolve questions of bodily identity into discrete and governable categories, which map onto the solidifying dichotomy between worthy and unworthy objects of charity (Carey 43; Trent 10). However, in *The Confidence Man* the perpetual shifting between real and fake, speech and silence, visually marked and textually produced bodies undermines any direct or straightforward reading of such a dichotomy. The novel thus demonstrates the complexities and uncertainties of mid-nineteenth-century stagings of fantasies of identification, and in particular the instability of the proposed link between body, text, and state authority that will eventually be codified into biocertificative law. We can also see the divergence of imaginative genres in staging the fantasy: while Melville's literary portrayal of the disability con resists the fantasy's reductive dichotomies, within a few decades the new medium of film appeared ideally situated to dramatically enact its division between real and fake, worthy and unworthy disabled subjects. In the next chapter we will explore these attempts to consolidate a fantasy of disability identification through filmic depictions.

3 /   The Disability Con Onscreen

*In 1896, the same year that Koster & Bial's Music Hall in New York,
equipped with one of Thomas Edison's Vitascopes, showed movies to
paying audiences for the first time, police in that city launched a major
crackdown on beggars pretending to be disabled. . . . [Within two years] a
New York audience viewed what may well have been the first storytelling
film with a disability theme: Thomas Edison's* The Fake Beggar.
                              —MARTIN NORDEN, *The Cinema of Isolation:
                              A History of Physical Disability in the Movies*

With the advent of the new medium of film, portrayals of the disability
con in American and British film became swiftly popular, perhaps due
to the suitability of the medium for dramatically "unmasking" the per-
petrator. The wheelchair-user walking, the blind beggar reading a newspaper, the twisted limb that suddenly straightens: all of these familiar
visual tricks were developed during the very earliest years of cinematic
invention. Short films such as *The Fraudulent Beggars* (1898), *The Beggar's Deceit* (1900), *The Fraudulent Beggar* (1900), and *Blind Man's Buff*
(1903) followed a stock formula of a fake-disabled beggar unmasked and
pursued by a policeman. Subsequently, as films became longer and more
complex, one-reelers such as *The Fake Blind Man* (1905) and *One of the
Finest* (1907) featured not merely a policeman but a "sizable crowd" pur-
suing the unmasked fraud, much like the crowd that surrounds the mute
and Black Guinea in Melville's novel (Norden 16). Thus the history of
film has always been deeply entwined with cultural mediations regarding disability, fraud, and social retaliation. As a result, one can hardly
point to a contemporary American film involving a con man theme
without finding the disability con somewhere in the mix, often as a key
ingredient. Some examples from the past four decades include *Trading
Places* (1983), *Dirty Rotten Scoundrels* (1988), *The Usual Suspects* (1995),
and *There's Something about Mary* (1998), all of which were box-office
and critical successes.

In this chapter I first consider those early silent films, in particular
Thomas Edison's 1898 *The Fake Beggar*, and then explore the evolution

of the disability con in American film and television in interaction with social, economic, gendered, and racial changes. I briefly diverge from the generally chronological progression of the book in order to draw parallels between the notable cluster of disability con films at the turn of the century and a second cluster that emerged in the 1980s and continues through the present day. I suggest that these elaborate filmic portrayals of "real" and "fake" disability, which seem to proliferate at times of social crises about disability rights and benefits, function to stage or forecast fantasies of disability identification and thus provide a crucial context for understanding modern efforts to define disability and its corresponding legal and economic structures.

To pursue such a discussion, however, it is necessary to first explore in more detail what exactly is meant by "real" and "fake" disability in film, where actual bodies enact impairment in order to convey disability's social meanings, with or without the audience's knowledge or complicity. Film reverses the literary hierarchy of narrative and appearance: even more than listening to what characters say, a film viewer must scrutinize the faces and bodies of characters and sometimes translate those bodies into speech, just as Melville's narrator translates the "dumb-show" of the sick man. Indeed Lloyd Michaels suggests that film itself may be viewed as a confidence game, in which the "images themselves remain inherently deceptive, inspiring false confidence in their reality and presence" (375–376). This dynamic becomes even more complicated when we consider how images of real and fake disability are mapped onto actors' bodies, which themselves are always already constructed according to social understandings of ability and deviance. The fantasy of verifiable and authentic disability as a deserving social category is tested and contested through these filmic portrayals in the deployment of multiple and overlapping categories of realness and falsehood.

Taxonomies of Real and Fake

In *The Ugly Laws: Disability in Public*, Susan Schweik examines the "dissimulations" underlying the unstable relationship between fake and real disability in relation to unsightly beggarhood. While I previously noted Martin Norden's claim that for many turn-of-the-century citizens, "beggars with feigned disabilities weren't all that different from those with real ones" (16), Schweik suggests that "many of us might nonetheless still want to make some kind of distinction between . . . genuinely fake unsightly beggars, on the one hand, and . . . the people whom they mimicked, on the other" (125). Reasons for making such a distinction seem obvious, yet, as Schweik goes on to provocatively suggest, if we ascribe to a social constructionist model of disability, many "disability imposters *were* disabled," since they were often subject to the same discrimination and barriers as those Schweik calls "for-real" disabled people (128).

I take this discussion in a somewhat different direction by interrogating what exactly constitutes the "disability faker" under discussion. In Jean Baudrillard's original writings on simulacra, he makes an intriguing distinction between simulation and dissimulation: "To dissimulate is to pretend not to have what one has. To simulate is to feign to have what one doesn't have. One implies a presence, the other an absence" (522). The question then arises, is a disability faker simulating or dissimulating? Is disability in this case a matter of having or lacking? The matter becomes more complicated, as Baudrillard goes on to explain, tellingly evoking the disability con: "Simulating is not pretending. 'Whoever fakes an illness can simply stay in bed and make everyone believe he is ill. Whoever simulates an illness produces in himself some of the symptoms'" (523). Where this distinction breaks down, I argue, is in that clause "make everyone believe he is ill." How does the disability faker so easily "make everyone believe"? Simply staying in bed cannot be enough; narratives of illness and disability must be produced, and signs and behaviors of disability must be inscribed and performed.[1] And in that process, are not some of the *symptoms* of disability produced in the disability faker?

According to the *Oxford English Dictionary*, the verb *fake* came originally from "thieves' or vagrants' language" and meant not only "to tamper with, for the purpose of deception," but also "to perform any operation upon . . . to plunder, wound, kill; to do up, put into shape." Thus in J. H. Vaux's *Flash* (slang) *Dictionary* of 1812, he explains, "To *fake* any person or place, [is] to rob them; to *fake* a person may also imply to shoot, wound, or cut; to *fake* a man *out and out*, is to kill him; a man who inflicts wounds upon, or otherwise disfigures, himself, for any sinister purpose, is said to have *faked himself*," and finally, "To *fake* your *pin*, is to create a sore leg, or to cut it, as if accidentally" (*OED*). If by the end of the century "faking" had become firmly associated with the idea of deception, I suggest its early connotation of violent intervention, and specifically of intervening upon the body to simulate disability, persists into later conceptions of disability fakery and its exposure.

With this context in mind, I will attempt to further elucidate real and fake with regard to the disability con. I draw on Stephen M. Fjellman's cultural study of Disney World, which utilizes four categories of analysis: the *real real*, the *fake real*, the *real fake*, and the *fake fake*. To illustrate this model, at Disney World "the real birds and the climate are real real; so is the limestone geology that underlies [it]. Hunger, thirst, crowds, trash, and sewage are real real" (255). By contrast, the fake fake is "the stuff of fantasy and commerce," such as dolls based on characters and the live cast members dressed as Disney characters who circulate and interact with visitors: "As an animated character," Fjellman explains, "Mickey is a real fake; as portrayed by a cast member, he is a fake fake" (256). The real fake is Cinderella's Palace or Alice's Tea Party brought to animatronic life; by contrast, the fake real is the "false turn-of-the-century facades on Main Street USA" or "the pagoda at the Japan Showcase" (256).

Using Fjellman's analysis as a starting point, I propose a taxonomy of the disability con in which the first term refers to the performative aspect of identity, the second term to its presumed "essence." In this taxonomy, the *real real* is the disabled person who performs disability as expected, transparently, legibly. The *fake fake* is the nondisabled actor, on stage or film, who performs disability with the audience's knowledge that it is a performance, in this case, a laudable deception. The wheelchair-using character on the Fox television show *Glee* is a current and controversial filmic appearance of the fake fake. Thus far, performance and essence are equivalent and identification remains a stable link between the viewer and the figure of disability.

What is more complex is teasing out the distinctions between the fake real and the real fake. The *fake real* emerges as the disabled person who deliberately shapes the performance of her disability, what Tobin Siebers has describes as the "disability masquerade" (96–104). This includes those who renarrate their disabilities to redirect prejudice into sympathy, such as the soldier of fortune in Melville's novel and the young Ray Charles played by Jamie Foxx in the 2004 biopic *Ray*, both of whom falsely claim to be disabled veterans to recast themselves as heroes rather than victims. The fake real also includes disabled people who deliberately "perform" their impairments in order to negotiate social prejudices about disability, as Megan Jones describes in her essay, "Why I Use a White Cane to Tell People That I'm Deaf." A fake real disabled beggar discussed by Schweik is Spike O'Day, an amputee who pawned his wooden leg every morning and "redeemed it at night from the proceeds of a day's begging in a sitting position on the sidewalk" (117).

Finally we come to the *real fake*, what I have been calling the disability con: the masquerade of a nondisabled person who deceptively and deliberately performs disability, often for material gain. As noted in the previous chapter, the idea of such real fake disability is an ongoing feature of European and American history and culture. However, there are notable clusters of its American filmic portrayal: one at the very inception of film, with the silent films described by Norden, and one beginning in the 1980s and continuing into the present. Perhaps the most intriguing point about the evolution of this category is that the fake beggar figure at the center of the first cluster has all but disappeared in the second one. When this figure does infrequently appear, as in a 2000 episode of *The Simpsons*, it is often marked as belonging to an earlier period, as could be seen in that episode's *TV Guide* advertisement, in which Homer Simpson is dressed as a turn-of-the-century "grifter," complete with pinstripe suit, bowler hat, and handlebar mustache. The headline reads, "Bart and Homer: Con Men. Tonight they're scamming their way through Springfield," while in the foreground Bart Simpson enacts the classic version of the fake beggar con, wearing dark glasses and wielding a cane while calling out, "Won't you help a poor blind boy?—Hey, you in the hat! I'm talking to you."

The *Simpsons* episode is the exception nowadays. Instead American filmic disability cons since the 1980s usually involve the faking of disability for more elaborate material ends: in criminal schemes, as in *Dirty Rotten Scoundrels*, when the con man played by Steve Martin pretends to be a disabled veteran to scam a wealthy heiress; or for benefits fraud, as in the character of Janice on *The Sopranos* who pretends to have chronic carpal tunnel syndrome from operating the steamed milk machine at Starbucks. Contemporary disability cons in film are also employed to conceal guilt, as in an episode of the TV show *Monk* when a woman pretends to be blind to conceal the fact that she shot Willie Nelson.[2] The contemporary disability con is even used to attract romantic interest, as in the character of Tucker in *There's Something about Mary*, who stumbles about inexpertly on crutches to garner Mary's sympathies.

Of course, there is often bleeding between the categories of this taxonomy, as well as ambiguous subjects who hover around its edges. Where, for example, would we put the deliberately impaired person, the one who "fakes a pin" or has such an injury inflicted by others? Where would we put those nondisabled fakers who then become "truly" disabled, such as the Jason Bateman character in the 2006 romantic comedy *The Ex*, who uses a wheelchair after a childhood accident, later doesn't need it but pretends he does, is then exposed as a fraud, and finally has another accident that lands him back in a chair? What about fake fake Laura Innes, a nondisabled actress who developed chronic pain from playing a crutch-using character on the television drama *ER* for years, (real) pain that was cured by having her (fake) character undergo surgery to eliminate her limp? And finally, where do we put people who identify as transabled, also sometimes called "wannabes" or "pretenders," people who simulate or produce actual impairments in themselves, and do we distinguish between the simulators and those who actually deafen themselves or amputate limbs?[3]

I raise these questions not to try to answer them but to reinforce the notion that attempts to describe exactly what we mean by "fake disability" will always be blurry, contingent, and incomplete—much like attempts to describe exactly what we mean by "disability." In fact I suggest it is difficult to talk about disability without talking about the disability con, as one cannot exist without the shadowy form of the other. This dynamic takes a visible form in the original disability con film, Edison's 1898 *The Fake Beggar*.

The Real "Fake" of *The Fake Beggar*

In Norden's encyclopedic *The Cinema of Isolation: A History of Physical Disability in the Movies*, he summarizes seven disability-con films appearing between 1898 and 1907, five American and two British. Their titles—*The Fake Blind Man, The Fraudulent Beggars, The Beggar's Deceit*, and so on—aptly convey their basic plot line of a fake disabled beggar who is unmasked and often pursued by an outraged crowd. It is not immediately apparent from Norden's book that he himself did not view these films but relied upon descriptions in catalogues and media notices. Only a small number of the films appear to have survived in archives, and none are yet available in digital or other readily accessible forms. Yet, as I argue in this chapter, viewing the films is important for our nuanced understanding of "fake" disability in all its manifestations and meanings and the implications of those meanings for broader understandings of bodily identities.

The Fake Beggar was made and released in 1898, only two years after movies first appeared in American theaters. Norden's discussion of the film is based entirely on filmographer Kemp R. Niver's catalogue description, which reads as follows:

The establishing scene is of a legless beggar leading a man with a
sign on his chest reading "Help the Blind." They stop near the camera and, as the film progresses, several people pass by and drop
coins in the blind man's cup. One passer-by drops a coin that hits
the sidewalk instead of the cup and a policeman standing nearby
notices that the blind man reaches out and picks it up. The policeman attempts to arrest the blind man and takes hold of his coat,
but the blind man wriggles out of it and runs down the street with
the policeman in close pursuit. (183)

This description outlines the stock plot of the fake-disabled beggar films.
Yet the film itself presents a far more intriguing and internally complicated portrayal of the relationship between real and fake disability.

The Fake Beggar is less than a minute in length and, as would be
expected in an 1898 film, is in black and white and rather blurry and
jerky. We first see a medium shot of what appears to be an urban street
corner, the foreground taken up by two figures, a white man in a dark
suit and a small white child in a white shirt and dark cap and pants. (The
child's gender is unclear, but the hat makes it more likely that he is a
boy.) Both characters appear to be kneeling and move toward the camera by hitching themselves along on mats with handles on the sides. As
they get closer we can see that the child is an above-the-knee amputee,
his stumps showing in a momentary glimpse. The man, however, is only
kneeling on the mat: he is the fake beggar of the title, and he also wears
dark glasses and a sign around his neck reading "Help the Blind" (Fig.
3.1). Various dark-suited men pass by and drop coins into his cup; we see
them from a kneeling perspective, so they are headless and faceless. The
child has neither sign nor cup and simply sits next to the man, smiling
and looking around. Some women pass but do not drop coins. A dark-
suited man's legs pause in front of the child, obscuring his white figure
into the white background, an effect heightened by the chiaroscuro effect
of the indistinct film. Another man apparently drops a coin (this part is
difficult to make out), and the fake beggar apparently reaches for it. The
other men begin to shift around and show agitation, and the fake beggar
stands up and begins to flee. There is a blink in the film then, a cut, and
after the cut the child has completely vanished. The fake beggar flees
toward the rear of the shot pursued by at least one man while others mill
about. The film ends.

Clearly there is a great deal in this brief film that Niver left out of
his catalogue description. Indeed in *The Fake Beggar* the real fake and

FIGURE 3.1. Still from *The Fake Beggar* (1898). Courtesy of the National Archives and Records Administration.

the real real collide in a kind of disability con big bang from which the real fake emerges as filmic victor, or at least survivor. The disabled child—who is all but invisible in Niver's description and goes unnoted in Norden's analysis, and who is apparently played by a for-real disabled child—can be read in a variety of provocative ways: as a haunting presence, who literally fades out ghostlike, a pallid real-real backdrop to the fake-real drama enacted by the dark-clothed, nondisabled adults; or as a near-literal narrative prosthesis that enables the successful performance of the disability con; or as the abject twin or double of the fake disabled beggar, or as his constitutive outside, the supplement that, unseen in itself, is added to the whole to make it legible.

My interpretation of the real-real disabled child as supplement has an additional etymological context. It is notable that this first disability con film is not called "The Fake Blind Beggar" or "The Fake Cripple Beggar" but simply *The Fake Beggar*. I have already addressed the first term of Edison's title, the "fake," with its connotation of interventional violence. Turning to the second term in the *OED*, we find that directly under the expected definition of *beggar* as "one who asks alms," the phrase "sturdy beggar" is given its own equivalent subentry and defined as "an able-bodied man begging without cause." Thus the idea of non-able-bodiedness as the only legitimate cause for begging is presumed in the definition of *beggar* itself. The real-real disabled child appears in the film as the phantasmic materialization of that parenthetical "disability" inherent in the word *beggar*.

If the disabled child is supplement, "the not-seen which opens and limits visibility" (Derrida 163), what happens to the meaning of the film when the child is cut out? This is an especially telling point when we consider that an editing cut like this in a film of this period is almost unheard of. The National Archives, where this film can be found, includes dozens of other short films by Edison of this period, not a single one of which contains such a cut. Blips or interruptions in the filming sometimes happened due to apparent technical difficulties but were never used to perform a visual effect such as the disappearing child. In fact when such deliberate effects first began to be used, after 1900, it was a matter of some note for filmographers.[4]

Of course, there is a practical aspect here as well: the child had to be removed so that the milling crowd chasing the fake beggar would not trample him. That matter in itself raises provocative and provoking questions regarding the deployment of real real and real fake disability in live-action films. But we must also consider what *else* was removed from the film when the real-real disabled child was removed, as well as when his presence was obscured or removed from subsequent discussions of the film. At the very least, the social existence of for-real disabled beggars is removed, not to mention the possibility that the fake disabled beggar is attached somehow to the child, perhaps begging to support him. Of course, that point in itself begs the question of why the disability con is happening here at all: why isn't the child the one soliciting alms on the basis of his real-real disability status?

I suggest that the "fake" of *The Fake Beggar* is not the beggar, who is, after all, not even a very good fake, not nearly as convincing as Eddie Murphy's fake-legless-on-a-skateboard beggar in *Trading Places* (1983), much less the wily disability fakers of history described by Schweik. Rather the fake of the film is that cut, that "tampering with, for the purpose of deception" that enacts a technological erasure of the inconvenient real-real disability to make room for the drama of the real fake. If the child had simply moved aside, his presence would still need to be accounted for. But by actually pausing the filming process in order to remove him, it is his *absence* that must be accounted for and, by extension, the hauntingly present absence of real-real disability in all depictions of the disability con. This is why I argue we cannot talk about disability, particularly on film, without talking about the disability con. Too often the realness of disability interacts with the fakeness of the filmic process itself to suggest that all disability is somehow fake, or at least fake real, and that thus the fake real *is* the real, the visible reality that remains when the real real has conveniently faded to white and been forgotten.

Screening the Disability Con Today

After the initial turn-of-the-century proliferation of disability con films inaugurated by *The Fake Beggar* and noted by Norden, few such films appeared in American cinema for the next seventy or so years.[5] Then, in the early 1980s, a new and ongoing cluster of such representations began to appear, both in feature films and on television. Following the unprecedented extension of social benefits and entitlements offered by President Lyndon B. Johnson's Great Society in the 1960s, these new portrayals of the disability con reflect similar concerns as those of the late nineteenth century about the problematic distinctions between worthy and unworthy recipients of assistance, producing a range of backlashes and damaging representations, such as the so-called welfare queen.[6] In particular the Reagan administration formalized the backlash against disabled Americans, denying or canceling Social Security Disability benefits for tens of thousands of disabled people throughout the 1980s, often in contradiction to legal rulings. The second cluster of filmic portrayals of the disability con both reflected and reinforced social policies and attitudes toward people claiming to be disabled.

A number of such portrayals were briefly mentioned earlier to illustrate the taxonomy of the disability con. Most of these merit little more than passing mention, impressive largely for their diversity and range. Yet several filmic examples are worth considering in more depth, particularly in relation to the earlier anxieties on display in Melville's novel, from the unreliability of identity to the constitutive exchange between body and text and the reconciliation of democratic and capitalist ideals.

A fairly clear-cut exploration of these themes appears in the 1988 comedy *Dirty Rotten Scoundrels*, which stars Steve Martin and Michael Caine as feuding con men who compete to romantically ensnare an heiress. Caine's debonair style seems certain to outshine Martin's more plebeian charms until Martin's character suddenly appears not only in a wheelchair but as a decorated disabled war veteran. The sympathy and admiration elicited by this masquerade enrapture the heiress, demonstrating the symbolic (if unrealistic) power of disability in the con game context. Much of the film's comic power is then evoked by the attempts of Caine's character to expose Martin's disability fakery, balanced by Martin's consummate ability to simulate real impairment. One notable scene involves Caine, posing as a miracle-cure doctor, whipping Martin's "senseless" legs with a crop, trying to provoke an outcry that will reveal the deception. The audience, privy to the secret of each man's chicanery, may indulgently enjoy the spectacle of the disability faker suffering for his crime, a scenario repeated throughout the film, as Caine earlier forces Martin to play the humiliating role of his cognitively disabled brother "Ruprecht" to fool various marks and, at the end of the film, silences him by imposing a new role as a "mute" sidekick. However, we then encounter the usual twist ending of the con man movie, in which we learn that the innocent and gullible heroine, played by Glenne Headley, is herself an "operator" who has succeeded in duping both the con men and us.

The disability con twist-ending device takes on a more complex significance in *The Usual Suspects* (1995), in which Kevin Spacey's character, Verbal Kent, fakes being disabled by cerebral palsy in order to construct a believable persona with which to con his criminal accomplices, the authorities, and, of course, the audience. Throughout the film Kent is defined by his disability, referred to most often as "the cripple from New York" but also as "the gimp" and "pegleg" (even though he does not have a prosthetic leg). The customs officer whose interrogation of Kent provides the narrative frame for the film's action explicitly connects Kent's disability with his role as both victim and narrator: "It's *because* you're crippled. It's *because* you're stupid . . . [that the supposed villain] programmed you to tell us just what he wanted you to." Kent's tears and groveling at this moment set up the audience for the subsequent revelation that he is in fact the master villain who has engineered the plot (in both senses) of the movie—a revelation conveyed visually as the camera focuses on Kent's twisted hand and foot, which have been lavishly displayed throughout the film, as they miraculously untwist and become "normal."

The dramatic untwisting of Kent's body is metonymically mirrored in the twist ending of the film, as the viewers' expectations and assumptions are suddenly revealed to be false. The twist ending, a hallmark of contemporary con game movies, essentially constructs the viewer as mark of the con man and moviemaker. Each of the films discussed earlier, like *The Confidence Man*, interpellates the reader or viewer into a system of suspicion and unstable reality, for, as Melville notes, "True knowledge comes but by suspicion or revelation" (78). In contrast, the final film of this discussion, *Trading Places* (1983), creates a comic world in which the instability of identity ultimately produces empowered subjects. Eschewing irony, except in its most blatant turning-the-tables form, this film functions almost as an optimistic sequel to *The Confidence Man*, examining many similar social issues and linguistic themes within a simplified framework that allows for both closure and morality, two elements carefully excluded from Melville's novel.

Trading Places tells the story of two social opposites: the homeless, streetwise, African American con man Billy Ray Valentine, played by Eddie Murphy, and the affluent, white, spoiled-boy stockbroker Louis Winthorpe III, played by Dan Aykroyd. The two men's lives are turned topsy-turvy when the Duke brothers, Winthorpe's eccentric upper-crustean employers, place a bet on whether, by switching the two men's circumstances, they can switch their characters as well. Ultimately Valentine and Winthorpe realize they've been duped and employ their own con, which succeeds in transferring the wealth of the Duke brothers into their own pockets.

This plot of class reversal fits nicely with the literary-historical argument that the confidence man emerged as a central figure in nineteenth-century America due to the changing nature of class structures and social relationships, such that class background was no longer fate for increasing numbers of socially mobile Americans. Since the early nineteenth century, "instead of relying on family background, class habits, inherited manners, many Americans have had to confront each other as mere claimants, who can at best try to persuade each other who they in fact are. It is easy to see how a con man can slip into such a situation and exploit it" (Lindberg 5). Indeed the film's central con, that of switching Winthorpe and Valentine, both relies on and undermines such observations. Since Valentine does in fact become refined, honest, and hard-working, while Winthorpe sinks into degradation and crime, it appears that neither man is defined by his background but only by his immediate surroundings. However, the film's ultimate message is that neither man's original position is real, since both men are pawns in the larger con game of the Dukes. Only when they reverse the con do the film's protagonists truly participate in the great American project of self-actualization through material gain.

Halttunen observes that "since the Revolution, Americans had stressed that what made a republic great was the character and spirit of its people. The ultimate threat of the confidence man was thus his power to subvert the American republican experiment" (9). The opening montage of *Trading Places*, consisting of scenes of 1980s Philadelphia, intersperses shots of various statues of and monuments to the "founding fathers" with carefully juxtaposed footage of poverty and wealth—a homeless man sleeping in a doorway and a butler serving breakfast in bed, for example—which represent the two worlds the film's protagonists will soon exchange. This montage evokes revolutionary ideals of democratic equality and self-determination, which are then undercut by the stark reality of extreme economic inequality, thus setting the scene for the advent of the con man who will demonstrate how to succeed in this modern democracy. In addition to the central con on which the film's plot turns there are numerous large and small cons throughout the film, many of which employ disguises that recall those used by Melville's confidence man. When we first encounter Billy Ray Valentine, it is in a guise that closely resembles the appearance of Black Guinea: African American, apparently legless, and dressed in rags, Valentine propels himself along the sidewalk on a wheeled platform, humorously accosting passersby with requests for money. While two policemen quickly see through this disability con, throughout the rest of the film a number of ridiculous and unconvincing disguises—culminating in an "African" Aykroyd sporting blackface and limp dreadlocks—appear surprisingly successful. This dynamic works as a comic device but serves as well to emphasize the theme, also central in *The Confidence Man*, that all identities are artificial and assumed and that social relations consist of recognizing and negotiating rather than unmasking these performed roles.

Complicating this theme is the film's plot trajectory, which requires that the "good" con men ultimately triumph over the "bad" con men. In this way the film reflects the historical progression from nineteenth-century condemnation of con men to twentieth-century approval and emulation: "After 1870, a new success literature was emerging that effectively instructed its readers to cultivate the arts of the confidence man in order to succeed in the corporate business world" (Halttunen 198). It is appropriate therefore that the setting of the triumph of the "good" con men is the futures market, a cousin of the stock market, which as early as 1849 had been called "the confidence-man on a large scale" (Lindberg 6). This triumph is portrayed as a moral victory, despite the heroes' employment of the same stratagems as their adversaries, a similarity emphasized when Valentine informs the Dukes that he ruined them to win a bet with Winthorpe for one dollar, which is the same sum that the Dukes originally wagered. Similarly the Black Rapids Coal Company transfer agent in *The Confidence Man* deplores the stock market manipulators, "destroyers of confidence . . . who trump up their black panics in the naturally-quiet brightness, solely with a view to some sort of covert advantage," even as he manipulates the youth into purchasing phony stock (41). By the end of the film, however, both protagonists are strong and upright millionaires, having reclaimed their subjectivity through the successful manipulation of the con man role. Thus the film can be seen as an optimistic sequel to Melville's novel, in which what matters is not so much society's lack of confidence as one's own confidence in oneself and one's abilities.

The evolution of the disability con on film shows a notable consolidation of a fantasy of identification between the original turn-of-the-century cluster of shorts and the cluster that began in the 1980s. While *The Fake Beggar* enacts, in a mere thirty seconds, the myriad complexities inherent in attempts to separate real and fake, worthy and unworthy disabled figures, *Trading Places* spends two hours exploring the instability of identity only to claim an absolute and fulfilling resolution at its close. This trajectory is a familiar feature of the fantasy in many cultural representations, as portrayals of ambiguous identification are tolerable only if contained and ultimately resolvable. We saw the foretelling of this dynamic in the retellings of Ellen Craft's story, as well as its wholesale rejection in Melville's novel. In part II, however, we turn to a broader cultural arena in which literary representations circulate with and begin to penetrate discourses in law, medicine, and policy—and fantasies about bodily identification begin to have material consequences for real, flesh-and-blood people. In these cases we will see that, while ambiguous bodies and identities continue to appear in both fictional and legal representations, those ambiguities are increasingly foreclosed or overwritten by the solidifying fantasy of strictly knowable bodily truths.

PART II

FANTASIES OF MARKING

4 / The Trials of Salomé Müller

If it were true that every individual had any peculiar mark or designation, natural or imposed, which once impressed were adherent and indelible, the possession of that peculiarity by the person in the case and the person in the evidence would conclusively prove them to be the same.

—JOHN HUBBACK, British legal scholar, 1845

The wistful jurist voices here the inadequacy of personal recognition in an increasingly diverse and urban British society, particularly in the colonial context.[1] This problem was even greater in the United States, due to rapid immigration, geographic expansion, and the lack of a centralized policing agency (S. Cole 17). Thus by the late nineteenth-century, a highly reductive—and seductive—fantasy began to emerge and compete for dominance of cultural discourses on identification. This new fantasy of marking—a persistently imagined belief in a single physical mark of identity, produced by nature and legible by the state—appears at first to be more focused on crises of racial rather than disability identification. Yet when we consider how disability by the nineteenth century had come to signify both physical immutability and the naturalized body, the idea of a "peculiarity" to be marked upon the body clearly evokes ideas about disability as the most "adherent and indelible" of bodily states. In part II we will see how racially ambiguous female bodies in particular became the grounds on which to figure this peculiarity, thus expanding our previous understandings of how race, gender, and disability in this period have been understood to "mark" bodies in various real and symbolic ways.

Fantasies of marking seek to resolve "the problem at the heart of the modern idea of race," the possibility that "legal, physical, and social identities might fail to coincide, leaving open the gaping question of where the truth of race in fact resides" (Kawash 125). In this chapter and the next, we will see how both cultural texts and legal verdicts attempted to answer that question by discovering, inventing, or simply recognizing the presence of bodily marks that could be read as the truth of racial and personal identity. From the 1845 trial of Salomé Müller to the fingerprinting prowess of Twain's Pudd'nhead Wilson, I trace an ongoing and internally dissonant discourse of marked bodies and marked births that attempts to resolve unresolvable questions of identity, race, and citizenship.

Birthing the Marked Body

In a 1997 episode of the popular television drama *Law & Order*, the discovery of a peculiar birthmark known as a Mongolian spot on a baby shockingly reveals that one of the baby's ostensibly white parents is actually black. Virtually simultaneously the mark reveals the clue to the criminal's identity, since his concealed racial background is the motive for the crime. Never mind that Mongolian spots, while most common among children of Asian and African background, can be found among a wide variety of racial and ethnic groups; scientific and medical reality are easily set aside in the service of dramatic effect.[2]

The purpose of this opening anecdote is to foreground the persistence of a cultural belief that birthmarks are permanent and incontrovertible clues not only to an individual's identity but also to his or her racial background—and indeed to the question of guilt or innocence. This chapter explores the roots of this belief in the American nineteenth century. If the first part of this book demonstrated that nineteenth-century America was deeply concerned with the mutability and deceptive potential of social-bodily identities, this chapter suggests one primary response to that anxiety: an increasing fixation on identifying marks located not merely *on* the body but inherent to that body.

Beginning in midcentury we find a notable literary preoccupation with birthmarks, a remarkable number of which involve some reference to hands, such as the "bloody hand" on Georgiana's face in Hawthorne's 1843 short story "The Birth-mark" (119). E. D. E. N. Southworth's heroine, Capitola, in her sentimental thriller, *The Hidden Hand* (1859), is recognized as an heiress by the overdetermined mark of a red hand *on* her hand, while in Thomas Fullerton's 1858 poem "The Birth-Mark" the narrator also has a "bloody" hand impressed upon his breast, supposedly caused by his mother's murder (412).[3]

In ongoing evidence of the fantasy of marking's penetrance from literary representation into the material world, we find the report of a conviction for assault in the *New York Times* of February 14, 1887, based on the marks of "four fingers" and "a thumb" that appeared on the neck of a baby whose mother was allegedly choked by the defendant while pregnant. The victim's accusation had been met previously with suspicion because she had no witnesses to the assault, but the presentation of the "startling and most extraordinary evidence" of the baby's birthmarks secured her assailant's conviction ("Convicted by the Baby"). The judge in the case apparently subscribed to the still widespread (though controversial) notion of "maternal impression," the belief that the experiences and emotions of a pregnant woman produce marks and other bodily changes in her infant (P. Wilson 1–2).[4] The seemingly obvious possibility of the baby's marks being faked was not apparently raised, so convincing was their physical presence. That these marks produced an actual conviction testifies to the material as well as symbolic power invested in the fantasy of bodily marks which can prove guilt or innocence as well as identity. Such fantasies become even more complicated and compelling when produced by the anxiety of a culture attempting to codify an increasingly ambiguous realm of racial identity in the context of "the rapid change caused by increasing industrialization and urbanization, as well as an influx of immigrants and a migration of southern African Americans from rural areas to urban centers in the North and South [which] created a fluid and highly mobile society" (Zackodnik 440–441).

"Marked" bodies in nineteenth-century America are often understood racially, as those bodies marked by dark skin or other phenological characteristics identified with nonwhite identity. In "Race and Nature: The System of Marks," Colette Guillaumin uses this conception to trace the history of bodily marks in relation to systems of slavery, arguing that "the mark *followed* slavery and in no way preceded the slave grouping" (33). The mark to which Guillaumin refers existed first as a system of externally imposed marks, such as brands and tattoos, and then evolved into a specific racial notion of marked skin, which she locates historically, observing that "the idea of visually making known the groups in a society is neither recent nor exceptional. However, the idea of classifying *according to* somatic/morphological criteria is recent and its date can be fixed: the eighteenth century. From a circumstantial association between economic relations and physical traits was born a new type of mark ('color'), which had great success" (32). Robyn Wiegman traces a similar progression, placing the shift slightly earlier, in the late seventeenth century.[5] She draws upon David Brion Davis's history of Western slavery to support the idea of this progression from "an imposed sign crafted by the master" to "a 'natural' sign based on skin" (24–25). Both Wiegman's and Guillaumin's analyses of the function of skin color as a naturalized social "mark" are useful and important; however, I disagree with their characterization of a broad shift from a pre-eighteenth-century emphasis on imposed, localized marks such as tattoos and brands to a post-Enlightenment reliance on skin color.[6] The actual social history, at least in the examples discussed in this chapter, appears considerably more invested in such localized marks than either of these critics' analyses allows. It seems that no sooner did skin color (and other supposedly reliable phenological racial marks such as hair, nose, etc.) emerge conceptually at the end of the eighteenth century as the dominant determiner of race than this model began to break down in the nineteenth century, in the face of increased racial mixing and the resulting racially ambiguous bodies circulating within and outside of the U.S. slavocracy.

Thus an entirely opposite progression emerges, moving *from* the idea of skin color as mark *back* to the need for a more localized and objective mark, but one that is inherent rather than imposed—and therefore "natural." In fact the very reliance on color seems to have produced the need for a more regularized form of marking, as Sterling L. Bland observes with regard to Ellen Craft: "Slavery and, by extension, its dependence on easily identifiable racial identity, argues for a view of race that emphasizes the truly arbitrary nature of racial identification and classification. . . . The distinctions involved in classifying black and white require a way of marking blackness as socially different. Ellen Craft's ability to pass, however, suggests that without some easily identifiable imprint of race, race itself turns into a socially inscribed marker in which the imprint has no true distinguishing content" (*Voices* 145). Yet, as Wiegman notes, "to mark the body is not the same as *being* a bodily mark. Each involves a vastly different understanding of the substance of the body, regardless of the extent to which a visible decoding has been brought to bear" (24–25). Contemporary critical discourse of racial marking often inscribes a slippage between literal marks—such as scars, birthmarks, and brands—and figurative conceptions of "marked bodies" as signifiers of cultural otherness. But as the figurative evokes the literal to achieve its symbolic power, the significance of the mark's physical reality often falls to the wayside, thus robbing such analyses of their full potential. Since this chapter is specifically concerned with such literal marks, we must be careful to avoid such slippages by closely examining how the terminology of *marking* is deployed in the nineteenth-century American context: When does it refer to specific, localized marks like birthmarks? When does it refer to other supposed physiological "signs" of race, such as skin color, hair, nose, and so on? And most important, what is the signifying connection between these two meanings? This question becomes even more complicated when we consider how, in pseudoscientific accounts of race in the eighteenth and nineteenth centuries, "black skin itself has been treated as something anomalous . . . something akin to an all-body birthmark" or a "universal freckle."[7]

Thus it is common parlance in nineteenth-century American literature, medicine, and law to speak of a person's African heritage as a "mark" or "imprint" on his or her body. The following are merely a sample of this dynamic. In *Uncle Tom's Cabin*, Stowe's heroine Eliza has the "impress of the despised race on her face" (chapter 9, 70). In the 1853 legal case of *Nichols v. Bell*, a man was freed from slavery because, in the judge's opinion, he did not have the "decided mark" of the African (Keetley 9). And while the Rev. Philip Slaughter inveighed against African American freedom by declaring that "Almighty God has placed between us and them, by a visible mark, an impassable gulf," the physician Samuel Latham Mitchell suggested that slavery would end if medicine could abolish the "sable mark of distinction between slaves and their masters" (Armistead, LAS 6; Martin 39). From a critical standpoint, contemporary scholars also speak of "marked" races, highlighting the neutral "unmarked" space of whiteness in order to challenge it.[8]

Yet "marking" is also used in both nineteenth-century and current discourse to refer to specific localized marks, including birthmarks, moles, and scars. In his *Confession* Nat Turner explains that "certain marks on his head and breast" led to his special destiny (31). We find another example in the Leeds Anti-Slavery pamphlet, "A Slave Auction in Virginia," which describes how "each scar or mark is dwelt upon with great minuteness—its cause, its age, its general effect upon the health, &c., are questions asked and readily answered" (Armistead, LAS 49). In this context such marks often refer to those bodily signs produced by the violence of enslavement. Moses Roper is one of many slave narrators who describe how the marks of ferocious beatings and torture "remain on my body, a standing testimony" to the truth of his story (56, 68).

Some of these marks are deliberately inscribed to identify potential runaways; in a macabre echo of Hawthorne's scarlet letter, many slave women and men were branded with letters, such as "Molly," branded "R" on the left cheek and the insides of both legs; "Mary," branded "A" on her cheek and forehead; and an unnamed woman branded "M" on the left side of her face, all named in an advertisement for fugitive slaves reproduced in the Leeds Anti-Slavery series (Armistead, LAS 23). Stowe drew on these real-life examples for her character George, branded on his hand with his master's initials (91). In a demonstration of the practical as well as semantic relationship between these types of marks and the idea of blackness as a mark, Roper explains that his master wished to tattoo his face with gunpowder "on account of my being too white," for better identification were Roper to escape (70). This example offers critical insight into how these several forms of marking have overlapped and become semantically blurred.

Carol Henderson's 2002 *Scarring the Black Body: Race and Representation in African American Literature* presents a comprehensive analysis of the violent marking of enslaved African Americans' bodies. She notes the disingenuous integration of such marks with "natural" forms of bodily marking in fugitive slave advertisements, in which "'African markings,' 'branded,' 'whip-scarred,' and 'smallpox-pitted' are just a few of the terms used to categorize the distinguishing marks present on the bodies of fugitive slaves" (26). Henderson also suggests that the marking of slaves, the violence of which often produced bodily differences that fit contemporary definitions of disability, served both to consolidate enslaved people's subjugated status and, conversely, to signify resistance, as "amputated limbs, disfigured body parts, welted backs—all were read as manifestations of a rebellious spirit. Moreover, the slave's body served as a billboard in another way, a 'visual aid' if you will, within the social structure of slavery, with these same marks serving as reminders to the black slave community of the consequences of rebellious action" (36). This production of the marked slave body as text was also present in antislavery contexts, as "a standard feature of abolitionist meetings . . . was what one commentator calls the 'Negro exhibit,'" in which the fugitive slave silently displayed the wounds and scars on his or her body (Baker 13).[9] Moreover Keetley suggests that this dynamic functioned narratively, noting that the amanuensis of Louisa Picquet's narrative "consistently draws attention to Picquet's beatings, asking her not only if her various masters whipped her, but how and where they whipped her, how she was dressed, and whether they whipped her hard enough 'so as to raise marks'" (7). This narrative exhibition of Picquet's marked body, Keetley notes, "brand[s]" the light-skinned Picquet both as "slave" and as "black" (8).

Henderson argues that the exhibition of marked slave bodies "set a framework for formulating a recognizable African American voice situated around the body and its scars" (40). Hortense Spillers more explicitly claims the centrality of bodily marking for African American identity, suggesting that the literal, physical marks of slavery's violence became a form of cultural memory internalized and passed down generationally as racial marks: "We might well ask if this phenomenon of marking and branding actually 'transfers' from one generation to another, finding its various *symbolic substitutions* in an efficacy of meanings that repeat the initiating moments" (67). This dynamic, I argue, underpins modern critical slippages between literal and figurative marks, as well as adding an important political context in which such marks might be recast as signs not only of past oppression but of future communal healing and resistance.[10]

This is a crucial point to keep in mind as we examine the function of bodily marking in two examples of literary-historical negotiations of racial identity. In each of these cases, gender and disability function as submerged yet crucial contexts for the contested fantasy of racial identification, figured through the bodies of African American woman. In the remainder of this chapter, through accounts of the trial of Salomé Müller, we will see how the merging of literal and figurative marks into the "birthmark" allows racial difference to be located in the interstices of meaning and thus to be produced through language even as it is insistently located in the physical body.

Natural Marks on Trial

> If, in truth, there is or was another person of the same age, with the same peculiar marks upon her person, and bearing such a strong resemblance in every feature, as to lead every witness who had ever seen her or known her parents, to swear unhesitatingly to her identity, it would be one of the most wonderful facts in history. ("The Case of Salomé Müller")

In a celebrated 1845 trial in New Orleans, Salomé Müller, an enslaved woman, sued for her freedom, claiming to be a white German immigrant kidnapped into slavery as a child. Her suit succeeded largely due to the evidence of her birthmarks, two coffee-colored dots on her inner thighs identified by witnesses from her infancy and authenticated by eminent white physicians who examined her under court order.[11] Descriptions of the case, both in the original law reports and in literary adaptations by George Washington Cable, William Wells Brown, and even William and Ellen Craft, reveal a complicated and conflicted discourse on the relationship of recognition to identification, including such issues as the reliability or "truth" of eyewitness testimony; the location of racial identity, as color, "blood," or reputation; and the role of language in fixing bodily identity. Ultimately the identification of Müller's birthmarks emerges in these narratives as a reassuring and exact solution to the indeterminacy and ambiguity of identity.[12]

While Keetley's analysis of the Müller case accurately posits racial identity "as both determinate *and* contested," both self-evident and requiring scrutiny, like many critics she overlooks the crucial function the fantasy of marking played in producing a supposed reconciliation of this contradiction; in fact she never even mentions the birthmarks in her analysis of the case (12). Instead she concludes that it was the "*prima facie* evidence of [Miller's] complexion—the fact that she is not visibly marked as an African," which ultimately led the court to its presumption of freedom (11). This statement, I contend, is both true and false; it is true that the court's decision, recorded in *Miller v. Belmonti*, makes clear that complexion played a key role in their decision making and that had Müller had darker skin or more tightly curled hair, her case might never have been considered at all. The justices write, "The first enquiry which engages our attention is, what is the color of the plaintiff?" (*Miller v. Belmonti*). However, the full text of their decision demonstrates a complex and often internally dissonant struggle to determine what forms of evidence—oral testimony, written records, bodily marks—are most likely to produce a reliable answer to the question "What is the color of the plaintiff?"

The complex interrelation of these factors is apparent in another passage from the judges' decision: "The proof in the record of the complexion of the plaintiff is very strong. Not only is there no evidence of her having descended from a slave mother, or even a mother of the African race; but no witness has ventured a positive opinion, from inspection, that she is of that race" (*Miller v. Belmonti*). Here we see the judges proceeding from complexion to heredity to reputation, and then back to the physical "inspection" of Müller, in a pseudo-logical progression that attempts to conceal its own incoherence beneath a proliferation of supposed "proofs." As Teresa Zackodnik notes in her review of nineteenth-century legal cases of contested racial identity, "we see a tension emerging in conceptualizations of race as discernible in the body's hidden interiors and their external expression or as evident in the social reputation and associations of individuals whose racial identity had come under question" (425).[13]

In efforts to resolve this tension, one technique frequently employed by the courts during this period was the physical "inspection" of plaintiffs:

> The usual procedure was for the claimant to stand in the well of the court under the gaze of the judge while their lawyer pointed out that their nose was thin and angular, or that their eyes were blue. He would ask them to bow their heads to display the straightness of their hair. Sometimes they would disrobe to show how pale their skin was. Next, physicians would come forward and provide opinions about the identifying features of the various races, and advise on what side of the line the claimant stood. (Bailey 150)

Such inspections did not follow any uniform format or employ regularized criteria but were determined in each case by the biases of the judge involved. The commonality of these cases was the perceived need for physical inspections, a need produced by an accumulation of legal precedents attempting to define race as biological.

The first statutory definition of race in the Union was Virginia's 1662 law, which "declared that the status of a child's mother determined the status of the child, breaking away from the English rule of determining inheritance status from the paternal line, and resolving the status of most mixed-race children by declaring them black" (Wright 164). The "condition of the mother" rule persisted into slavery to ensure slave owners' profits from the rape of female slaves (Roberts 187). However, as Luther Wright Jr. explains, legal definitions of race (as opposed to slave status) developed according to diverse criteria:

> Early statutes in Virginia and Arkansas used a physical appearance approach, defining negroes as those with visible and distinct admixtures of African blood. Later, other states defining race would adopt one-fourth, one-sixteenth, and one-thirty-second rules which declared that people with these fractional quantities of black ancestry were black under the law. . . . As the likelihood that more biracial people could be classified under existing laws increased, the laws became more restrictive. . . . By 1910, almost all southern states had adopted the "one-drop" rule. (164–165)

At the time of Salomé Müller's trial in 1845, both physical appearance and bloodline rules were applied to determine race, although not with any consistency. We see the slippage between these two conceptual frameworks in the judges' opinion quoted earlier, which moves from "the proof in the record of the complexion of the plaintiff" directly to the statement that there is "no evidence of her having descended from a slave mother," as if there is a clearly logical progression between the two. Yet in the judges' own daily existence, such supposed logic was clearly and repeatedly undermined by the presence of white-appearing slaves like Müller; thus they find it necessary to proceed further to adduce the evidence of physical inspection.

In doing so the judges are drawing upon a legal precedent originally set in the 1806 case of *Hudgins v. Wright*, in which three generations of enslaved women sued for freedom in a Virginia court, claiming to be American Indians rather than African American. The women were ultimately freed based on the judges' inspection of the "complexion of their faces, the texture of their hair, and the width of their noses" (Haney López, "Social Construction" 163–164). In their decision the judges "articulated rules to govern future cases in which a claim of mistaken racial identity might be made as a defense to being enslaved" (A. Davis 232): "In the case of a person visibly appearing to be a negro, the presumption is, in this country, that he is a slave, and it is incumbent on him to make out his right to freedom: but in the case of a person visibly appearing to be a white man, or an Indian, the presumption is that he is free, and it is necessary for his adversary to shew that he is a slave" (*Hudgins v. Wright*). The judges deciding Müller's case clearly drew upon *Hudgins v. Wright* to support their decision that, because Müller appeared white, she could not be a slave ("The Case of Salomé Müller" 204–205). Less obviously, however, the judges' emphasis on the identifying power of Müller's birthmarks also evoked the reasoning of *Hudgins v. Wright*, in which the justices declared that "the distinguishing characteristics of the different species of the human race are so visibly *marked*, that those species may be readily discriminated from each other by mere inspection only" and that "Nature has stampt upon the African and his descendants two characteristic *marks*, beside the difference of complexion, which often remain visible long after the characteristic distinction of color either disappears or becomes doubtful: a flat nose and wooly head of hair" (*Hudgins v. Wright*, my emphasis).

These contradictory legal claims—that race is apparent from immediate inspection and that race consists of a specific mark that must be looked for—resulted in such arbitrary-seeming legal decisions as the case of Abby Guy, who sued for her and her children's freedom in 1857 and was finally victorious based upon the jury's inspection of their feet, for, as the appeals judge wrote in 1861, "The experience of every intelligent observer of the race, whether in the instances of mixed or unmixed negro blood, will doubtless attest the truth of the professional witnesses. No one, who is familiar with the peculiar formations of the *negro foot* can doubt, but that an inspection of that member would ordinarily afford some indication of the race" (*Daniel v. Guy*). This reasoning would appear simply ludicrous were it not for the knowledge that five people's freedom hung in the balance. As the *Guy* decision indicates, the courts hedged their bets by appealing at once to the pseudoscientific expertise of professional witnesses, like the surgeons who examined Müller's birthmarks, and to the experience of the "intelligent [white] observer." As Ian Haney López has documented, well into the twentieth century American courts have relied upon these two rationales, "common knowledge" and "scientific evidence," to "justify the various racial divisions they advanced." And while contemporary legal discourse tends to avoid common knowledge and rely more on "knowledge of a reputedly objective, technical, and specialized sort," contradictory definitions of race persist to the present day ("White by Law" 628).[14]

In courtroom inspections of the Hudgins family, Guy, and Müller, "the literal body often constituted the body of evidence" (Keetley 5), reinscribing the "negro exhibit" in a form that the historical record tends to render passive, if not entirely mute. Lesser-known historical examples, however, can crucially remind us that the body under inspection belonged to a speaking subject who often spoke back, as in the case of Cyrus Clarke, brother of the slave narrators Milton and Lewis Clarke, which was reported in the Leeds Anti-Slavery series. Clarke's exchange with the New York judge questioning his petition to vote demonstrates his articulate challenge to the arbitrariness of physical inspection:

[CLARKE]: "I am as white as you, and don't you vote?" . . .

JUDGE E.: "Are you not a coloured man? And is not your hair curly?"

[CLARKE]: "We are both coloured men; and all we differ in is that you have not the handsome wavy curl."

Eventually "the board came to the honourable conclusion that, to be a coloured man, he must be at least one-half blood African. Mr. Clarke, the SLAVE, then voted, he being nearly full white" (Armistead, LAS 75).

Unfortunately challenges such as these did not have a transformative impact on the power of courts claiming, "as an objective legal standard, the individual judges' subjective perceptions of racial distinction" (A. Davis 232). In particular, from the mid-nineteenth century onward, we see "the court's inability to address questions of racial identity with any consistency and . . . the schism that develops in conceptualizations of whiteness and blackness" as corporeal or social, visible or invisible (Zackodnik 425). While both Zackodnik and the legal historian Ariela Gross emphasize the role played by the social, figured as "reputation" or "association," in cases such as Guy's and Müller's I contend that the court's very inability to reconcile the social and the biological produced its increasing reliance on a discourse of marking that purported to resolve racial contradictions with a simple, visible solution.

That the birthmarks emerged as the most solid form of evidence in Müller's case is made clear by the closing page of the decision, where the justices observe that, while "numerous witnesses swore positively to their undoubting conviction of her identity, . . . the proof does not stop at mere family resemblances and recognitions. It is shown by evidence which is not impeached, that the lost child had certain natural marks, or moles, on the inside of her thighs" (*Miller v. Belmonti*). The suggestion that mere oral testimony is subjective and liable to be "impeached," while "natural marks" are objective and unimpeachable clearly privileges empirical physical data over personal observation or recognition.

Yet there is a glaring flaw in this self-fulfilling logic of bodily determinism: the "unimpeached evidence" of the birthmarks is actually only as valid as the verbal testimony of the various witnesses can make it. No written records or pictures of Müller's birth are offered to prove that the German girl was born with such marks, only the verbal testimony of various women who knew the real Salomé as a child: her godmother, Eva Schubert; her cousin Madame Karl; her aunt Mistress Schultzeheimer; and Eva Schubert's mother, Eva Kropp. All accounts of Müller's story agree on this point, yet the possibility that these women may be lying is never raised by any party, even the vitriolic defenders of Müller's slave status.[15] Cable's account, in his 1889 story "Salome Müller: The White Slave," is typical: "'If ever our little Salomé is found,' Eva Kropp had been accustomed to say, 'we shall know her by two hair moles about the size of a coffee-bean, one on the inside of each thigh, about midway up from the knee. Nobody can make those, or take them away without leaving the tell-tale scars'" (178).[16] This passage embodies its own unacknowledged contradictions: the roots of the evidence are discursive (the witness "was accustomed to say"), yet its validity is seen as rooted in the physical body—the moles that "nobody" can make or take away. The very phrase "tell-tale scars" signifies this merging of language and body, which Cable, like the justices, appears ultimately to reject in favor of the fantasy of incontrovertible bodily evidence that exists outside the subjective realm of discourse. Yet in Cable's story, discourse cannot be so easily suppressed, emerging repeatedly, as in another telling passage about the marks: "But another confirmation was possible, far more conclusive than mere recognition of the countenance. Eva [Schubert] knew this. For weeks together she had bathed and dressed the little Salomé every day. She and her mother and all Henry Müller's family had known, and had made it their common saying, that . . . if ever Salomé were found they could prove she was Salomé beyond the shadow of a doubt" (166). Again we see the discursive nature of truth, as that which is said over and over until it becomes true ("their common saying"), bracketed within the supposed totalizing power of the physical, which is "far more conclusive than mere recognition of the countenance" and "beyond a shadow of a doubt." Alice Petry argues that Cable's tale of Müller, unlike the official court documents, is an exploration of the idea that "'truth,' far from being hard and fast, is elusive, subjective, and quite possibly untenable as either a label for experience or an abstract concept" (25).[17] Thus we may find in Cable a more ambivalent negotiation of the relationship between body and text than in the related legal and historical documents, demonstrating the importance of reading the fantasy at this time through the interplay between cultural forms. Yet unlike Melville's *The Confidence Man*, which in both intention and reception dissociated itself from any extraliterary application, Cable's story drew directly on, corresponds quite closely with, and is often treated like other historical sources, such as the legal reports on Müller's case. Indeed as the fantasy continued to penetrate the cultural sphere, its very insistence upon certainty seemed to produce a greater blurring of the boundaries between history and fiction, bodies and the stories told about those bodies.

Thus we find in all accounts truth-claims based on marks that have, so to speak, a history with two ends—their presence on the infant Salomé Müller and their appearance on the adult claimant to that identity—and for some reason, the first end is considered by all sides to be affirmed simply by oral testimony. The other end, however, must be scientifically examined and validated in order to be true, hence the summoning of "eminent members of the medical profession" to give their opinion that the marks are in fact "*noevi materni*" and could not have been faked by any means (*Miller v. Belmonti*). (Again, the reasonable possibility of a conspiracy among the four witnesses to claim such marks for the infant Müller once they were discovered on the adult "Müller" is never raised or even implied.) In his story Cable reproduces a portion of the original handwritten opinion of the physicians, ostensibly in service of historical truth but also perhaps as an oblique comment on the discursive nature of even this "objective" evidence (180).

In fact, as Petry notes, Cable's preface to *Strange True Stories of Louisiana* places great emphasis on his story's grounding in historical research, in the "court records," "old newspaper files," and "great heap of papers," as well as the extensive interviews he conducted with "Salomé's still surviving friends and relatives" and other New Orleans residents familiar with the case (Cable 3–4). Yet the product of all this research is unconvincing, producing not a coherent tale but "dates, statistics, details, definitions, and an avalanche of German names—who married whom, who knew whom, who lived in what district . . . presented in such a flurry that they overwhelm rather than enlighten" (Petry 23). Petry suggests that this incoherent flurry of details does not comprise an aesthetic failure on Cable's part but is an integral feature of his interrogation of the limits of truth, particularly "the limitations of . . . the primary recorder and conveyor of truth: the words themselves, and the frail humans who use them for good or ill" (28).

The limitations that Cable registers are signaled in other accounts of Müller's case, I suggest, by the emphasis placed on a particular fantasy of identification in which the truth of identity is immediately and fundamentally visible. We see this fantasy played out most dramatically in the account printed in the 1845 edition of the Boston law journal the *Law Reporter*. This account, "The Case of Salomé Müller," repeatedly emphasizes personal recognition, as in its description of Müller's first discovery on the street by Madame Karl: "So instantly was she attracted by her peculiar features . . . that she entered the shop, and immediately began to question the young woman. . . . She carried her to the house of her cousin and god-mother, Mrs. Schubert, who instantly and unhesitatingly recognized her . . . exclaiming, 'My God! here is the long-lost Salomé Müller'" (197). This moment of immediate and perfect recognition is echoed in the *Law Reporter*'s account by a number of other German immigrants who appeared at the trial to obtain the girl's freedom: "The family resemblance in every feature was declared to be so remarkable, that some of the witnesses did not hesitate to say that they 'should know her among ten thousand'; that they were 'as certain the plaintiff was Salomé Müller, the daughter of Daniel and Dorothea Müller, as of their own existence'" (197). Drawing on the *Law Reporter*'s account, John Bailey's 2003 novelistic retelling of the case reinscribes this fantasy of recognition, even as it undermines it in Bailey's final, unconvincing claim that Müller was an imposter (257).

Yet all these accounts also acknowledge that testimony of recognition was not enough to obtain Müller's freedom. It was necessary that she also be recognized racially as white—for otherwise she had no grounds on which to sue—and finally, for her identity to be fixed through the medical verification of her birthmarks. Yet, as noted earlier, the evidence of the birthmarks itself rests on the testimony of the same women who claimed such immediate and perfect recognition of Müller's face. Here we see how discourse and bodily inscription function to reinforce one another in a tautological process whose unifying principle is the upholding of the fantasy that race is knowable.[18]

Ironically Müller's brown birthmarks stand in for and metonymically realize her whiteness, anchoring racial and personal identity in the physical against their threatened unmooring into the social and discursive field. Thus the trial of Salomé Müller demonstrates the deep imbrication of race with the fantasy of identification, a connection that solidifies at the site of the marked body. Yet this particular fantasy of marking had limited scope, since not all ambiguously raced subjects could be expected to have conveniently unique birthmarks, much less a bevy of mnemonically gifted women to authenticate them. Thus fantasies of marking continued to circulate unevenly throughout the second half of the nineteenth century, until they were at last provided with the necessarily universal and "scientific" mode of deployment. Fingerprints, true "physiological autographs," seemed to be the perfect answer to the desire expressed by John Hubback at the opening of this chapter. In the next chapter we will explore some notable fissures in that perfect solution, already prefigured by our consideration of the fantastical case of Will West. Additionally, we will see how disability provides a key trope with which Twain explores racial ambiguity even as he provides the most famous and influential example of the fantasy of marking with his introduction of fingerprinting to the American imagination.

5 /   Of Fiction and Fingerprints

In the introduction to this book, the case of Will West richly demonstrated the fantastical status of fingerprinting in modern culture, exposing its material effects as well as its mythical origins. In this chapter I argue that the power of fingerprinting to realize the fantasy of identification stemmed largely from its imagined power to mark and control racial and disability identities. This analysis assumes that race and disability must be read as mutually constitutive and imbricated, as "the colonial encounter and the series of migrations that it triggered in its wake served to displace the discourse of disability onto a discourse of otherness that was correlated to racial difference" (Quayson 10). The relationship of fingerprinting to racialist science has been well established, yet the role of disability in anchoring that relationship through its signification of natural physical immutability remains largely unexplored. By examining that role through Mark Twain's 1894 novel *Pudd'nhead Wilson* and its accompanying short story, "Those Extraordinary Twins," as well as critical responses these works have evoked, I demonstrate that the race-disability connection is fundamental to the emergence of fantasies of marking.[1] By the end of the nineteenth century such fantasies had achieved significant penetrance into legal and bureaucratic spheres but were not yet deployed in an organized institutional fashion. Twain's novel marks the turning point in this process, as, through the reversal of cause and effect previously discussed, a work of literary invention becomes the means by which fantasies of marking make their first institutional claims to truth.

Twain's deployment of fingerprinting as trope and plot device through which to explore race is crucially mediated through the evocation of physical disability, which stands for the *truly* absolute bodily difference. This connection becomes clear when we consider Twain's first use of the plot device of a bloody thumbprint, in his 1881 *Life on the Mississippi*. In the brief tale "A Thumb-print and What Came of It," the narrator tracks down and identifies two murderers—one, painstakingly, through his thumbprint; the other, immediately, through the fact he is missing his thumb. The implication that this physical disability—the missing finger—is semantically and practically equivalent to the textual mark of the fingerprint introduces the connection of disability to fingerprinting through their signification of a fixed and legible physical identity.

The literary historian Ann Wigger confirmed in 1957 that Twain had learned about fingerprinting by reading Sir Francis Galton's 1892 work *Finger Prints*, and many critics have commented on the relationship between Galton's racial biases and Twain's novel.[2] What has not yet been explored is how the connection between race and fingerprinting is mediated in the novel, other than through our knowledge of Galton's racialist, eugenic agenda. I suggest that disability functions as a necessary supplement in this significatory process, representing the "natural" physical body against which race may be shown as a construct, exposed as such by the technology of fingerprinting, which, like disability, is rooted in "nature" and the body's immutability: "The immediacy of fingerprinting suggests the 'naturalness' of symbolic forms in general, forms upon which the society depends" (Fredricks 496).

In Twain's novel the protagonist, lawyer David "Pudd'nhead" Wilson, solves a murder and a case of identity-switching by taking fingerprints from the residents of the town of Dawson's Landing, which he demonstrates dramatically during the climactic trial that closes the novel. Wilson discovers that Tom Driscoll, heir of one of the town's foremost white families, was switched in infancy by his nurse Roxy for her own son, a slave. The spurious Tom eventually murders his guardian, leaving a fingerprint on the weapon that Wilson is able to identify, during which he also exposes Roxy's deception by comparing infant and adult fingerprints.

During that climactic murder trial, Wilson makes a famous speech explaining fingerprinting:

Every human being carries with him from his cradle to his grave certain physical marks which do not change their character, and by which he can always be identified—and that without shade of doubt or question. These marks are his signature, his physiological autograph, so to speak, and this autograph cannot be counterfeited, nor can he disguise it or hide it away, nor can it become illegible by the wear and the mutations of time. This signature is not his face— age can change that beyond recognition; it is not his hair, for that can fall out; it is not his height, for duplicates of that exist; it is not his form, for duplicates of that exist, also, whereas this signature is each man's very own—there is no duplicate of it among the swarm- ing populations of the globe! (*Pudd'nhead Wilson* 108)

This speech is an ideal realization of the fantasy of identification, recasting the body as a text "autographed" by nature and readable by the state expert, here represented by the lawyer-scientist-detective character of Wilson.[3]

In fact this speech is frequently cited and reproduced in contempo- rary fingerprinting textbooks and histories and has been repeatedly cited in actual court decisions to support the reliability of fingerprint evidence (Beavan ix; Rowe 233n51). In the 1911 burglary trial of Carlo Crispi, for example, Lieutenant Joseph Faurot of the New York Police Department borrowed explicitly from Twain during his expert testi- mony, which included examples of twins' fingerprints and the gim- mick of identifying anonymous fingerprints on the courtroom win- dows (S. Cole 181–184). Two decades later a decision by the Criminal Court of Appeals in Oklahoma cited *Pudd'nhead Wilson* to support the reliability of fingerprint evidence (S. Cole 208). Like the Will West leg- end, "in law-enforcement folklore, Twain's novel helped transform the popular conception of fingerprint evidence as a hoax or fad. Its court- room scenes seemed to affirm the transcendence of fingerprinting over earlier kinds of physical identification, and this affirmation carried the aesthetic and cultural force of an authentic American voice" (Rowe 160). I contend that the startling and repeated use of Twain's satirical work of fiction to make serious arguments in law-enforcement settings is difficult to comprehend except through the powerful lens of the fan- tasy of identification, which uses fiction to both validate and create itself as a state apparatus.

Yet only a greatly oversimplified and selective reading of Twain's novel can render it as a wholesale endorsement of either the means or the goal of the fantasy of identification. Instead Twain's "complicated and contradictory attitudes toward fingerprinting" reflect his ambiva- lence about "systems of knowledge . . . that create fixed boundaries and thereby control human beings" (Gillman 80). Thus Twain "celebrates the new technology [of fingerprinting] anxiously, suspicious of the institutional interests it serves" (Rowe 167), and this anxiety primarily emerges through his depictions of race slavery (Berkson 316; Cox 1; Gillman 55; Robinson, "The Sense of Disorder" 34). In the case of the switched babies, for example, Twain plays repeatedly upon the failure of identification, both personal and racial, that enables the switch, commenting that even the heir's father could only distinguish the two babies, with their "blue eyes and flaxen curls," by their clothing (*Pudd'nhead Wilson* 9). Similarly the end of the novel produces not the restoration of a moral universe, as in the classic detective novel, but a satirical and racialized failure of justice, as the false Tom is sold down the river, the very fate his mother hoped to avert by switching the babies (Cox 19–20; Gillman 93; Whitley 69). Rather than wholesale endorsement, then, Twain's text is a complex and ambivalent exploration of the fantasy through the shifting meanings of race and disability, enabled in part by the complicated textual history of the novel and story.

Monstrous Identities

The novel now known as *Pudd'nhead Wilson* began in 1892 as a short story about a pair of conjoined ("Siamese") twins (*Pudd'nhead Wilson* ix). Also set in the town of Dawson's Landing, this comic tale told of the townspeople's awed reaction to the twins, who had two heads, four arms, two legs and one torso. However, the original subplot of racial switching, with its minor characters of Wilson, Tom Driscoll, and Roxy, grew and took over the tale until it was necessary to separate them in what Twain famously referred to as a "literary Caesarean operation" (*Pudd'nhead Wilson* 119). The result was the current novel, *Pudd'nhead Wilson*, and a concurrently published, raggedly edited compilation of the excised material, known as "Those Extraordinary Twins."[4] (For clarity, in the remainder of this chapter I refer to these two works as "the novel" (*Pudd'nhead Wilson*) and "the story" ("Those Extraordinary Twins"), although I acknowledge that the textual history is somewhat more generically complicated.) In the revised novel, the twins Angelo and Luigi still exist as very minor characters, but they are no longer conjoined. However, in a textual move that has been read as both careless and intriguing, "ghostly remnants" of the twins' original conjoinment remain in the novel (Fredricks 484): the twins speak at one point of having been exhibited in a circus, and later are referred to derogatorily as "side-show riff-raff" and "dime museum freaks" (*Pudd'nhead Wilson* 28, 83).[5]

Thus any reading of disability in *Pudd'nhead Wilson* must also include consideration of "Those Extraordinary Twins" and of the intertexuality between the two works, for "the image of the tangled twins represents an origin for the text of *Pudd'nhead Wilson*—an origin that, despite the attempts of the author, stubbornly refuses to be erased" (Fredricks 486). When we consider that Twain wrote the conjoined twins material first, as the foundation, so to speak, and constructed the eventual text of the novel atop that foundation, we can see how considerations of disability become crucial to reading the novel's mediations of bodies, texts, and power. This is true both in analyzing the novel itself and in responding to the body of criticism it has produced. Many critics have read the novel as critiquing the social construction of race, what Twain calls the "fiction of law and custom" that makes Roxy and her son black although they appear white, and several have pointed out that Twain also portrays gender as highly constructed and contingent (*Pudd'nhead Wilson* 9).[6] Disability, however, remains an apparently fixed and naturalized category that resists—and thus enables—other embodied social identities like race and gender to be exposed as constructions.

One way to understand this process is through the deployment of terms such as *freak*, *monster*, and *unnatural*. In the world of Twain's stories—and in the critical responses to the stories—race slavery perverts human relations and character to an extent that can be represented only by comparisons to disability, the ultimate state of unnature. Put simply, slavery is *monstrous*; the twins are an actual *monster*, functioning, in Foucault's terms, as "the principle of intelligibility" of all other forms of abnormality (*Abnormal* 56). This abnormality makes itself felt at the cultural level of the novel, which reverses proslavery rhetorical and legal assertions that racial mixing was itself "abominable," "unnatural," and "monstrous."[7] As monsters, the twins are placed outside the realm of signification, as reflectors rather than producers of meaning. This process, described by David Hevey as "enfreakment," is integral to Western cultural definitions of the "human" and more specifically to nineteenth-century American definitions of the citizen-subject (Hevey 335; Garland Thomson *Extraordinary Bodies* 10).

Writing of the hugely popular freak shows in the United States from midcentury through the early 1900s, Rosemarie Garland Thomson argues that the display of freaks served to fashion the "self-governed, iterable subject of democracy—the American cultural self . . . at a time when modernization rendered the meaning of bodily differences and vulnerabilities increasingly unstable and threatening" (*Extraordinary Bodies* 10–11). The

American subjects of Twain's novel and story struggle with problems of identity, autonomy, and will that are represented through race but mediated through a process of enfreakment that at once submerges and solidifies the disabled presence in the text. Critical responses to *Pudd'nhead Wilson* have generally mirrored and extended this process. Critics such as Forrest Robinson, Myra Jehlen, Nancy Fredricks, and Eric Sundquist repeatedly refer to aspects of the novel and story as "unnatural," "freakish," and "monstrously deformed." Tom Driscoll, for example, is described as both an "unnatural" and "monstrous" son to Roxy, since even after learning she is his mother, he contemplates selling her down the river. These critics also use terms of enfreakment to describe the system of racial slavery, and Sundquist extends the metaphor to include the 1896 *Plessy v. Ferguson* decision, in which "the Court left equal protection, like Twain's mulatto, and even more, like his Siamese twins, monstrously lodged in two bodies, neither of which had full responsibility for its legal or moral guarantee" ("Mark Twain" 56).

I wish to emphasize that Twain himself never actually describes Tom Driscoll or slavery as monstrous or unnatural; these critics are not adopting the language of the novel but rather are transcribing its submerged meanings, meanings that are driven by the haunting presence of the freakish bodies imperfectly excised from the novel's racial narrative. In other words, while these critics accurately perceive the racial metaphorics of Twain's monstrous bodies, they do not pay heed to the actualities of those bodies, their material and historical particularities. Yet such particularities are both meaningful and provocative in the resonance they add to critical understandings of Twain's explorations of race, agency, and American selfhood.

We can begin by exploring the historical sources of Twain's portrayal of his original conjoined twins, Angelo and Luigi. In 1869 Twain published a humorous sketch about Chang and Eng Bunker, "Personal Habits of the Siamese Twins," as well as a lesser-known piece about another famous pair of conjoined twins, Millie and Christine McKoy, which appeared in the *Buffalo Herald* (Gillman 58; Cox 14). However, when embarking on his tale, Twain based Angelo and Luigi not on either Chang and Eng or the McKoys but on the Italian brothers Giacomo and Giovanni Tocci. He refers to the Toccis in his essay that connects the novel and the story: "I had seen a picture of a youthful Italian 'freak'—or 'freaks'—which was—or which were—on exhibition in our cities—a combination consisting of two heads and four arms joined to a single body and a single pair of legs—and I thought I would write an

FIGURE 5.1. Chang and Eng Bunker. Courtesy of the State Archives of North Carolina.

extravagantly fantastic little story with this freak of nature for hero—or heroes" (*Pudd'nhead Wilson* 119). The differences between these twins' bodily configurations is important: while Chang and Eng Bunker had two distinct and "normally" configured bodies merely connected by a band of tissue, the Tocci brothers' bodily configuration presented a far more challenging blurring of boundaries of body and self, for they

FIGURE 5.2. Giacomo and Giovanni Tocci.

shared a single set of legs and lower torso, only dividing midchest into separate upper bodies (Fig. 5.1 and Fig. 5.2).

On the choice of the Toccis as Twain's model, Gillman observes that "the crucial distinction is the shared body, which heightens the dilemma of whether the twins should be accorded individual or collective status" (60). Sundquist similarly suggests that the "more physiologically apt Tocci brothers were an even better model" for signifying the doubling of Tom and Chambers, as well as Tom's dual racial status ("Mark Twain" 67). Gillman's and Sundquist's observations are certainly valid, yet they leave a great deal unexplored regarding the twins' historical models and fictional presentation. I would like to highlight three largely unexplored issues here: the choice of the Toccis rather than Chang and Eng or other contemporaneous models; the differences between Luigi and Angelo and the Toccis; and the critical reception (or elision) of these differences. I will briefly explore each issue with a view toward demonstrating how the depiction of the twins crucially engages with issues of racial identification through the trope of the immutable (disabled) body.

The choice of the Toccis over Chang and Eng, Millie and Christine, or other conjoined twins of Twain's era certainly points to a desire to signify a more profoundly merged and ambiguous bodily condition than that of two bodies merely connected, as in Chang and Eng's case. (Millie and Christine, while more extensively joined than Chang and Eng, had discrete torsos and two separate sets of legs and arms.) In his earlier sketch Twain had played upon the recent strife of his "conjoined" nation by humorously (and falsely) claiming that Chang and Eng fought on opposite sides during the Civil War, took each other prisoner, and were then exchanged when an army court could not determine "which one was properly the captor and which the captive" ("Personal Habits" 297). This scene foreshadows a farcical trial in "Those Extraordinary Twins" in which Luigi and Angelo are acquitted of kicking Tom Driscoll since the court cannot determine which of them was controlling the legs, as well as the story's denouement, in which both twins are hanged for Luigi's crime (*Pudd'nhead Wilson* 146–148). However, bodily configuration produces an important difference: while Chang and Eng are *inseparable*, Luigi and Angelo are *indistinguishable*. In other words, the rhetorical and practical dilemma for Chang and Eng is that one twin's movements mirror the other's. In the case of Twain's fictional twins, however, their actions are not mirrored but merged: in the extended comic scene of the twins' trial,

Wilson challenges witness and court alike to tell the difference between a kick by Luigi and one by Angelo.

Gillman and Sundquist both suggest that the merged twins' bodies better represent the racial entanglement of Twain's America, a claim that my argument does not contradict but rather strengthens through nuance. In 1869 Twain used the connected bodies of Chang and Eng to sketch the absurdity of a nation recently divided against itself; in 1892 he chose the merged bodies of the Tocci brothers to explore the dilemma of a postbellum nation attempting to reimagine itself as a unified, indivisible whole entering a new century.[8] Yet he sent his twins to the antebellum South, to the world of the slavocracy, whose dark doings gradually transformed his tale of bodily confusion into one of racial contention, entangling his narrative to a point where he had to take an authoritative surgeon's scalpel to separate his conjoined tale.

I suggest that Chang and Eng's bodies may be read to signify the *imagined* slavocracy, in which black and white, slave and master, inhabit distinct but intimately connected worlds: neither can survive without the other, but each stays in its socially and physically demarcated arena, and separation—if contemplated—involves a quick and authoritative snip of the connecting ligature. Luigi and Angelo's merged bodies, however, metaphorically enact the *reality* of antebellum America: the races merged by decades of rape and sexual intermingling and the crumbling distinction between black slave and white master upheld by elaborate and increasingly threadbare social and legal fictions based on bodily configuration in name only. Thus Twain's choice of the Tocci brothers as his model logically connects to his seemingly irresistible need to explore the slaveholding world of his boyhood in terms at once more grisly and complex than those of Huck Finn. In this context, making the twins Italian rather than Asian (like Chang and Eng) or African American (like Millie and Christine) foregrounds his troubling of the category of whiteness, which is the true race "problem" at the heart of his tale.

Such a claim is bolstered by the significant changes Twain did choose to enact upon his twins, changes that largely cluster around issues of agency and monstrosity. In the first place, he made his twins even more "freakish" in configuration than the Toccis by placing two arms on each of their outside shoulders, a configuration not only inaccurate but physiologically impossible (Fig. 5.3). In fact parapagus twins (joined at the pelvic region) have either one arm on each outside shoulder and one on the inside shoulder (like the Toccis) or one on each outside shoulder while the inside shoulders are merged, like twenty-first-century twins Abigail and Brittany Hensel (Dreger, *One of Us* 28–29). Placing two arms on each shoulder allows Twain to exaggerate the enfreakment of the twins through the townspeople's reactions to them, as in their landlady Aunt Patsy's first horrified impression of a "wormy squirming of arms in the air" (*Pudd'nhead Wilson* 126) and descriptions of the twins as nonhuman objects, such as a "tarantula" (127), a "philopena" (double-kernelled nut; 125)," a "pair of scissors" (145), and "one of those pocket knives with a multiplicity of blades" (130).

As a result of the placement of the twins' arms, Aunt Patsy is mystified by the question of the twins' agency, as evinced by her internal monologue at the breakfast table: "Now that hand is going to take that coffee to—no, it's gone to the other mouth; I can't understand it; and now here is the dark-complected hand with a potatoe [*sic*] on its fork, I'll see what goes with it—there, the light-complected head's got it, as sure as I live!" (*Pudd'nhead Wilson* 131). This confusion is figured racially as well, as a matter of "dark-complected" hands feeding "light-complected" heads, a depiction that hardly needs glossing in the context of race slavery. Aunt Patsy's confusion is mediated through the enfreakment of the twins, their unnaturalness standing in for the supposed normalcy of the other "dark" hands feeding "light" mouths at this table: the hands of the enslaved woman, Nancy, who is serving the food during this scene. Here we see how exaggerating the twins' monstrosity serves Twain's racial critique of the slave system while simultaneously undermining it by separating "normal" and "abnormal" problems of agency. If agency, and by extension control of the body's actions, lies at the heart of the system of slavery, it is vital to note that it is virtually impossible to represent problems of physical agency without referencing disability. A consideration of the particularities of disability representation enables us to appreciate the particular aspects of enslavement being represented and, in Twain's case, ironically critiqued. If the novel turns upon Tom Driscoll's deceptive duality, in which "his second (slave) self is internal but also unwilled, an unwanted identity imposed by society's racial classification" (Gillman 71–72), the story mirrors that duality through the ambiguous agency of the twins.

The second alteration performed by Twain, also predicated on agency, is the invention of another historically and physiologically inaccurate feature: the "switching" of control of the twins' legs, which plays a key

FIGURE 5.3. C. H. Warren and F. M. Senior, original 1894 illustration for "Those Extraordinary Twins." Courtesy of the Mark Twain Papers and Project at the University of California, Berkeley.

role in the story's plot. Angelo explains: "By a mysterious law of our being, each of us has utter and indisputable control of our [legs] a week at a time, turn and turn about" (*Pudd'nhead Wilson* 139).[9] This alternation, said to occur precisely each Saturday at midnight, is presented as the solution to the dilemma of merged agency, in which the twins would be immobilized by the need to agree: "We should always be arguing and fussing and disputing over the merest trifles. We should lose worlds of time, for we couldn't go down stairs or up, couldn't go to bed, couldn't rise, couldn't wash, couldn't dress, couldn't stand up, couldn't sit down, couldn't even cross our legs without calling a meeting first, and explaining the case, and passing resolutions, and getting consent" (138). This comically ironic description bypasses the fact that the conjoined twins on whom Luigi and Angelo were modeled did not have the problems so eloquently imagined by Twain, a fact of which Twain must surely have been aware through his encounters with them. While many real-life conjoined twins make agreements as to which of them will make decisions on certain days, these are voluntary arrangements, not an actual physiological mechanism (Dreger, *One of Us* 40). Yet Twain chose to create such a mechanism for his twins, substituting for a socially constructed, negotiated, and discursive solution one that is involuntary, physically based, and supposedly "natural"—like the fantasy of identification.

As a result Twain is able to predicate his plot upon the mystery of the twins' agency, a mystery founded in their unreadable, inseparable body. From the "Who is kicking?" trial to the final solution of hanging both twins to keep Angelo out of town meetings, the plot of "Those Extraordinary Twins" turns upon the impossibility of determining who is acting through the twins' shared body (Fig. 5.4). This impossibility is presented both ironically and straightforwardly as a social threat. The judge who presides over the "kicking" trial melodramatically proclaims that the acquittal of the twins sets "adrift, unadmonished, in this community, two men endowed with an awful and mysterious gift, a hidden and grisly power for evil—a power by which each in his turn may commit crime after crime of the most heinous character, and no man be able to tell which is the guilty and which the innocent part in any case of them all. Look to your homes—look to your property—look to your lives—for you have need!" (*Pudd'nhead Wilson* 154). The judge's impassioned warning, which echoes antebellum white fears of slave rebellions, ironically describes not the twins but their symbolic corollary in the novel, Tom Driscoll, whose racial identity is "hidden" and who proceeds to commit "crime after crime," all the while secure that he cannot be found out due to his many disguises and his "innocent" status as a white gentleman. After murdering his uncle, for example, Tom reflects complacently, "All the detectives on earth couldn't trace me now; there's not a vestige of a clew left in the world" (*Pudd'nhead Wilson* 95).

Wilson's ability to pin the crime on Tom through fingerprinting suggests that the solution to the problem of agency presented by the conjoined twins is a new definition of identity as rooted in the normative body. I agree with Katherine Rowe that "the Siamese [*sic*] twins represent the nightmare of a legal apparatus unable to make their physiology testify for them," but not with her conclusion that the "extraordinary, radical uniqueness of their body" precludes the usefulness of fingerprints to determine their agency (193). Rather I suggest that the twins' body stands in for the "extraordinary, radical uniqueness" now discoverable in *all* bodies through their fingerprints, as well as demonstrating the problems of agency inherent in

FIGURE 5.4. C. H. Warren and F. M. Senior, original 1894 illustration for "Those Extraordinary Twins." Courtesy of the Mark Twain Papers and Project at the University of California, Berkeley.

that technology. Thus I move now to the second point of my argument, the metonymic and historical connection between disability and fingerprinting which is then used, ironically, to disconnect racial difference from the physical body.

Fantasies of Fingerprints

It is well established that Galton spoke for most early European and American fingerprint researchers when he wrote in 1891 that fingerprint identification was most needed "in our tropical settlements, where the individual members of the swarms of dark and yellow-skinned races are mostly unable to sign their names and are otherwise hardly distinguishable" ("Identification by Finger-Tips" 303). What is usually omitted in discussions of Galton's racialist agenda is that disability was as crucial as race to his interests, and in fact the two are deeply imbricated in both his research and its later applications.[10] Galton not only made a point of fingerprinting people of different races but also collected prints from the "lowest" and "worst" "idiots" in London (*Finger Prints* 19, 197). Again Galton was disappointed in his eugenic hopes, for he found "prints of eminent thinkers and of eminent statesmen that can be matched by those of congenital idiots" (197).

One would think, from Galton's acknowledged failure at finding racial or mental distinctions in fingerprints, that the idea would have stopped there. But here is where the power of fantasy comes into play again, producing social imperatives that masquerade as science even when blatantly contradicted by science. Thus Galton can write that, having compared fingerprints from English, Welsh, Basque, "Hebrew," and different groups of "Negro" peoples, he finds that "no very marked characteristic distinguished the races" (*Finger Prints* 195) but then continue in the same breath, "Still, whether it be from pure fancy on my part . . . or from some real peculiarity, the general aspect of the Negro print strikes me as characteristic. The width of the ridges seems more uniform, their intervals more regular, and their courses more parallel than with us. In short, they give an idea of greater simplicity" (196). What Galton calls fancy, we may understand to be fantasy—a fantasy that has persisted for a hundred years in research by experts seeking to demonstrate racial and mental differences through fingerprints. Such research peaked during the eugenic frenzy of the early twentieth century but still persists to this day and usually manifests in entanglements of racial difference and mental disability, as in Harold Cummins's 1943 work, *Fingerprints, Palms, and Soles*, which made claims of discernible patterns in the fingerprints of different racial groups, schizophrenics, and epileptics (S. Cole 114).

Cummins's work is cited in a 1987 article in the trade journal *Identification News* titled "Disease Inheritance and Race Determination by Fingerprints," whose author, FBI fingerprint specialist Donald F. McBride, devotes a paragraph to a study on "Mongoloids," referring to people with Down syndrome, a group who in Galton's day would have been referred to as "Mongolian idiots" and who very likely comprised a large number of the "idiots" he fingerprinted at the Darenth Asylum (McBride 1). At the time of Galton's writing, Dr. John Langdon H. Down had already popularized the term "Mongolian idiot" in medical circles (Bérubé, *Life* 25; Jackson 168). Whether or not the widely read Galton was familiar with Down's "Observations on the Ethnic Classification of Idiots," published in 1866 (Jackson 170), he is certain to have encountered such racialized classifications in his visits to the Darenth Asylum in the late 1880s and early 1890s.[11] Thus we may uncover the submerged enmeshment of race and disability in Galton's work, which has persisted, despite ostensible scientific disproof, into present-day professional identification circles. I would argue in fact that just as it seems impossible to disentangle race and disability in the history of eugenics, it is equally impossible to do so with regard to the early history of fingerprinting. Attempts to do so in order to counter racism, such as Stephen Jay Gould's well-known *The Mismeasure of Man*, unfortunately themselves rely on a stabilization of "real" disability against the "false" and oppressive disabilities ascribed to people of color.

To note the problems of this dynamic is not to deny the pervasively destructive scientific racism directed against people of color, nor to claim for disability some kind of originary or hierarchical status as the ultimate, grounding category of oppression. Rather it is to foreground the necessity of a fully integrated analysis that proceeds from the central understanding that race and disability are mutually constitutive and inseparable. Such an understanding is necessary to see that Galton did not just happen to fingerprint nonwhite people and "idiots" but that the two groups were integrally merged for both his peers and his followers. As Mark Jackson observes, "Medical constructions of idiocy were not merely derived from debates about racial inferiority and the origins of racial difference but were also a principal ingredient of those debates" (172).

Thus when we consider Twain's literary representations of fingerprinting, we can see even more clearly the impossibility of separating race from disability. Here is where the metonymic importance of the conjoined twins to mediate this connection becomes apparent. If by "drawing connections between fingerprinting and the economics of possession expressed in race slavery, Twain shows their paradoxical dependence on a pervasive loss of self-control" (Rowe 180), he most clearly depicts this dilemma of self-control through the twins' extraordinary body and its social effects.

The twins' symbolic function as signifiers of bodily immutability (fingerprinting) and bodily immobility (slavery) can be read through their contaminating influence upon the normate characters they encounter. Angelo and Luigi's presence produces multiple impairments as they move through the town of Dawson's Landing, leaving in their wake a slew of characters described as "paralyzed," "petrified and staring," "tottering," "tongue-tied and dazed," "silent," "unconscious," "faint," and "blind" (*Pudd'nhead Wilson* 124–125, 131–134). Even "the city government stood still, with its hands tied," when one of the twins was elected as alderman while the other was excluded (169). This effect is parallel to that which Sarah Chinn sees produced by the evidence of his fingerprints upon Tom Driscoll during the novel's climactic trial: "In the moment of revelation . . . Tom is rendered mute and immobile. . . . These prints speak for themselves, removed from his body and erasing Tom as a speaking subject" (26). Indeed from the moment of Wilson's identification of him, Tom never speaks in the novel again; in our last glimpse of him, he "made some impotent movements with his white lips, then slid limp and lifeless to the floor" (*Pudd'nhead Wilson* 113).

Here we see again a symbolic and causative corollary between the effect of encountering the freakishly disabled body and the effect of encountering the bodily authority of fingerprints. Both produce muteness and immobility in the subjects they encounter, signifying the location of identity in the fixed, involuntary body. The translation of this effect from the story to the novel suggests that Twain's efforts to excavate disability from the novel by removing the conjoined twins material and to focus instead on race produced a kind of palimpsestic haunting which rewrote disability insistently into his revised text, including his treatment of race. We can see this dynamic most clearly when we consider the two African American characters with disabilities who appear in the novel: the bell ringer and Roxy.

The Haunting Presence of Disability

Thus far my discussion of disability in Twain has centered on the extraordinary figures of the conjoined twins. But there are two notable characters in *Pudd'nhead Wilson* who have more commonplace physical debilities, and not coincidentally both are African American. The bell ringer appears in the novel's fifth chapter, when the young people of Dawson's Landing, fed up with Tom Driscoll's eastern finery and airs, arrange a prank so that Tom is followed by an "old deformed negro bell ringer straddling along in his wake tricked out in a flamboyant curtain-calico exaggeration of his finery, and imitating his fancy eastern graces as well as he could" (*Pudd'nhead Wilson* 24).

This figure, who shadows Tom, obviously represents another instance of ironic doubling in the novel, which suggests, in Eric Lott's words, "that Tom's whiteness is itself an act, a suggestion that is truer than either the bell ringer or Tom can know, since Tom's identity is precisely a black man's whiteface performance" (145). In this context, some critics have read the bell ringer's disabled status metaphorically, as symbolizing Tom's "'deformed' black nature" (Berkson 314). Linda Morris suggests, however, that "to assume the joke is somehow on Tom because he is 'really' black but does not know it misses the point. Lott's notion that

Tom's whiteness is itself a performance comes much closer to the mark; nonetheless, his analysis stops with this observation, thereby missing the opportunity to investigate the convergence of a racialized *and* gendered performance" (44). Morris argues instead that the scene is an example of Bakhtinian carnivalesque, "with the most lowly member of the community, the deformed Negro bellringer, dressed in clothing intended to mock a member of the town's most privileged class" (43–44). As in this excerpt, Morris's essay centers on the use of clothing to anchor Twain's unsettling of race and gender identities, and as far as it goes, her argument is compelling. However, even she seems aware that there is a missing term in her equation, as she poses a final unanswered question in her discussion of the bell ringer: "We might wonder why this scene has such a haunting quality about it" (43). Jehlen similarly characterizes the bell ringer scene as semantically mysterious: "It is unclear just what is being satirized" (110).

These critical reactions highlight the necessity of theorizing the representation of disability, not merely as an additive component but as a key to a text's range of meanings, including its raced, gendered, and classed meanings. I suggest that the haunting quality of the scene indicates not only the hidden "truth" of Tom's race but also the anchoring of that racial identity in the fixed physical body, here as elsewhere signified by the disabled body. Furthermore the bell ringer's shadowing of Tom evokes the "ghostly remnants" of the conjoined twins found elsewhere in the novel, suggesting that removing that "deformed" body from the text has left semiotic gaps that necessarily evoke another, similarly marked body. We are never told the nature of the bell ringer's "deformity"; our only textual clue is that his manner of walking is described as "straddling along" (*Pudd'nhead Wilson* 24). Thus we are left to visualize his bodily appearance by drawing upon an imaginary realm already aggressively haunted by the image of the imperfectly excised "monstrous" body of the twins. This connection is further reinforced by the fact that the bell ringer scene immediately precedes the first appearance of the (separated) twins (27).

Another symbolic corollary to the bell ringer is marked by his costuming in "flamboyant curtain-calico," the same material donned earlier by Roxy, Tom's enslaved mother, just before switching the babies. Roxy comically dons her "new Sunday gown—a cheap curtain-calico thing, a conflagration of gaudy colors and fantastic figures," as a preparation for drowning herself and her baby to avoid being sold down the river (*Pudd'nhead Wilson* 13). But when she completes her toilette by switching the babies' clothing, she realizes their physical resemblance and so conceives the plan of making the switch permanent. By doing so, she inscribes the mirroring relationship already represented by the two babies in their wagon, "one at each end and facing each other," an image that also evokes the split-mirror twinning of the conjoined Luigi and Angelo (8). Yet the physical exchangeability of Tom and Chambers is contradicted by their legal and social distinction, and so Roxy's actions produce a representational double, a "shadow," that later returns to haunt Tom in the form of the disabled bell ringer, the figure of bodily irreducibility.

Thus far these dynamics demonstrate the supplementary role played by disability in constructing racial and gender performativity. However, in Twain's novel it becomes clear that the reverse dynamic is true as well—namely, that evoking disability also necessarily evokes race, particularly in the nineteenth-century American context of scientific racism. This dynamic is apparent in Twain's depiction of the twins, who in the novel are strangely colorless characters stripped of their freakish connection as well as their racial duality: "One was a little fairer than the other, but otherwise they were exact duplicates" (*Pudd'nhead Wilson* 27). Ironically, though, while singleton twins can be either fraternal or identical, conjoined twins, formed from the incomplete division of a fertilized egg, are always necessarily identical. Yet in the original conjoined versions in "Those Extraordinary Twins," Luigi is "dark-skinned" (*Pudd'nhead Wilson* 125), while Angelo is "blonde" with a "fresh complexion" (126). Their different coloring is reflected in their cravats, "a delicate pink in the case of the blonde brother, a violent scarlet in the case of the brunette" (127). The racialization of this color contrast is clear in an earlier version's sentence that Twain later deleted, in which Luigi pleads with Angelo, "Be humane, be generous—don't carry me in there before all those people in this heart-breaking costume which offends against every canon of harmony in color and will make everybody think we have been brought up among African savages" (*Pudd'nhead Wilson* 184). The "violent scarlet" of Angelo's cravat clearly evokes Roxy's flamboyant dress, which includes a shawl of "a blazing red complexion" (13). Furthermore the twins' costume produces a sartorial equivalent of miscegenation, since "as a combination they broke all the laws of taste known to civilization. Nothing more fiendish and irreconcilable than those shrieking and blaspheming colors could have been contrived" (*Pudd'nhead Wilson* 127). Thus we see how Twain's exploration of the paradox of individuality and duality embodied by the conjoined twins was inevitably represented in terms of racial difference and racial anxiety.

We can further explore this question by examining the semantic connection between the twins, the bell ringer, and Roxy. It would seem that Roxy's final appearance in Twain's novel reinforces the power of fingerprinting to establish "indisputable racial difference" (Rogin 85). The free play of race, and its haunting echo in disability, which has circulated throughout the novel, is brought to a crashing halt in the climactic trial scene when the secret knowledge that gave Roxy power is usurped by the white lawyer's technological mastery. Once Wilson has revealed Tom's true identity through fingerprints, Roxy loses her strength: she "[flings] herself upon her knees, cover[s] her face with her apron, and out through her sobs the words [struggle]—'De Lord have mercy on me, po' misable sinner dat I is!'" (*Pudd'nhead Wilson* 113). Yet a full reading of Roxy's character reveals a more complex dynamic at work.

It is virtually unnoted by critics that Roxy becomes disabled in the course of the novel and that her disability plays a key role in the unfolding of the plot. Roxy is "crippled" by "rheumatism in her arms" after working for eight years of freedom as a chambermaid on a steamboat (*Pudd'nhead Wilson* 22, 33). She refuses to beg, as she believes that a lifetime of hard work merits a disability pension. Tom Driscoll doesn't agree, and his refusal seals his fate, for Roxy has the power of her knowledge of his true identity. Morris's observation that "this moment represents the most powerful embodiment of [Roxy's] strength" demonstrates a possible reason for the critical silence about Roxy's disability status (46–47). It is politically as well as semantically difficult to reconcile "powerful embodiment" with the usual understanding of disability as the ultimate in power*less* embodiment. Thus, like Morris's, even critical analyses explicitly focused on the character of Roxy emphasize her "force and shrewdness," her "courage," her strong will and "calculating mind," and never get around to mentioning that she has a disability (Jehlen 109; C. Porter 125).

This is not to say that I disagree with these characterizations of Roxy, for I believe that it is possible to be strong, shrewd, *and* disabled. Rather I am suggesting that it is not incidental but crucial that Roxy is disabled and that her return to play a pivotal and powerful role in the plot is driven by her disability status. Indeed in the moment in the text when Roxy is most powerful, she manipulates the power of marked bodies to reverse the master-slave relationship. While before becoming disabled she despaired that "she could prove nothing" about Tom's true identity and raged at herself for "not providing herself with a witness," *after* she becomes disabled she easily persuades Tom of the untruth that "all dis is down in writin', en it's in safe hands, too" (*Pudd'nhead Wilson* 22, 41). The novel presents no explanation for this change, but I contend that Roxy's physical disability, even as it produces her as the object of identification, also enables her to see beyond the fictionality of objectification, to see that identification can be discursively manipulated.

Thus the ending of the novel, which leaves the reader with a feeling of uneasy satisfaction at the unmasking and subsequent enslavement of Tom, may also be seen as a foreclosing of the possibilities of greater freedom briefly glimpsed through Roxy's exercise of power. Such freedom is portrayed as residing in the manipulable relation between body and text, identity and proof, which so powerfully shaped understandings of disability and racial difference in nineteenth-century America. Thus the fantasy of marking, while powerfully penetrating into the wider cultural sphere, in the novel remains in a complex tension with questions of text and body, and through this tension, figures of resistance may emerge. Yet as we have seen in the real-life deployments of Pudd'nhead Wilson's fingerprinting expertise, such ambivalences are not to be found in the legal sphere's wholesale adoption of the fantasy. As we turn now to the twenty-first century's institutionalization of fantasies of identification, we will find fewer and fewer examples of the fantasy itself within literary texts, as it continues to migrate from the realm of imagination to those of policy and law. Instead, as heralded by the figure of Roxy, creative works will increasingly become sites of counterdiscursive and resistant refigurings of the fantasy and its claims to power.

PART III

FANTASIES OF MEASUREMENT

The overmastering fantasy of modern disability identification is that disability is a knowable, obvious, and unchanging category. Such a fantasy permeates all levels of discourse regarding disabled bodies and minds, even as it is repeatedly and routinely disproved by the actual realities of those bodies' and minds' fluctuating abilities. As we will see, individuals whose lives are shaped by such disability identifications often experience a kind of bodily/textual dissonance, in which their experiences are displaced and superseded by a written authentication that palimpsestically overwrites their own bodily knowledge. Carrie Sandahl, a disability scholar and performer, challenged this dynamic in her art-life piece *The Reciprocal Gaze*, in which she "attempted to make clear the medical and social metaphors that had been inscribed on my body by directly acknowledging and confronting them" (26). I begin part III with Sandahl's piece to frame my discussion of the institutionalization of fantasies of identification as always already accompanied by acts of creative resistance and bodily reclaiming.

For one day of working and teaching, Sandahl wore a white lab jacket and white pants on which she had written notes from her medical records and marked the locations of her scars and "abnormal" x-rays along with dates of surgeries, as well as quotes from feminist psychoanalytic performance theory and questions people have asked her about her body: "Is one leg shorter than the other?" "Will this surgery cure you?" "Were you born this way?" (26–27). Whenever she met the eyes of people looking at her, she offered them a handout chronicling her medical history. In *The Reciprocal Gaze*, Sandahl materialized the submerged process of medical identification that shapes the lives of many people with physical disabilities, while foregrounding the extent to which such identifications take place not only in the medical setting but in everyday social interactions. The white lab coat and pants became textual surfaces overlaying her body and functioned as a kind of "paper suit" encasing her actual experience of her body.[1] Following Sandahl, I suggest that each modern subject is, in a sense, an individual wearing a "paper suit," our bodies contained and constrained by medical and bureaucratic authority, and each of us may seek at times to tear open that suit while remaining aware of the material consequences of such a rupture.

I call this process *biocertification*, a neologism that draws upon and expands Foucauldian notions of biopolitical citizenship. Biocertification describes the many forms of government documents that purport to authenticate a person's social identity through biology, substituting written descriptions for other forms of bodily knowledge and authority. Biocertification materializes the modern belief that only science can reliably determine the truths of identity and generally claims to offer a simple, verifiable, and concrete solution to questions of identity. Yet in practice biocertification tends to produce not straightforward answers but documentary sprawl, increased uncertainty, and bureaucratic stagnation.

Defining Disability in the Age of Biocertification

> The science of counting "cripples" throws into relief battles over the delineation of "disability" in an environment where people are turned first into objects and then into numbers. For administrative purposes, it is imperative that the (real) disabled person is made visible through the processes of calculation and therefore can be made governable. The obsession with "disability fraud" induces such questions as "who is the genuine disabled person and how many of them are there?" (Campbell 128)

People with disabilities in the present-day United States and other industrialized countries must provide a nearly endless series of medical certifications in a number of settings, including (but not limited to) school, work, travel, insurance, court, taxes, and sports. In this process the form becomes "*inform*ational, reproductive of a social formation as it institutes and applies its assumptions. . . . The form furnishes uni*form*ity—regularity, repeatability, reiterability, predictability—to identity, rendering it accordingly accessible to administration" (Goldberg 31). Even those with permanent and unchanging impairments, such as loss of a limb or irreversible paralysis, must often file form after form, year after year, to maintain their legal and economic status as disabled.

The 1994 documentary film *When Billy Broke His Head* features "Kay," a former concert pianist who has permanently lost her sight yet must repeatedly certify her impairment to keep receiving benefits: "I have to have an affidavit stating that yes, I am legally blind. Now they have known this for seven years, but I still have to verify every year, or every six months, that I can't see. Now it's never going to get better, my particular condition will never get better. And I cannot read a single word of print of any kind, of any size, and yet, this is my task," she concludes, holding up the thirty-four-page form sent by the Social Security Administration. Kay's experience is a commonplace within the American disability community.

Clearly the vectors of power that produce the current proliferation of overlapping and often tautological disability biocertifications in the United States are hardly driven by efficiency or ease. Rather the overriding concern is the determination of the "truth" of disabled bodies and the subsequent validation and documentation of those supposed truths. This "medico-administrative" (Foucault, *Power/Knowledge* 176) truth-making is predicated upon the belief that disability can in fact be measured, named, and quantified. Yet such an assumption is far from empirically verifiable. Modern biocertifications of disability, like the discourses of sexual deviance described by Foucault, constitute their own regulatory targets, outlining parameters that must be constantly shored up through new claims of measurability, difference, and expertise. As Alison Kafer observes, the "governmental and non-governmental groups alike [that] frequently issue definitions of who is disabled . . . would not have to be so precise in defining 'disability' if such definitions were without controversy; the very fact that so much energy is funneled into defining disability and impairment suggests the fundamental instability of the terms" (78).

Such definitions proliferate and vary across localities, nations, and histories. Currently global definitions include that of the United Nations, recently updated and codified in the UN Convention on the Rights of People with Disabilities, and of the World Health Organization's International Classification of Functioning, Disability, and Health.[2] Both of these definitions show the influence of the social model of disability in their attempts to separate the biological and social components of disablement, yet both still rely on medico-administrative methods to produce knowledge about disability that determines policy and resource allocation. In the United States the most prominent operative definitions include those of the Americans with Disabilities Act (ADA), which speaks of disabilities in terms of essential functions, reasonable accommodations, and major life activities; the Social Security Administration, which defines disability purely in terms of full-time gainful employment or the lack thereof; and Workers Compensation, Veterans Administration, and other disability insurance schemes that measure the percentage of ability lost through injury.

These competing definitions can produce moments of profound material and significatory paradox, such as that described by Connie Panzarino in her 1994 memoir, *The Me in Mirror*. Panzarino relies on an attendant to turn her in bed, lift her into her motorized wheelchair, help her bathe and use the toilet, and perform other intimate and essential activities of daily survival. Thus her experience clearly fits into medical, social, and ADA-based definitions of disability. Yet her ability to work and earn a living ironically disqualifies her from receiving the Social Security–reliant benefit of a personal care attendant. She describes a confrontation with a worker at the Social Security Administration:

> The man behind the desk read my application and laughed. "What is this, a joke? You're not disabled. You're working full time at DSS [Department of Social Services]!"
>
> "What are you, blind?" screamed Mickey. "Can't you see she's in a chair?" she said, rapping his desk with her white cane. . . .
>
> I tried to remain calm while Mickey began cursing and swearing.
>
> "Connie, don't let these assholes screw you over. Quit your job and go on disability. You have to have attendant care or you're going to die."
>
> The man at the desk cleared his throat. "I'm sorry, but since we know that you're *able* to work, we would have to deny you benefits even if you quit your job." (175)

Appeals to common sense—"Can't you see that she is disabled?"—ironically voiced here by the "unseeing" blind woman, Mickey, sometimes support and sometimes clash with medico-administrative definitions of disability, a point to which I return below. What is clear in this example is that such definitions, developed and implemented in isolation from one another, are often violently contradictory in ways that severely impact disabled people's access to employment, social participation, and even the basic needs of survival.[3]

We can see a similar dynamic in a very different cultural and geographic realm in Matthew Kohrman's study of disability in post-Maoist China. Kohrman relates the story of Ma Zhun, a woman who lost the toes on one foot from an industrial accident. Her employer tells her that, due to her impairment, she will be laid off unless she can obtain a state-issued disability ID card in order to count toward a national employment quota. However, Ma Zhun is denied this biocertification because she does not meet the standards to be considered *canji* (disabled). Much like Panzarino, Ma Zhun reacts with frustration and even removes her shoe in the government office to show her injured foot (213). This appeal to common sense has no effect on the clerk, however, because her impairment still does not correspond to one of the categories of *canji* defined by the Chinese government in 1987.

In his exploration of the codification of those categories, Kohrman notes that researchers wished only to include disabilities that were "not only permanent but easy to grasp and control" (226), clearly demonstrating the influence of a fantasy of identification. Although, like other modern disability regulatory structures, *canji* is supposed to be based on medical science, Kohrman discovered that members of China's Disability Leadership Council adjusted their definitions of *canji* in attempts to produce numbers that would reflect well on China in the international arena—ironically shaping their findings to the oft-repeated claim that 10 percent of the world's population is disabled, a claim known to be invented simply to impress the importance of disability on a United Nations audience (Kohrman 223–229). Like the legal use of racialist claims about "Indian hair," "Negro feet," and "Anglo-Saxon noses," such deployments of pseudo-empiricism can seem laughable until we remember that they have real and often devastating effects upon the people trapped in their interstices of meaning. From enslavement to the loss of services needed to literally survive each day, intolerable consequences loom behind each social policy that uses claims of science to bolster fantasies of bodily identification. In the case of disability, supposedly the most fully biological—and thus measurable—of embodied social identities, we come up repeatedly against catachresis, in which "as soon as we discursively interrogate 'disability,' its meaning loses fixity, generality, and ultimately collapses" (Campbell 127). Yet that fact does not discourage attempts to define disability, but rather, through the fantastic process discussed throughout this book, produces an ever growing body of such attempts, an industry of disability definitions, a macro- and micropolitics of knowledge proliferating in both local and global settings.

States of Impairment

In the remainder of this chapter I explore the paradoxes of biocertification through the local example of disabled parking permits in the United States. This particular and paradigmatic disability certification process richly demonstrates that the idea of physical disability as fixed, knowable, and describable far exceeds any material reality—that this idea in fact constitutes one of the most powerful and fundamental fantasies of identification in the modern world. This point is foundational to further understanding the biocertification of gendered and racial identities, a process that relies both ontologically and practically on the concept of a knowable physical essence historically materialized through the disabled body.

This case of disabled parking is especially illustrative due to its peculiar combination of homogeneity and difference. All fifty states issue disabled parking permits, which utilize similar certification structures, grant similar privileges, and are reciprocally honored across state borders. In that sense, disabled parking permits constitute a kind of national disability certification program. However, each state utilizes different medicolegal criteria for establishing eligibility for disabled parking permits, criteria that are often both internally dissonant and strikingly inconsistent from state to state.[4] In twenty-two states, for example, being legally blind is grounds for a disabled parking permit (to be used as a passenger). In twenty-eight states, however, blindness is not included as a qualifying condition, and in Arizona and Hawai'i blindness is specifically excluded. Thus, as a given blind person moves across state lines, while her impairment (to use social model distinctions) remains constant, her disability, as socially and legally defined, may change quite dramatically. If she holds a permit in Massachusetts and visits Arizona on vacation, she could use her permit due to interstate reciprocity rules. But if she likes Arizona so much she decides to relocate there and then applies for a permit in her new home state, she will be denied.

A fairly typical list of qualifying conditions can be found on New York State's application:

Uses portable oxygen.

Legally blind.

Limited or no use of one or both legs.

Unable to walk 200 feet without stopping.

Neuromuscular dysfunction that severely limits mobility.

Class III or IV cardiac condition (American Heart Assoc. standards).

Severely limited in ability to walk due to an arthritic, neurological, or orthopedic condition.

Restricted by lung disease to such an extent that forced (respiratory) expiratory volume for one second, when measure by spirometry, is less than one liter, or the arterial oxygen tension is less than sixty mm/hg of room air at rest.

Has a physical or mental impairment or condition not listed above which constitutes an equal degree of disability, and which . . . prevents the person from getting around without great difficulty.

Some version of this list of *conditions*—conveying the double meanings of medical diagnoses and eligibility requirements—appears on every state disabled parking application in the United States. One of the most striking aspects of such lists is their combination of extreme medical specificity and objectivity with commonsense or "obvious" descriptions of bodily limitation that are more subjective in nature. Thus while it is very common (thirty-four states), to delimit qualifying lung disease within identical numerical limits of spirometry and arterial blood tension, or to require that cardiac conditions fit the AHA's Class III or IV criteria (thirty-three states), there are also statements such as "limited or no use of one or both legs." Unlike the previous conditions, this statement relies on a presumed shared understanding of its meaning and thus does not include quantitative measurements such as tensile strength, range of motion, level of paralysis, or other theoretically available objective criteria. The same may be said for the conditions of being "severely limited in ability to walk" or "getting around without great difficulty." As Susan Wendell points out in her discussion of the cultural relativism of impairment, a woman who can walk only short distances but needs to walk several miles each day to fetch water would be disabled in a way a woman in an urban setting would not (14). Certainly, within the U.S. context, the extent to which a problem with walking might become an impediment to daily life varies widely by region, lifestyle, and socioeconomic class.

The "200 feet" clause is prevalent on disabled parking applications, appearing on twenty-seven out of the fifty states, most often with the conditional "without stopping to rest," but sometimes "without assistance," and occasionally, as in New York, simply "without stopping." How this particular distance emerged as the delimiter of sufficient mobility disability is obscure. That it is not an empirical, research-based criterion, like the AHA guidelines or the measurement of arterial blood tension, is clear, especially as a minority of states require smaller numbers of feet: 100 in Arkansas, Kansas, New Mexico, and South Carolina, and only 50 in Missouri, deviations that appear to have no relation to the size or urbanization of the states in question.[5] Rather such criteria rely on supposed commonsense understandings of how far a "normal" person can or needs to walk, and as such are open to contestation and debate.

Indeed several state applications now explicitly exclude "being unable to walk 200 feet" as a sufficient condition in itself for needing disabled parking. The assertion on Florida's application that, by law, being "'unable to walk 200 feet' is no longer a qualifying disability," indicates a legislative and discursive struggle over this criterion, with the implication that too many people are unable to walk 200 feet, and thus the qualifying criteria needed to be narrowed further, a debate that we might speculate was driven by the large proportion of older residents in Florida. But then, why does Illinois's application contain an identical statement indicating a similar concern? And what contentious debates and uneasy compromises produced these criteria on Minnesota's application?

7. Because applicant has a condition that would be aggravated to such an extent that walking more than 200 feet would be life-threatening.

8. The applicant cannot walk more than 200 feet without stopping to rest.

If common sense presumably governs such nonscientific certification criteria, then it would also seem to dictate that a person whose life is threatened by walking 200 feet would (hopefully) have stopped to rest at a somewhat shorter distance, thus qualifying her under criterion 8 without the need for including criterion 7. Clearly this instance of redundant extremity reflects a submerged struggle over the meanings of various impairments and the ability of the medical-bureaucratic state to adequately measure and label their impact upon an individual body. As Julia Epstein observes, "Cultures produce explanatory stories about the human body in order to contain human beings safely within recognized social norms, to hold their anarchic potential in check, and to underwrite sanctioned cultural expectations" (4). The stories told in disabled parking permit applications indicate an extreme anxiety regarding the inchoate and unstable nature of disability and an insistent concern that unqualified bodies be excluded from the privileged position conferred by the parking permit: "Beneath every set of figures, we must seek not a meaning, but a precaution" (Foucault, *Discipline and Punish* 139).

Perhaps the most cogent signifier of this concern is the deployment of the term *severe* on the applications. Thirty-four out of fifty forms contain the word at least once, and many of those repeat it multiple times, sometimes in the actual title of the permit, as in New York's "Parking Permit or License Plates for Person with Severe Disabilities" and Pennsylvania's "Severely Disabled Veteran's Placard." In many cases, "severity" is deployed almost as punctuation throughout the applications and their supporting documents, as if to keep the applicant and medical certifiers constantly alert to the danger of such privileges being granted to those only moderately afflicted by their disabilities. For example, from Missouri's application:

> The term "physically disabled" means . . . a person with medical disabilities which prohibits, limits, or *severely* impairs one's ability to walk . . . as follows:
> 1. The person cannot walk 50 feet without stopping to rest due to a *severe* and disabling arthritic, neurological, orthopedic condition, or other *severe* and disabling condition. (my emphasis)

The *Oxford English Dictionary* offers a variety of definitions for the adjective *severe*, of which several refer to illness, describing it as "attended with a maximum of pain or distress, violent," and "grievous, extreme." Other definitions also appear relevant, however, to the particular insistency with which *severe* is deployed in these applications, which, while "imposing rigorous conditions," seek to be "rigidly exact or accurate, not leaning to tenderness or laxity; unsparing." Again, it is clear that the concern here is to distinguish the truly deserving—defined by the extremity of their suffering—from those undeserving claimants who experience only mild or moderate distress. Here is where examining the actual certification process reveals that more is at stake than simply creating a screening process to keep out fraudulent claims. For it is not likely that the repeated insistence upon severity in such certifications would discourage any deliberate falsehoods from nondisabled applicants or their colluding physicians. Rather the discourse of severity is deployed to create doubt in the minds of disabled applicants and their doctors—Am I (Is she) really disabled enough to need this?—and to reassure legislators and bureaucrats that they are not contributing to the growth of a population of weaklings spoiled by privileges that they don't really "need."[6]

The legal scholar Fiona Kumari Campbell makes a similar observation in her examination of rhetorical strategies in court cases regarding the Americans with Disabilities Act, noting that "to limit 'disability' under the ADA to significant or severe impairment ensures that this population stands out and is delineated from the general American population. . . . By including so-called minor impairments, however, the danger is that disability becomes a normative and not unusual experience for the general population" (125). One assumed consequence of such a normativizing of disability, in the context of the ADA, is that employers and the courts would be swamped by demands for accommodations for even the mildest of impairments. In the case of parking permits, one can certainly argue that there is a limited number of disabled parking places to go around, and these should be reserved for those who truly need them. Under such utilitarian thinking, it is reasonable that definitions of "true need" should be closely contested and kept as narrow as possible. However, I argue that utilitarianism is only one of the operative logics governing the cultural construction of this category of the "truly disabled parker" and as such exists in uneasy tension with logics predicated upon moral judgments and stereotypical understandings of disabled bodies. In particular, stereotypes of physical disability as both permanent and obvious shape both disabled parking permit applications and the social policing that surrounds disabled parkers, a policing that underpins and reinforces the state bureaucracy of biocertification.

Stereotypes, Surveillance, and Citizenship

One of the most powerful cultural assumptions underlying the fantasy of disability identification is that a person's state of impairment must be absolute and unchanging and that even the slightest hint of "normal" function renders both the individual and her social categorization suspect, even criminal in nature. How else to interpret the language of many disabled parking applications, which do not simply ask if the disability is permanent or temporary but demand that the applicant "[have] a total or lifelong condition of mobility impairment from which little or no improvement or recovery can reasonably be expected" (Louisiana), be "permanently and totally confined to a wheelchair" (Tennessee), and have "no prognosis for improvement" (Delaware)? Connecticut's form warns that "additional certification may be required at the time of the original application or any time thereafter if there is cause to believe that the ability to walk is not seriously and permanently impaired," while South Carolina nuances the usual requirement of a class III or IV cardiac condition with the note that "if the person's status improves to a higher level, for example as a result of bypass surgery or transplantation, he no longer meets this criteria [sic]." If the emphasis on severity suggests that the boundaries of privilege must be policed against the less disabled people out there looking to take advantage, the discourse of permanence implies that a person who did improve in health or function, rather than responding with excitement, relief, or joy, would be maliciously preoccupied with maintaining her parking privileges.[7]

Severity and permanence are complemented by perhaps the most vexing rhetoric of disability definitions, that of "obviousness." I have already noted the dissonance in permit applications between those conditions defined by more objective medical criteria and those that rely on more subjective and flexible criteria. Supplementing these two versions of biocertification is a third method of bodily validation: a minority of states allow the applicant to bypass the need for medical certification altogether if her disability is visible and obvious. In some states, the applicant must appear at the Department of Motor Vehicles (DMV) in person, where the clerk may issue the disabled permit under certain conditions of impairment: in California, if the person has "lost a lower extremity or both hands"; in Connecticut, Indiana, and the District of Columbia, if he is "missing a lower extremity or unable to walk without the aid of a motorized wheelchair"; in Maryland, "if [he] has lost arm, hand, foot, or leg." In some states such an applicant may self-certify in person at the DMV, but in others a government official must sign the form, as in California's inclusion of the section "Certification of Readily Observable and Uncontested Permanent Disability" with a signature line labeled "DMV Employee." In Pennsylvania a police officer may certify in cases where the applicant is blind or "does not have full use of a leg or both legs as evidenced by the use of a wheelchair, walker, crutches, cane/quad cane, or other prescribed device." In Kentucky a county clerk may sign the statement "I hereby attest that the applicant is obviously disabled and should be issued a special parking permit."

In all of these cases, the condition of obviousness substitutes for the medical certification, which can now be left blank. Yet far from bypassing medical authority, this process functions to extend and solidify that authority by imbuing the government official with the diagnostic gaze. The DMV worker, county clerk, or police officer is both authorized and required to scrutinize the body of the applicant to determine the validity of her disability. Rather than drawing on a body of scientific knowledge to make this determination, these lay diagnosticians presumably employ a shared understanding of what constitutes disability, even as the multitude of dissonant criteria on the form testify to the lack of any such common definitions. Like other powerful modern ideologies, this idea of easily identifiable disability works at an unconscious level, both evoking and enforcing "obviousnesses as obviousnesses, which we cannot *fail to recognize* and before which we have the inevitable and natural reaction of crying out . . . : 'That's obvious! That's right! That's true!'" (Althusser 172).

I return here to the themes raised in part I regarding the cultural investment in distinguishing between real and fake disabilities, authentic and fraudulent bodily claims. We saw how these anxieties deepened in the mid-nineteenth century and intersected with similar concerns regarding transgressively gendered and raced bodies, and how they reemerged in the post–Great Society era to again reflect fears over entitlements and national character. In the twenty-first-century context of disability certifications, these anxieties have become both institutionally sedimented and widely diffused throughout our culture, and the advent of the information age has served to recruit a wide swath of the population into the ranks of lay diagnosticians and enforcers of disability identification.

Again, disabled parking is the most prominent cultural locus for this apparatus of surveillance. Every nonvisibly disabled person has a host of stories of being challenged by strangers in parking lots with statements like "You don't look disabled to me" and "You should be ashamed for taking a place from someone who really needs it." Even when such suspicions are not directly voiced, they are communicated by the act of pausing and watching the disabled walker exiting the car, often focusing on the legs in a pseudo-diagnostic attempt to determine if the person's parking is legitimized by subtle aspects of bodily appearance. In reaction to such surveillance, it is not surprising that many disabled parkers engage in what Tobin Siebers describes as the "masquerade" of disability: exaggerating a limp, carrying a cane not strictly needed, or otherwise performing to stereotypical expectations of disabled bodies in order to deflect the suspicious gaze (96–104). Here we clearly see that "the exercise of discipline presupposes a mechanism that coerces by means of observation; an apparatus in which the techniques that make it possible to see induce effects of power" (Foucault, *Discipline and Punish* 170–171).

Such spontaneous, individual acts of lay surveillance have recently found an organizational home in cyberspace, on the website Handicappedfraud.org. Founded in 2007 by the nondisabled sister of a disabled man, the site's mission statement explains that it

> was launched as a community service effort to end the misuse
> of handicapped parking spaces and placards. The disabled have
> run out of places to park, as their designated handicapped park-
> ing spaces are being taken by fraudulent individuals. Our cities
> are being robbed of serious metered parking revenue [due] to this
> abuse as well. The police are far too valuable and busy to stake out
> parking lots to ticket handicapped parking violators. The abusers
> go largely unpunished. It's time for our community to become the
> ambassadors for our cities, and report handicapped parking viola-
> tors when they see it.[8]

The basic assumptions encoded in the disabled parking applications are apparent in this statement, for example, in the opposition between the deserving "disabled" and the "fraudulent individuals" who are "robbing" the larger society both financially and morally. But Handicappedfraud.org goes further by insisting that it is not enough for either the city or the police to enforce this distinction: it is up to a presumed "us," the "community" that illogically must act as ambassadors within our own cities, extending the apparatus of the state with each individual act of surveillance and "punishment."

The mechanism of this surveillance is the Abuse Board on the website, on which individuals can report incidents of parking violations, known or suspected. Anyone can post an anonymous report, recording the date, city, license plate number, and (if displayed) disabled parking permit number of the suspected violator. The site states that this information will be communicated to local law enforcement and, if a violation is confirmed, citations may be issued or permits revoked. However, it is unclear how much information is actually being sent to local law enforcement and how much is simply staying in cyberlimbo on the site.

Furthermore there is no evidence that law enforcement entities are able or willing to take action based on reports from the abuse board. The site's home page reports that officials in San Francisco have been appreciative and have said that parking violations have decreased since the site began its activity. The only other evidence of interaction with government entities consists of two letters from the DMVs in Hawaii and Florida posted in 2007, neither of which indicates that information from the abuse board will be implemented in any way.[9] Furthermore, the site does not appear to have been updated or maintained since 2008. For all of these reasons, it seems unlikely that violations reported on the abuse board are producing material changes on any institutional level.

Nevertheless the abuse board is consistently and widely used, with over thirteen thousand postings since its initiation on January 7, 2007.[10] Postings come from nearly all of the fifty states, and there are new postings every week. The frequency of postings may perhaps be traced to an iPhone app, available through a link on the site, which allows reports to be sent from a smartphone, potentially with accompanying pictures of vehicles. The site also offers for sale Post-it notes to be left on the vehicles of violators, announcing, "You've been reported at Handicappedfraud. org" (Fig. 6.1). Thus surveillance and discipline of supposed violators is "organized as a multiple, automatic and anonymous power" (Foucault, *Discipline and Punish* 176).

On the site's home page the founder of Handicappedfraud.org asks that participants "report handicapped parking violators respectfully. Remember that we cannot know somebody's personal situation. Many handicapped people are hassled over their lack of a visual [visible] disability by well meaning citizens."[11] She suggests that if a genuinely disabled person using a valid permit is reported, nothing will happen to him because the DMV will verify that he is a legitimate user. (Of course, there is no evidence that anything is happening to illegitimate users reported through the site either.) "We are not qualified to know if someone is healthy or not," she insists, rejecting the idea that these community ambassadors can claim the medico-administrative authority of the diagnostic gaze.

Despite this well-meant plea, the abuse board has quickly become a forum for vociferous fantasies of disability identification. This problem is aggravated by the fact that the reporting structure makes no distinction between people who park in a disabled place *without* a permit and those who display a permit but whose bodily appearance and behavior do not accord with onlookers' assumptions about the legitimately

FIGURE 6.1. Post-it image from the home page of Handicappedfraud.org.

disabled body. Reports on the abuse board are almost evenly divided between these two very different categories. To be clear, I too consider violations in the first category to be inexcusable and believe that there is a great need for more stringent enforcement of disabled parking, particularly in congested urban areas. The second category, however, is far from clear-cut and is deeply fraught with dynamics of surveillance, moral judgment, and entrenched assumptions about the identifiability of the disabled body.

Each abuse board report includes space for a brief comment, and these comments make it clear that the bodies of suspected violators are under close and hostile scrutiny. Of the approximately six thousand comments relating to suspects who display disabled parking permits, the vast majority make a statement about their appearance and behavior.

Often pseudo-medical language is used, as well as the terse style of an imitative police report:

> 2/15/11. Las Vegas, NV. "Approx. 35 yo blonde female, 5'5", 110 lbs, able to pass 3 other shoppers in line with ease to exit Costco. She was alone on foot, had a steady gait, no limp, no SOB, no cast, no obvious injuries."

> 12/04/08. Clayton, NC. "VA Plate U6854, Red Hyundai Santa Fe, WM & WF appears walking at quick steady pace moving all extremities well without difficulty. No physical handicaps noted. No other passengers noted."

Evoking the rhetoric of common knowledge and obviousness, statements such as "from all outward appearances, he is not handicapped," "no obvious handicaps," and "looks perfectly healthy" are frequent. There are also many comments regarding the amount of movement and activity shown by the suspect, reflecting assumptions about the necessary severity and permanence of a valid disability. With descriptions of drivers as "walking briskly," "bounding," "bouncing," "sprinting," and even one who "practically leapt out of the car before dancing down the street," reporters emphasize that real disability involves the consistent performance of slow, painful, and hesitant movement. Seemingly unrelated comments, such as the fact that suspects are "laughing," further emphasize the necessity of unmitigated suffering to qualify as a deserving disabled person.

Many such comments also reflect assumptions about gender and class: comments about women are far more likely to mention seemingly extraneous details about appearance:

> 9/13/07. Palo Alto, CA. "These two ladies were not only young and very healthy looking but very athletic looking also (actually quite hot)."

> 2/9/11. Frankfort, KY. "She was a well dressed lady and had absolutely NO obvious physical impairment."

> 5/30/07. Oakland, CA. "This woman literally had on 4 inch stiletto heels, as she hurried from her car."

These comments confirm the oft-shared advice in the disability community that, when applying for benefits or accommodations of any kind, it is best to appear ill-groomed, unattractive, and generally impoverished. For women in particular, this means performing a nonfemininity that precludes makeup, fashionable clothes, high heels, or styled hair.[12] Terry Galloway describes struggling with this form of disability masquerade in order to obtain badly needed hearing aids from a state rehabilitation center. Worried that she didn't look "disabled enough to deserve the help" because she had a "great haircut, a sex life, and interesting shoes," Galloway narrates how she prepared for her appointment:

> I dressed in the drabbest clothes I could dig out of my closet. . . . I didn't gel my hair up but let it adhere, naturally, flatly to my skull. I left my contacts in their case, my funky glasses by the bedside, and dug up the ghost of three prescriptions past—a hoot-owl-shaped pair with finger-thick lenses I didn't bother to clean, thinking the scratches and smudges would add to the overall effect. . . . I did feel a residual bit of shame. But I needed those hearing aids. That's how I thought I had to act to get them. And that's how I got them. (169–170)

Logically neither gelled hair nor "funky glasses" should affect whether Galloway could receive aids for her documented hearing loss. However, such "performances of proving" disability often have more to do with perception and stereotype than with rationality.[13]

Unlike the scenario described by Galloway, the procurement of a disabled parking permit does not involve a material or monetary transaction. A mobility-impaired millionaire has the same right to accessible parking as does a person living off an SSI pittance. Yet abuse board comments frequently reflect the sense that affluent parkers must be engaged in fraud, as in the case of the "young person, stylish, going to pre–Academy Awards event down the street. Driving brand new Porche [sic]." Even more than affluence, the mere fact of youth is frequently presented as a suspicious quality in disabled parkers, along with the related factors of parenthood, exercising, and even owning a motorcycle. Many comments cite the suspect's entering a gym or health club as proof of fraudulent status, despite the fact that disabled people use gyms regularly for exercise and physical therapy. There are also frequent comments about "holding a baby" or "carrying a toddler" as markers of suspicious behavior, reflecting widespread assumptions about the inability of disabled people to bear or care for children.

The legal and social dissonances of competing disability definitions also emerge in comments suggesting that being able to work automatically disqualifies a person from the disability category: "I found out she works at K-Mart. I'm sorry, if you are disabled you should not be working.

This is fraud at its finest," and "Blonde female, possibly teacher or staff. If on disability how does she hold a job and be on permanent disability?" Reminiscent of the stories of Panzarino and Ma Zhun, these comments indicate that the effects of dissonant definitions extend beyond the institutional sphere to influence social attitudes, provoking cultural hostility and suspicion toward disabled people caught within their contradictory matrices.

Cal Montgomery describes the contingent (in)visibility of disability produced by social confusion about incongruous definitions and behaviors:

> The person who uses a white cane when getting on the bus, but then pulls out a book to read while riding; the person who uses a wheelchair to get into the library stacks but then stands up to reach a book on a high shelf; the person who uses a picture-board to discuss philosophy; the person who challenges the particular expectations of disability that other people have is suspect. "I can't see what's wrong with him," people say, meaning, "He's not acting the way I think he should." "She's invisibly disabled," they say, meaning, "I can't see what barriers she faces."

We can see this dynamic on the abuse board, even in cases where supposedly obvious signs of disability are present, as in the report of a woman who "manually unloaded and set up motorized wheelchair, loaded it up with things, and motored into the hospital." The reporter adds, "If you can do all of that, are you handicapped?" Yet again assumptions about the static nature of disability can both support and override commonsense perceptions of its appearance.

Despite the founder's request that reporters remain nonjudgmental and avoid interaction, many of the comments on Handicappedfraud.org indicate that reporters engaged in lengthy and repeated surveillance, following and sometimes confronting their suspects. Reporters frequently state the names of suspects in their comments and add information such as "this permit belonged to her deceased husband," or "this woman brags that she is using her mother's permit," indicating a broader social interaction than merely spotting and reporting an offender. Comments such as "I have been watching my neighbor for a while and he looks perfectly healthy," "I watch them come and go each day and there is NOTHING handicapped about them," and "She walks her dog for about 1 to 2 city blocks several times a day" indicate prolonged and persistent surveillance of suspects. Those suspects observed parking outside of gyms appear especially likely to be followed, resulting in comments about their incongruous exercise behavior—"lady parks outside gym does exercise for 45 min including 30 mins on tread mill"—which imply near-stalking behavior on the part of the reporter, apparently poised near the treadmill, stopwatch in hand.[14]

A subset of comments take this surveillance further, describing real or imagined hostile confrontations, often with overtones of violence and moral condemnation: "I found it rather difficult to keep pace with his youthful stride. I immediately became enraged. . . . I will be taking matters into my own hands." One thread of these comments will ironically suggest that the suspects are disabled by their inability to respect the law, being "too blind or illiterate to read the sign," or suffering from the handicaps of "laziness and inconsideration." A few commenters then take this thread to its supposedly logical conclusion, wishing "real" disability as retribution upon imposters: "People like this SHOULD end up in a wheelchair." Here the destructive power of the fantasy of identification comes to fruition, as we see how a biocertification process meant to create a peaceful alliance between the legislating state and the law-abiding citizen results instead in discourse and practices that construct disability as the punishment for the crime rather than the subject being defended from crime.

In response to this onslaught of reports, a few commenters have urged reporters not to "jump to conclusions." One woman writes, "I'm a female in my 20s, a mother & uses a handicap plate. I don't always look handicapped but I have fibromyalgia & MS. If someone reported me it would cause major problems because I truly do need the plate. Before you report someone please get your facts!" Sometimes these comments evince a defensive hostility: "You jerks should realize you don't have to be missing an arm or leg to be handicapped. I am handicapped with a lung disease. I can't walk far, but when I do walk, it's not noticeable to you nosey A-HOLES!" The defensiveness felt by those who recognize themselves as suspects due to the nonvisible or contingently visible nature of their impairments is produced in direct proportion to the sheer magnitude of the comments, which themselves provide merely a sample of the verbal and nonverbal suspicion that surrounds the ambiguously disabled subject on a daily basis.

Many of these same subjects, of course, are materially affected by *actual* violations of disabled parking. Yet rather than seeing their needs reflected at Handicappedfraud.org, these disabled people find themselves described as the objects of its intervention. Here the dissonance produced by the layering of biocertification over bodily experience is expanded and solidified in cultural cybersphere, once more demonstrating the power of fantasy to exceed and obscure both material conditions and the means of their regulation and indicating the urgent need for further artistic and political challenges to biocertification such as Sandahl's *Reciprocal Gaze*. As I turn in the next chapter to another key local example of biocertification's institutional power, I will also note a range of resistant counterdiscourses produced when targeted individuals and groups reclaim the right to define their bodily and cultural identities.

7 / Revising Blood Quantum

*Whenever I must present my "CDIB" identification card from the
Department of the Interior in order to authorize my identity biologically
in terms of racial purity—my "certified degree of Indian blood"—I am
reminded that the United States polices my Native identity.*
　　　　　　　　　　—TEUTON, Red Land, Red Power: Grounding Knowledge
　　　　　　　　　　　　　　　　　　　　in the American Indian Novel

*Power, after investing itself in the body, finds itself exposed to a counter-
attack in that same body.*
　　　　　　　　　　　　　　　　—FOUCAULT, Power/Knowledge

Like the fantasies of marking discussed in part II, fantasies of measurement also rely on a merging of expert and lay assessment of bodies;
however, even more than in the case of marking, identifications based
on measurement produce vast bureaucracies and systems of biocertification. Perhaps the most powerfully entrenched example of such a system
can be found in the institutionalization of blood quantum identification for Native people of the United States. Blood quantum refers to the
amount of Native or Indian heritage possessed by an individual residing
in the United States, measured by genealogical inheritance: one parent
equals one-half blood quantum, one grandparent equals one-quarter,
and so on.[1] Blood quantum is employed as regulatory device and cultural
trope by the federal government, various tribal authorities, and many
individuals within Native communities.[2] Some American Indians are
extremely critical of its use, seeing it as a colonialist and Eurocentric
imposition, while others feel it is a necessary and important means by
which to preserve tribal culture, language, land, and resources.[3] While
mainstream American culture remains largely ignorant of the existence
and enforcement of blood quantum requirements, in Indian communities the issue looms extremely large. James Hamill, for example, observes
that, in Oklahoma, "it is rare and remarkable to have a conversation with

a Native American in which the topic of Indian identity and blood quantum does not come up in one way or another" (268).[4]

Scientifically exact as the term sounds, blood quantum functions merely as a symbolic abbreviation for ancestry that can be traced through documentary evidence such as birth certificates, genealogical records, and tribal rolls.[5] As in the trial of Salomé Müller, blood quantum certification works tautologically, document to document, invoking the biological (or "natural") to obscure the pure discursiveness of the supposed proof. Such biological framing is especially notable as numerous critics have pointed out that the documentary proof available, especially that of tribal rolls from the nineteenth century, is incomplete, flawed, or unreliable.[6] Yet despite these acknowledged problems, Congress and the courts have repeatedly upheld the enforcement of definitions of *Indian* based on these tribal enrollment records (Spruhan, "A Legal History" 43; Barker 31). Thus blood quantum is one of the most powerfully institutionalized—and controversial—fantasies of identification at work in the United States today.

American Indian writers and scholars often refer to the multiple, sometimes paradoxical ways in which the Certificate of Degree of Indian Blood (CDIB) is deployed within Indian Country.[7] "This small white card, so critical to an individual's legal and political recognition" (Sturm 87), can be invoked in both formal and informal settings, as in one Cherokee woman's response to strangers claiming Indian ancestry: "Yeah, yeah, show me your CDIB" (qtd. in Hamill 280). Joanne Barker observes that "the certificate is so widely accepted as proof of identity among indigenous people that individuals are often asked to show it to get into Indian-only events, to receive discounts at tribally owned businesses, or to gain access to tribally restricted areas" (31). A similar dynamic is described by Terry P. Wilson, some of whose friends "miniaturized and laminated their blood quantum certificates, which were drawn from purses or wallets at appropriate or, as it seemed to me, inappropriate times" (122).

On the other hand, Hamill observes that "many Indian people in Oklahoma today believe that the CDIB means nothing about Indian identity. One woman who is active in the affairs of her tribe once told me that the CDIB makes a very good 'scraper for your windshield but it is not enough to be an Indian.' To her, true Indian identity came from participating in the community, speaking the language, and attending the rituals" (280). Scholars researching from within and outside tribal communities, as well as Indian writers and artists speaking from personal experience, emphasize the importance of culture and kinship in shaping contemporary Indian identity.[8] Many also criticize the incorporation of the CDIB into daily community life. In Hulleah J. Tsinhnahjinnie's film *NTV*, she "includes a hilarious scene between two Indian women who won't even talk to each other until they see the certificate, and then embrace one another as 'sisters'" (Barker 71), to satirize the way this fantasy of identification has displaced traditional notions of identity based on kinship and shared experience.

Yet the CDIB is often represented as a kind of necessary evil, especially due to histories of racial mixing such that many Indians may not "look Indian." Such "nonrecognizable" Indians may face stigma within tribal communities and are "particularly suspected of falsifying indigenous identity" (Allen 97).[9] In such cases documentary proof of identity may be prized by those who seek tribal acceptance and validation of their internal identifications. The tension this dynamic produces is described by Circe Sturm:

> [In Oklahoma] they often refer to other nonrecognizable Chero-kee citizens, particularly those who are not socially or culturally accepted by a Cherokee community, as "card-carrying Indians" or "those Cherokees who'll be needing their white card." Obviously, *white* in this instance is a double entendre, referring both to a certificate degree of Indian blood, which is literally a white card, and also to white-Cherokees who need proof of their Indian identity and status and must document their Indianness through genealogical research. (138–139)

Indeed the history of racial mixing combined with complex negotiations of tribal sovereignty, enrollment, and entitlements means that challenges to self-identification proceed as vigorously (if not more so) from within tribal communities as from the state.[10]

Furthermore although federal law since 1905 has officially held that only tribal authorities have the right to determine membership, the actual process of determining identity has evolved in a far more complicated and enmeshed fashion. Most federally recognized tribes require some level of blood quantum for membership, and while "the federal government does not force tribes to implement blood quantum criteria and clearly states tribal authority in enrollment . . . the BIA [Bureau of Indian Affairs] provides patronizing step-by-step process guidance on tribal enrollment, emphasizes federal review of tribal law, and even provides charts on how tribes should determine blood quantum" (TallBear,

"DNA" 89). The most recent version of these step-by-step guidelines, available on the BIA website, refers exclusively and extensively to *documentary* evidence of identity, requiring the applicant to claim "relationship to an enrolled member . . . of a federally recognized Indian tribe or [relatives] whose names appear on the designated base rolls of a federally recognized Indian tribe."[11]

Such a relationship must then be proved through certified copies of birth and death certificates. The form itself requires names, maiden names, birth and death dates, tribal affiliations, and roll numbers for parents, grandparents, and great-grandparents, thus imposing a significant burden upon the applicant in gathering accurate information, while ironically implying a positive value placed on ancestry and kinship connections absent in much of mainstream American culture. While the words *Indian blood* appear six times in the instructions—in such tautological phrases as "your degree of Indian blood is computed from lineal ancestors of Indian blood"—the form itself is entirely discursive in nature, substituting names, dates, and numbers for the physical substance it claims to be measuring.

In this way the CDIB materializes a powerful and totalizing fantasy of identification that obscures not only its discursive roots but also the multiplicity of definitions of *Indian* that have existed historically and into the present day. In 1934 John Collier, U.S. commissioner of Indian affairs, complained in a memo that "determination of the degree of Indian blood is entirely dependent on circumstantial evidence; there is no known sure or scientific proof. Nor has any legal standard of universal applicability been set up by statute for the determination of who is, and who is not, an Indian" (qtd. in Brownwell 288). By 1977 the *Final Report of the American Indian Policy Review Commission* noted that the BIA had over three hundred different definitions of Indian identity, and in 1991 federal legislation contained over thirty-three different definitions of the term *Indian* (Barker 32; Brownwell 278; see also Miller 7). "Thus, under certain federal programs, an Indian person of one-fourth blood quantum may be considered Indian and is entitled for certain benefits, yet under a different program that requires one-half blood quantum, the same person would not be considered Indian since they would be ineligible for that program's benefits. On the other hand, a member of a federally recognized tribe, regardless of whether they were 1/8, 1/4, or 1/2, could benefit from certain programs since they would all be considered Indian" (Desjarlait 2). Some of the most prominent official federal definitions deployed today are those of the

1934 Indian Reorganization Act (IRA), which takes a relatively inclusive approach, considering Indian descent, tribal rolls, personal testimonies, findings of an anthropologist, and "a considerable measure of Indian culture and habits of living"; the Federal Acknowledgement Process (FAP), which uses similar criteria; the Indian Health Service, which requires only tribal enrollment; and the Census Bureau, which relies wholly on self-identification.[12] Most recently the Indian Arts and Crafts Act of 1990 (IACA) has provoked controversy with its requirement that "for art to be 'Indian art,' the artist must prove Indian ancestry and must be 'certified as an Indian artisan by a [federally recognized] Indian tribe'" (Nagel 243; see also Barker 25–26).[13] Notably, as discussed further below, while none of these federal definitions explicitly includes blood quantum requirements, in practice blood quantum is both pervasive and fundamental to each.

The multiplicity of federal definitions of Indian status is certainly a product of the proliferating nature of modern bureaucracy, but it is also heavily determined by shifting economic, political, and historical factors. During the original turn-of-the-century enrollments, it was in the state's interest to recognize fewer Indians for land allotment, since all "surplus" lands would become available for white settlement. At the same time, since the signatures of the majority of adult males in a tribe were necessary to go forward with land distribution, the government also explicitly pushed for the recognition of mixed-blood Indians, who were perceived as more likely to vote in favor of land distribution than the supposedly more traditional full-blooded Indians.[14] On the other hand, when mixed-blood members have supported antifederal political positions, the BIA has sought more stringent blood quantum requirements in order to exclude these disruptive elements (T. Wilson 120–121). Currently the perception of Indian blood as a lucrative commodity once again gives the state an interest in imposing more restrictive blood quantum requirements so that fewer individuals will be eligible for government-funded services and entitlements.

Not only the federal government but also individual tribal authorities have expanded or contracted definitions of *Indian* according to economic and other pressures. In the 1930s, for example, when the Osage tribe had dwindled to small numbers due to low birth rate and intermarriage with non-Indians, they "broadened their political base by identifying as 'full blood' all tribal members of one-half or more blood quantum (and in some instances even less if the person's physical appearance seemed to warrant the designation)" (T. Wilson 120). Similarly after the Sault Ste. Marie Tribe of Chippewa switched from a blood quantum to a lineal descent requirement in 1975, its population increased from 1,300 to 21,000 members (Brownwell 310). Tribal blood quantum requirements also change in response to outside pressures: in the 1950s, when federal officials pushed to terminate the Flathead tribe of Montana due to their perceived acculturation, the tribe tightened their blood quantum requirements (Nagel 243). On the other hand, the loosening of blood quantum requirements by the Cherokees of Oklahoma in the 1970s forced an improvement of federal services: "The Cherokee Nation originally used the one-quarter blood cutoff for IHS [Indian Health Service]. But Hastings [the local Indian hospital] was overloaded with just one-quarter people. The old facilities were a joke. Everyone was overworked and it was just a mess. So, they opened up the rolls and soon there was a flood on the hospital. This forced the hand of the IHS. Now, we have a brand new hospital facility" (Sturm 96). Melissa Meyer observes that tribes with greater assets tend to have more stringent membership requirements, especially if they have a reservation land base, while those "without reservation land, like those of Oklahoma and California, tend to have more inclusive blood quantum requirements that underscore a concern with demographic survival" (241–242). In recent years membership requirements have also fluctuated in response to new casino revenues and monetary settlements for land occupied by the U.S. government.[15] The common factor uniting these tribal adjustments of membership requirements is the constant pressure from the federal government with regard to recognition, entitlements, and resource allocation. As Bonita Lawrence cogently argues with regard to similar dynamics for Native people in Canada, it is not that Indian communities are "brainwashed" by the federal government into accepting biocertification but that "real, tangible assets," including "cultural survival," often rest upon their flexible deployments of blood quantum (12).

Yet the question remains as to the ultimate efficacy of blood quantum in promoting Indian survival and growth, particularly when its very flexibility has produced rampant inconsistency within both tribal and federal policies. Not only is "inconsistency . . . the main theme in federal applications of blood quantum" (Spruhan, "A Legal History" 9), but even within a single federal entity marked differences in both definitions and applications of blood quantum are rife. By examining one local example of such internally dissonant governmental discourse through the current use of blood quantum by the Indian Health Service, we can see how the power of this fantasy penetrates and shapes even those discourses and entities supposedly defined in opposition to it.

Officially the IHS has had no blood quantum requirement since 1977, when the Cherokee Nation successfully challenged the one-quarter requirement previously in place (Sturm 96).[16] Instead the IHS currently states a flexible and notably nonbiological definition of eligibility, providing services to any person who:

Is of Indian and/or Alaska Native descent as evidenced by one or more of the following factors:

(1) Is regarded by the community in which he lives as an Indian or Alaska Native.

(2) Is a member, enrolled or otherwise, or an Indian or Alaska Native Tribe or Group under federal supervision.

(3) Resides on tax-exempt land or owns restricted property.

(4) Actively participates in tribal affairs.

(5) Any other reasonable factor indicative of Indian descent. (*Indian Health Service Manual* 2–1.2)[17]

Such a definition shares with the IRA, the FAP, and the IACA an apparent respect for tribal sovereignty and self-determination, with a conscious effort to avoid imposing blanket or reductive definitions of Indian identity.

However, this seeming disavowal of blood quantum as determinant of identity is markedly contradicted by the coexisting bureaucratic requirement that all registered patients be assigned a "Blood Quantum Code" which becomes part of their permanent medical record. The current (2013) edition of the *Indian Health Service Manual* glosses this requirement with the explanation that "blood quantum refers to the percent of Indian ancestry. Blood quantum is not an IHS criteria for eligibility for Direct or CHS [Contract Health Service] services. However, many tribes have established a blood quantum criteria for their tribal membership. This decision then does affect eligibility for care" (2–6.3). The illogic of this statement is striking: if tribal membership is the only pertinent factor for IHS eligibility, and the tribes themselves make that determination using blood quantum and/or other criteria, then what possible valid reason could the IHS have for *also* collecting information about blood quantum, much less recording it according to the elaborate coding system shown in this IHS table?[18]

BLOOD QUANTUM

1   Full
2   Greater than or equal to ½ but less than full
3   Greater than or equal to ¼ but less than half
4   Indian but less than ¼
5   Non-Indian
6   Unspecified
7   Unknown

The urgency of this bureaucratic marking of patient bodies with degrees of Indianness is apparent in the annual reports of the IHS to the National Patient Information Registry Services, which enumerate for each IHS point of service how many patients have "missing" or "invalid" blood quantum codes.[19] This information is collected and tracked, despite the fact that patients are also coded for tribal affiliation and community of residence, thus radically undermining the nonbiological, flexible terms of eligibility outlined in official IHS policy.[20] As Margot Brownwell notes, "In its eagerness to apply the blood quantum, the BIA has time and again proceeded without formally publishing its certification procedures as is required under the Administrative Procedures Act. Even more seriously, it has repeatedly exceeded its administrative authority by imposing a blood quantum where the authorizing statute provided for a different, and often more generous definition of 'Indian'" (290). Rather than interpreting this administrative excess merely as a product of over-bureaucratization or a holdover of racialist attitudes—though it may indeed signify both of these—I suggest it is best understood as testifying to the power of the fantasy of identification manifested through blood quantum. In chapter 9 I discuss how this fantasy has recently taken on a new form through attempts to use DNA analysis to verify tribal identity, despite the lack of a sound scientific basis or cultural context for such claims. Yet understanding blood quantum purely as a totalizing fantasy of identification does not fully account for its function as a location of cultural identity and pride for many Native people, nor for the complex range of Native resistance often deployed in response to blood quantum. Thus I turn now to consider how blood quantum discourse is transformed by artistic and literary works in which Native artists challenge, resist, and refigure the fantasy's bureaucratic forms.

Imagined Identifications: Blood Quantum and Native Artistry

> In the works of many American Indian writers produced dur-
> ing the contemporary American Indian renaissances, the issue
> of blood quantum or degree of Indian blood is a site of personal
> and social conflict, opening upon their pages as painful wounds
> inextricably personal—"Are you a real Indian?"—and political—
> "How much Indian blood do you have?" Perhaps paradoxically,
> in many of these works blood quantum is a source of potential
> power. (Allen 98)

In the context of identification crises, those whose identities are under
attack or rendered socially unstable often engage in resistant practices
both to validate their self-identification and to ensure cultural survival
linked to those identities. Such resistant practices may consist of direct
counteridentifications and what José Esteban Muñoz calls "disidentifications": "Disidentification is about recycling and rethinking encoded
meaning. The process of disidentification scrambles and reconstructs
the encoded message of a cultural text in a fashion that both exposes
the encoded message's universalizing and exclusionary machinations
and recircuits its workings to account for, include, and empower minority identities and identifications" (31). While I have hitherto considered
the largely destructive fantasy of identification operating through state
deployments of blood quantum, I will now turn to examples of largely
productive counter- and disidentifications produced by Native artists
and writers. In response to the omnipresence of blood quantum within
Native culture, these artists have "appropriated it, recreated it, fashioned
it into an image of themselves—imagined it" (Momaday qtd. in Teuton
1). Such reimaginings simultaneously resist the reductive alienating
nature of blood quantum discourse and celebrate alternative sources of
heritage, community, and identity—sources that also notably draw on
the trope of blood, thus enacting the sometimes paradoxical relationship
of tribal communities to blood quantum requirements as both external
imposition and internal desire.[21] This discussion also touches upon the
controversial deployments within Indian literature—most notably by N.
Scott Momaday—of "blood" as a source of pride, memory, and ancestral
connection, a move that has been both celebrated and condemned for its
apparent adherence to notions of biological identification.[22]

In the late Blackfoot artist Joane Cardinal-Schubert's 1990 mixed-
media installation *Preservation of a Species: DECONSTRUCTIVISTS*

(*This is the house that Joe built*), viewers must peer through tiny peep-holes to see chalkboards covered with painted and photographed images, surrounded and often overwritten by chalked text. Among these "lessons" is a board that combines photographs of the artist, her father (Joe Cardinal), and other members of her family with the hand-written text "What does part Indian mean? (Which part?) you don't get 50% or 25% or 16% treatment when you experience RACISM—it is always 100%" (Cardinal-Schubert 132). In this critique of the reductive nature of blood quantum, Cardinal-Schubert "realizes . . . the horror of being torn apart and defined as a fragment" (Strong and Van Winkle 551). On the other end of the board, the same chalked letters counter-act this fragmentation with the statement "I would like to think that I made a difference." The juxtaposition of the artificial and meaning-less nature of blood quantum with the assertion of positive difference reflects Cardinal-Schubert's stated purpose of counteracting the "pow-erlessness" of having "absolutely no control over your identity" (132). In her artist's statement she describes the challenge her installation poses to the "deconstructivists (viewers)":

> There is a choice being offered to the viewers as to how they wish to look at Native people. Do they wish to look at their skin colour and thereby colour what knowledge they possess of Native people? Do they wish to look at a different view of history? Do they wish to look at a more personal examination of the individual and the contribution of that person on an individual level? Do they wish to look at the ancestors to prove their theories about Native people are misinformed? Do they believe a fenced-off area is all Native people want out of life? (133)

Cardinal-Schubert opposes the individual Native person or artist, whose ancestors provide unifying knowledge, to the state fantasy of Native identity as biologically quantified and divisible, "fenced-off." As Eva Marie Garroute observes, "One either belongs to the ances-tors or one does not, and the notion of fractionating one's essential substance, as the terminology of blood quantum presupposes, is untenable" (124). To the government that "declares by number who is Native and who is not" (Cardinal-Schubert 132), *Deconstructivists* responds that its arithmetic is flawed: identity is defined by culture and experience, by "making a difference," rather than setting differ-ence aside.

Identity Genocide, a 2012 exhibit by the photographer Tom Jones, similarly critiques blood quantum as a "white way of thinking" that is leading toward "self-imposed tribal eradication and assimilation" by his tribe, the Ho Chunk Nation.[23] Several of the pieces in Jones's exhibit respond to the historically imposed separation between the Ho Chunk Nation of Wisconsin and the Winnebago Nation of Nebraska, which are federally recognized as two distinct tribes but which share a common tribal origin that was fractured by removal in the 1830s. As Jones explains in the note accompanying his portrait of Fernando Hazic Ontiveros, "Since the beginning of the removals, many families were separated and would travel back and forth between Wisconsin and Nebraska. There are constant marriages that continue between the two groups then and today. Fernando's grandmother is ½ Winnebago and ½ Ho-Chunk, making him ¼ Ho-Chunk blood. Since the tribes are considered two distinct nations he is only 1/8 of each nation. This does not qualify him for the blood quantum of ¼ for each nation."[24] The portrait (Fig. 7.1) shows a young boy against a white background, reminiscent of a catalogue advertisement, with lettering superimposed over his body that reads "1/8 Winnebago + 1/8 Ho Chunk = 1/4 Ho Chunk = 0% Indian." Like Cardinal-Shubert's work, Jones's piece opposes the destructive arithmetic of blood quantum with intimate portraits of individuals whose tribal identity is deeply rooted in kinship and culture.

Multimedia artist Hulleah J. Tsinhnahjinnie (Taskigi/Diné) makes a similar critique of the depersonalizing effect of state regulations of Indian identity in her 1993 installation *Nobody's Pet Indian,* which "include[s] three replicated 40"x 30" photographed self-portraits with her enrollment number and bar codes printed across her face" (Barker 43). As Barker observes, in Tsinhnahjinnie's piece, "instead of giving her the freedom to represent herself, the number and codes gag and label and market her as an Indian, constricting her to perform to federal definitions of Indianness as a specimen or as a testament of their authority to name her" (43–44). The bar codes further materialize the destructive commodification of Tsinhnahjinnie's identity as an Indian artist who was subject to additional government scrutiny through the recently passed IACA. She juxtaposes the two forms of state codification of identity, through enrollment number and bar code, with her self-portraits to "reinforc[e] her important criticism of the ways that federal policies catalog her as an artifact of their authority to name her" (Barker 44).

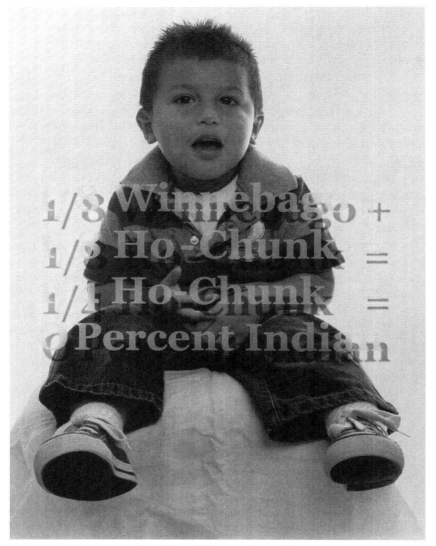

FIGURE 7.1. Tom Jones, detail from *Identity Genocide*. Courtesy of Tom Jones.

This criticism is also pointedly expressed in a piece from Tsinhnahjin-nie's 1994 series, *Photographic Memoirs of an Aboriginal Savant*, a poster loosely modeled on American Express credit card advertisements (Fig. 7.2). Under the headline "Don't leave the Rez Without It," Tsinhnahjin-nie places six mock-identification cards. Each card is headed with the

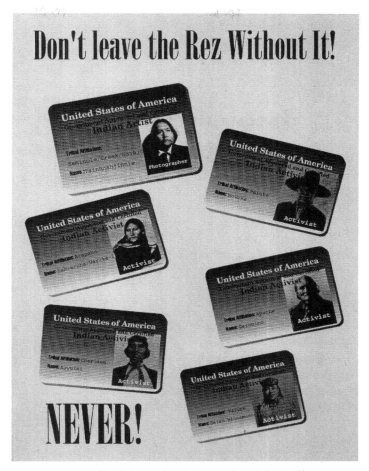

FIGURE 7.2. Hulleah J. Tsinhnahjinnie, detail from *Photographic Memoirs of an Aboriginal Savant.* Courtesy of Hulleah J. Tsinhnahjinnie.

official logo "United States of America / Government Approved and Certified." The top card, which carries Tsinhnahjinnie's name and photograph, lists her as a certified "Indian Artist," again critiquing the federal government's move to regulate "authentic" Indian artistry through the IACA. The other five cards are for certified "Indian Activists" and include the names and images of historically notable Native activists and warriors: Geronimo, Ayywini, Zah-e-cha/Har-ke-i, Wgwoka, and Sarah Winnemucca. By framing these resistant figures within the structure of a modern identification document, Tsinhnahjinnie exposes the contradictions at the core of federal identificatory practices toward Native peoples whose original identifications and structures of self-government have been violently disrupted by the same entity now claiming to protect their "true" selves. In the bottom left corner of the poster, the word "NEVER!" appears as a multifaceted warning against trying to exist as a mobile Native subject in the modern state without the necessary state certification, as well as a statement of profound resistance to the idea that such certification will ever truly reflect or contain Native identity.

Elizabeth Woody's 1993 poem "Translation of Blood Quantum" similarly testifies to an experience that exceeds and challenges reductive measurements of tribal identity. The opening lines of the poem inscribe the government-approved and -certified version of the speaker as "31/32 Warm Springs–Wasco-Yakima–Pit River–Navajo / 1/32 Other Tribal Entity Number 1553." The next two stanzas translate this quantification of "THIRTY SECOND PARTS OF A HUMAN BEING" as:

> SUN   MOON   EVENING STAR   AT DAWN CLOUDS
> RAINBOW   CEDAR   LANGUAGE
> COLORS AND SACRIFICE LOVE THE GREAT FLOOD
> THE TORTOISE   CARRIES THE PARROT   HUMMINGBIRD
> TRILLIUM   THE CROW RAVEN   COYOTE
> THE CONDOR   JAGUAR GRIZZLY TIMBER WOLF
> SIDEWINDER THE BAT CORN   TOBACCO   SAGE
> MUSIC DEATH CONSCIOUS OF THE SPIDERWEB
> RESURRECTED PROPHETS   RECURRENT POWER OF
> CREATION   IS FUELED BY SONG

The staggered format of this stanza separates its series of images into thirty-two phrases, "parts" of the speaker, while simultaneously undermining that quantifying move through both the organic naturalism of many of the words—"EVENING STAR, THE GREAT FLOOD, CORN TOBACCO SAGE"—and the enjambments that require the reader to make visual and conceptual linkages belying the false separations between phrases: "THE TORTOISE CARRIES THE PARROT," "RECURRENT POWER OF / CREATION." Like the "sidewinder" and the "spiderweb," the poem materializes a nonlinear, interconnected notion of self that powerfully contradicts the government version of that self.

These three artists—Cardinal-Schubert, Tsinhnahjinnie, and Woody—draw upon their experience and heritage to critique the state fantasy of identity as measurable through blood quantum. While Cardinal-Schubert's *Deconstructivists* notably evokes family relationships as a source of alternative identity and strength (as do works by Tsinhnahjinnie), none of these artists suggests that "blood" itself can be recuperated imagistically as a source of such identity. In her 2002 installation *Resisting Acts of Distillation*, however, Tlingit artist Tanis Maria S'eiltin expresses a powerful critique of the deployment of blood quantum in the Alaska Native Claims Settlement Act of 1971 (ANCSA) and invokes blood as an enduring trope of community survival.

Resisting Acts of Distillation is a three-room installation in which the viewer encounters a variety of elements combining sacred tribal tradition with contemporary politicized imagery. In a pointed critique of the role of oil interests in shaping the ANCSA, S'eiltin installs a series of shelves along one wall, each labeled with the name of a village, and supporting a vase of water in which floats a vial of petroleum oil, such that "the properties of the water and beeswax cork hold the petroleum oil perfectly upright in a delicate balance of innate nature" (Passalacqua 102). This balance between oil and water, two elements that symbolize the impossibility of mixing, reflects both the balance of power between corporate and Native interests in Alaskan land and the history of racial mixing that has produced a Native population who may now be disenfranchised of that land through the imposition of blood quantum requirements. In her artist's statement, S'eiltin also points out the unjust inconsistency of such requirements, such that her son, born in 1971, receives land title through the ANCSA, while her daughter, born in 1974, does not receive title, despite having the same blood quantum. She asks viewers to consider whether the ANSCA represents "termination in disguise" through the "social and legal dilution of a tribe" (S'eiltin 3).

In counterpoint to this critique, S'eiltin interpellates the viewer into a dialectic between oil and blood, state and tribal forms of identification, by placing a curtain through which viewers must walk in order to approach the wall of shelves. As pictured on the cover of this boook, this curtain is made up of strings of glass vials filled with red fluid, which "serve as a metaphor that cancels out the measurements of blood quantum and represents innate knowledge that remembers our past. . . . The vials represent our strength in terms of number and attitude" (S'eiltin 3). By requiring viewers to physically walk through and brush against these vials, S'eiltin surrounds them with the tangible power of communal identity rooted in the blood, an identity also materialized by images of a sacred T'lingit war helmet; the *Tinnah*, or copper shield; and the imprint of a hand.

Yet there remains a tension in the use of the "blood vials" as positive counterpoint to the suspended vials of oil. In a 2005 interview S'eiltin explains that each vial is filled to the top "to represent that despite all the things that have happened to us, and the corporations, that *we can still identify ourselves*," thus making a powerful statement of imagined identification as community survival (Passalacqua 107, my emphasis). Yet the interviewer, Veronica Passalacqua, pairs that quotation with the suggestion that "the vials evoking laboratory analysis [bring] the inequities of blood measurement from paper documentation to lifesize proportions" (107), thus interpreting the blood vials as a negative critique of blood quantum. I suggest that both these meanings exist in productive tension, a tension also reflected in the placement of the glass vases of oil and water against a red background such that the transparent water containing the petroleum vials appears blood-red.[25] This visual blurring of separate fluids and meanings enacts S'eiltin's resistance to "distillation," a scientific process for separating and purifying liquid elements, while also suggesting the violence of that process through the "bloody" history of colonization and resource theft. This blurring is furthered through various interpretations of the exhibit, as some viewers describe the vials as filled with "rich deep-red wine" (Passalacqua 107), while others see them as filled with "red-tinted oil symbolizing the blending of petroleum and the heritage or 'blood quantum' requirements for natives to share in the oil profits" (Kangas 1). (In her original artist's statement, S'eiltin refers only to "vials filled with red fluid" [2].)

This tension represents one artist's working through of what Circe Sturm calls the "circular logic" of the "cultural production of bloodedness." Sturm describes this logic in terms that evoke S'eiltin's piece:

> One way to conceptualize this process is to think of a Cherokee individual as a metaphorical container, a microcosm of the tribal body as a whole, that can be filled with blood, culture, or both. At the most basic level, it would seem that if individuals had less Cherokee blood, then they would need more cultural capital to achieve social recognition as Cherokee; at the same time, if they possessed less culture, they would require more biological capital. However, the process is not that simple. Since blood stands for culture and culture stands for blood, there is a circular logic behind Cherokee practices of social classification. (140–141)

The use of fluid and vials in *Resisting Acts of Distillation* suggest that, for S'eiltin, Native identity is defined at once in terms of blood and in defiance of attempts to quantify or commodify that blood as "capital." Thus both the fantasy of identification and its imaginative counterpoint are realized through a complex artistic gesture of disidentification, in which "the affirmation of that slippage . . . is itself the point of departure for a more democratizing affirmation of internal difference" (Butler , *Bodies That Matter* 219).[26]

This gesture can be understood in terms similar to those that Chadwick Allen suggests are crucial for understanding how Momaday develops his trope of "blood memory" as a productive alternative to blood quantum, for example, in his 1976 memoir *The Names*, by juxtaposing a quotation of government documents establishing his official blood quantum with a description of the day he received his Kiowa name (Momaday 42): "It is not Momaday's blood quantum, inscribed by the U.S. government in official documents, that confers his Kiowa identity; rather, it is his blood memory, the story of his being situated in ongoing Kiowa narratives of their identity as a people in the American landscape" (Allen 105). Such a perspective resonates with that described by Alexandra Harmon in her historical account of the Colville tribal enrollment councils, which spoke in terms of "blood" but resisted government pressure to enforce particular blood quantums, since for the tribal authorities, "'Indian blood' connoted not so much a quantifiable biological heritage, essential for Indian identity, as a conscious and sincere affiliation with indigenous people" (188). Sturm similarly observes that among the Cherokee people of Oklahoma, blood is "a social and cultural category as often as it is a biological one" (137).

Just as the social model of disability has allowed disability scholars to separate physical impairment from the social and identificatory effects of that impairment, social understandings of "blood" enable Native artists, scholars, and citizens to negotiate a complex fantasy of identification which at once reifies and denigrates ideas of identity based on kinship: "The blood of a Cherokee is not just a biological thing, but a lot of heritage. There are a lot of real Cherokee people running through our veins. There's cultural heritage in there" (qtd. in Sturm 98). Yet it is also true that, just as the social model of disability has been challenged and complicated by those who point out the social construction of impairment and the material effects of impairment as ontological experience, so do attempts to recuperate blood as a source of positive Native identity evoke challenges regarding the possible essentialism of such moves, as well as the complex blurring of boundaries between government and artistic deployments of "blood."[27]

Momaday, for example, has been particularly criticized for his genetic refiguring of blood memory, as in a 1989 statement, "Each of us bears in his genes or in his blood or wherever a recollection of the past," which would seem to reinscribe and strengthen biologically deterministic notions of identity (qtd. in Strong and Van Winkle 561). Pauline Turner Strong and Barrik Van Winkle make a compelling argument for the difference between Momaday's statement and the reductive uses of blood quantum: "Momaday's use of blood imagery aims not to differentiate but to relate; not to administer but to imagine; not to impose quantified identities upon others but to make sense of the intersubjective quality of his own experience. . . . Momaday's 'memory in blood' becomes a refiguring of 'Indian blood' that makes it a vehicle of connection and integration—literally, a re-membering—rather than one of calculation and differentiation" (562). This argument is predicated upon the idea that "blood" has so deeply permeated discourses about Native identity that it is impossible to speak of one without invoking the other.[28] Thus any reading of representations of identity by Native artists and writers must negotiate both oppressive and liberatory discourses of blood, since "it is a far from straightforward matter to rupture the 'grammar' of these discourses once they have been put into place" (Lawrence 21).

Strong and Van Winkle see the idea of blood memory in Momaday's work as a productive example of such ruptured grammar. I suggest that the work of S'eiltin similarly seeks to evoke a multilayered exploration of metaphorics of blood through disidentification. The writings of Gerald Vizenor also offer a "remaking and rewriting of a dominant script" (Muñoz 23) through his parodic literary portrayals of blood quantum politics and, more recently, of genetic discourses. In protesting what he has called the "perverse arithmetics" of blood quantum, Vizenor appears to reject the metaphorics of blood memory as well, a move that some perceive as politically dangerous in its potential undermining of stable Indian identity.[29] In his 1981 *Earthdivers*, for example, one of Vizenor's characters proposes "an organization of mixedblood skins which demands one-fourth degree of tribal blood or less, to be enrolled as a member," while another suggests a scheme in which "tribal faculties and students would be paid a basic wage according to their volume of tribal blood," based on a color wheel offering a "scientific approach to blood volume, degrees, and quantities of tribalness" (qtd. in Strong and Van Winkle 563). Both of these characters function to satirically expose the absurdity of blood quantum requirements, not only as governmental imposition but also as an integral part of tribal discussions of identity and belonging.

In his 1991 novel, *The Heirs of Columbus*, Vizenor incorporates genetic language into another complicated disidentification with discourses about blood, memory, and community. He portrays a crossblood, trickster community of genealogical heirs of Christopher Columbus and an Anishinabe woman, who are empowered to heal Indian children and the natural world through their "genetic signatures," the "stories in their blood" (4). In this sense genes and blood are merged into a spiritual heritage that enables community. However, the novel also presents a robust rejection of "the racist arithmetic measures of blood quantum," and the Heirs of Columbus will accept "anyone who wants to be tribal 'no blood attached or scratched'" (162).

Here genetics is invoked to mock biologized definitions of identity, through farcical claims by tribes suspicious that the Heirs "have established the genetic signatures of most of the tribes around the country, so that anyone could, with an injection of suitable genetic material, prove without a doubt a genetic tribal identity. Germans at last could be genetic Sioux, and thousands of coastal blondes bored with being white could become shadow tribes of Hopi, or Chippewa, with gene therapies" (162). Through the absurdity of suggesting that gene therapy could make a German into a Sioux, Vizenor destabilizes notions of Indian identity based on strictly biological heredity. Yet, as Lawrence observes, "no risk-free space exists in which to explore Native identity" (22), and Vizenor's satirical critique of blood quantum appears to run the risk of destabilizing the entire idea of identity as the basis for community or rights. A similar risk arises when the social model of disability is taken to its apparent logical extremes, in which any difference from the normate may be construed as "disability," obscuring the historical and lived particularities of disabled experience.

If the fantasy of identification often functions in a negative manner to supersede self-identification, substituting documentary proof for a false biological certainty, it also serves what many see as a necessary function, shoring up the boundaries of identity and experience. Thus critics of such fantasies are often challenged to propose alternative systems of identification, or else to reject the entire concept of identity. As discussed earlier, many critics of blood quantum propose alternatives through traditional systems of kinship and culture yet ironically employ a metaphorics of blood to ground such arguments. Kinship and culture, supposedly unlike blood, are neither quantifiable nor measurable. Similarly a strict social model of disability often obscures the extent to which the lives of disabled people are regulated by the quantification of impairment. In both cases there is a state interest in defining, measuring, and certifying identities that drives these particular fantasies of identification. In the next chapter I discuss how this state interest, and its modern deployment through structures of biocertification, evolved in an intersecting and mutually constitutive fashion for both people with disabilities and Native peoples in the United States.

8 / Realms of Biocertification

We have seen how blood quantum constitutes a powerful historical and current fantasy of identification, as well as the resistant counter- and dis-identifications realized through artistic revisions of blood quantum discourse. Yet this discussion remains incomplete without a consideration of the enmeshed histories of blood quantum and disability categorization in the United States. Such a consideration allows us to understand why, in the United States today, both Native and disabled people are required to carry and produce government certification that purports to validate their biological being in order to access certain rights and resources.[1] Such biocertification has become a persistent and powerful version of the "interventions and regulatory controls" characterizing the modern biopolitical state (Foucault, *History of Sexuality* 139). In this chapter I explore the shared origins of disability and Native biocertification in the United States to demonstrate that a comparison between the two goes far beyond analogy and into the realm of mutual constitution, and thus a resistant response will be most effective if structured to address that mutuality.[2]

The framework of biocertification explains why the Certificate of Degree of Indian Blood is not instead named the "Certificate of Tribal Membership" or even the "Indian ID Card." As biocertification, the CDIB symbolically provides a window into the very arteries and veins of the card's possessor, and thus imbues the civil servant checking the card with the pseudo-authority of the diagnostic gaze. Similarly the numerous certificates of impairment that people with disabilities must obtain throughout their lives depend upon a metonymic and actual link between the diagnostic authority of the medical practitioner and the regulatory authority of the bureaucrat. Just as the discursive stability of the CDIB can be disrupted when the person receiving (or being denied) certification has a physical appearance interpreted as Indian or non-Indian, the power of the medical certificate is at once displaced and reinforced by the occasional willingness of the state to accept the appearance of certain bodies as evidence of impairment.[3]

Yet my point is not to draw a simple analogy between biocertifications of disabled and Native people, thus running the risk of conflating their crucially different (though sometimes intersecting) histories of colonialism, institutionalization, and resistance.[4] Rather I seek to redirect one likely critique of this comparison—that biology is simply more fundamental to definitions of disability than it is to Native status—by exploring the hitherto unremarked origins of blood quantum certification in the same historical, legal, and cultural processes that produced modern understandings of "disabled" and "normal" bodies and minds. I seek to demonstrate a deeply embedded and mutually constitutive relationship between the emergence of biocertification for Native and disabled people in the United States in order to draw new insights and suggest future coalitions for these groups, as well as to shed light on the pervasive and multilayered functionings of fantasies of identification in the current day.[5]

Counting Competency

While blood quantum has been used since the 1930s to delimit which individuals can claim tribal membership and access to various tribal and federal rights and resources, its original institutionalization in the tribal enrollment records produced in the period following the General Allotment Act (often referred to as the Dawes Act) of 1887 was quite different.[6] The Dawes Rolls, as the first mass recordings of blood quantum, were part of the federal effort to divide the lands formerly held in common by various sovereign Indian tribes, for the stated purpose of better integrating Indian peoples into an American society based on principles of private property and individual agency. As many historians have noted, allotment also served to free up large parcels of land for sale to white interests and settlement by white Americans, and thus is often highlighted as a central device by which Indians were disempowered in the late nineteenth century.[7] Since the Dawes Act allotted 160 acres of land to each recognized Indian, it became necessary for the first time to create formal records of "official" Indians. The Dawes Rolls, along with subsequent enrollment documents, still serve today as a documentary basis for validating blood quantum and tribal membership, despite a variety of acknowledged flaws and omissions.[8]

The primary purpose of the blood quantum records compiled during the enrollment period, however, was not to distinguish between valid and invalid Indian claimants. Nor were land allotments determined by degree of Indian blood: a full-blooded Indian received the same 160-acre allotment as an Indian defined as half- or quarter-blood (LaValle 9). Rather blood quantum was used in the allotment process to distinguish between those "competent" and "incompetent" to have complete legal control of their land allotment, including the right to sell land without judicial approval (Gross 165). It was deemed that only a sufficient percentage of *white* blood conferred competence upon the Indian landholder, such that "those enrolled with less than 50 percent Indian blood and who spoke English were taken to be assimilated enough into U.S. society that they no longer required federal guardianship and were issued full land title and U.S. citizenship, while those enrolled with 50 percent or more Indian blood and who either did not speak English or English was their second language were assumed to be still too much tied to their tribal customs so that that they were in need of federal protection and were issued trust patents" (Barker 30). Barker further observes that, as the rolls did not record language ability, blood quantum quickly became the determining factor in whether land grants were issued in title or in trust. This attribution of competency to degree of white blood was affirmed by legislation and judicial acts in the following decades. The Burke Act of 1906 empowered the secretary of the interior to issue a title "whenever he is satisfied that any Indian allottee is competent," but two years later Congress held that if any Native allottee was of one-half degree Indian blood or more, his or her allotment would be held in trust (Beaulieu 290; Sturm 79). In the 1913 White Earth Chippewa case, Judge Page Morris ruled that at least one-eighth white blood was required for legal competence, as a lesser amount "would not affect [i.e., improve] the capacity of the Indian to manage his own affairs" (*United States v. First National Bank*).[9] Property rights were thus carefully predicated by blood quantum, despite ongoing disagreements among lawmakers as to the exact percentage of white blood needed to mark the line between competency and incompetency.

In 1908, for example, after the passing of an act to release certain allotments from trust, the commissioner of Indian affairs reflected that

in view of their white parentage and of their opportunities for education, all Indians of less than one-half blood could be intrusted
with the untrammeled management of their lands. It was also
believed that Indians of less than 75 percent Indian blood should
be authorized to sell their surplus lands, because as they too had
had opportunities for education, very few would have any excuse for
making a foolish use of the privilege, and if they did sell their land for
less than it was worth or make improvident use of the proceeds, they
would still have their homesteads to fall back upon and would have
learned a needed lesson. (*Reports of the Department of the Interior* 102)

As Paul Spruhan observes, the decisive and patronizing calculus of competency in this statement obscures the fact that members in the House
and Senate had previously disagreed quite strongly on the exact amounts
of blood quantum to apply in the act ("A Legal History" 42). Similarly, as
discussed in more detail below, pressure from powerful sugar companies
led Congress in 1921 to redefine the blood quantum boundary between
competent and incompetent Native Hawai'ians from one-thirty-second
to one-half, thus greatly reducing the number of Native people eligible
to claim homestead land (Gross 201; Kauanui 8, 89).[10] This move was bolstered by increasingly confident claims regarding the obviousness of such
distinctions, as in Senator Key Pittman's assertion that "*everybody knows
that any part Hawaiian is capable of taking care of himself*" (*Hawaiian
Homes Commission Act* 124, my emphasis). Here we certainly see a fantasy of identification at work, papering over the messy indeterminability
of identity with claims of absolute and quantifiable knowledge.

In this original deployment of blood quantum, then, Indian and white
blood were each commodified, but on crucially different planes: a substantial degree of Indian blood was required to *receive* a land allotment,
but a majority of white blood was required in order to have full legal *control* over that allotment. Thus in addition to the many other inaccuracies
of the Dawes enrollments, there was an incentive for allottees to report
a larger percentage of white blood than they might actually possess—a
practice that ironically might serve to disqualify their descendants in
the present day, when a minimum degree of *Indian* blood is generally
required for tribal and federal recognition.

The assumption that white blood was necessary for legal competence
emerged from a long history of characterizations of Indian people as inferior to Euro-American citizens. Such characterizations drew upon not
only discourses of morality and civilization but also quite centrally ideas

about disability and dependency, constructing Indian tribes as "wards" requiring the guardianship and guidance of the federal government. As Supreme Court Justice Samuel Miller wrote in 1886, "These Indian tribes are the wards of the nation. They are communities dependent on the United States.... From their very weakness and helplessness ... there arises the duty of protection, and with it the power" (*United States v. Kagama*). Characterizations of Indians as "weak" and "helpless" justified state intervention and, in many cases, were used as determinative of Indian status itself. Thus in 1869 the Supreme Court of New Mexico Territory excluded the Pueblos from Indian status because they were "honest, industrious, and law-abiding citizens," and the U.S. Supreme Court agreed with this conclusion, finding the Pueblos to be "a peaceable, industrious, intelligent, honest, and virtuous people" (Brownwell 279). As William T. Hagan wryly observes, this conclusion presumes its opposite: that if the Pueblos had been "militant, indolent, stupid, dishonest, and immoral, they would have qualified as Indians" (310). Yet many of these moralizing dichotomies—weak/strong, dependent/independent, stupid/intelligent, indolent/industrious—were shaped not only by racialist thinking but also inextricably by the social construction of categories of disability/ability. This connection was made explicit in a court decision of 1912 which stated that a family having one-eighth Indian blood possessed "sufficient Indian blood to substantially handicap them in the struggle of existence" (*Sully et al. v. United States et al.*).

The disability language used to characterize this early blood quantum discourse may be contextualized through the complex history of the notion of "competency," developed in American jurisprudence primarily in relation to mental disability. As Barbara Welke observes, what "counted as evidence of mental capacity and incapacity ... must be historicized" and thus denaturalized, both in the nineteenth century and the current day (7). The decades preceding allotment were marked by intense efforts to delineate and manage a newly legible population, which by the end of the century came to be known as the "feebleminded." The U.S. census began counting "idiots" and "the insane" for the first time in 1840, and eight years later institutions for "idiots" and "epileptics" began to appear and multiplied rapidly enough that the Association of Medical Officers of American Institutions of Idiotic and Feeble-Minded Persons was founded in 1876.[11] Feeblemindedness emerged as a flexible category within which to encompass a broad range of subjects perceived as unfit for or dangerous to American selfhood, a dynamic that crystallized in 1882 with the first eugenic immigration law, the Undesirables Act, which

barred "convicts, paupers, the insane, and idiots" (Trent 86). The conflation of "socially" and "biologically" produced categories in this act testifies to the mutually constitutive and indeed inseparable nature of such
categories at the turn of the century.

Allison Carey explains that such restrictive groupings "did not derive
simply from new understandings of feeblemindedness but relied heavily on meta-narratives of citizenship and rights that accepted incompetence, dependence, and immorality as legitimate reasons for exclusion"
(72). Furthermore "because of the loose definition of feeblemindedness
and the intersection of stereotypes and exclusions, individuals within
other marginalized groups could be labeled feebleminded and similarly
restricted" (72). Indeed many scholars have pointed out that John C.
Calhoun and other supporters of slavery manipulated the flawed results
of the 1840 Census to claim that free African Americans in the North
had higher rates of insanity and idiocy than those enslaved in the South
(Goldberg 38; Carey 46). This is an important point to make, both historically and politically; however, such arguments draw much of their
power from the unquestioned assumption that such racist distortions
falsely contaminated the black population with the stigma of real mental
disability. An analysis that incorporates both critical race and disability
studies approaches, however, reveals that the category of "real mental
disability" was as malleable and contested, and had just as tenuous a relationship to the biological, as did racial difference in this period.[12]

An enormous number of feebleminded Americans were newly discovered by medical and social reformers in the late nineteenth century, just
as these reformers sought greater legitimacy and state support for their
institutions (Carey 56; Trent 79). James W. Trent observes that many of
the people defined as feebleminded after the Civil War would not have
been considered so before the war, as diagnostic criteria loosened and
expanded during the postwar era (20). This trend continued into the
twentieth century, as "in the context of new social aspirations and fears,
mental defectives in the first decade of the new century began to be seen
in more places, in greater numbers, and associated with more and more
social problems" (140), such that some estimates identified as much as
30 to 40 percent of the U.S. population as feebleminded (Carey 63). By
broadening the criteria, medical reformers and the burgeoning eugenics
movement could justify both their own importance to the nation and
their increasingly stringent programs of control, confinement, and ster-
ilization of people marked as feebleminded. This violent history intersects with that of similar state programs targeting Indian populations in

the United States, and like those programs it is both shaped by and constitutive of power inequalities based on race, class, and gender. As Carey observes, "Individuals within marginalized groups, especially poor sexually deviant women, were particularly likely to be labeled feebleminded" (63). Such conflations were supported by racially charged associations of feeblemindedness with animalism, brutishness, and primitiveness, qualities also inherent in many Euro-American characterizations of Indians (Carlson 140). Indeed "in the context of the emerging national discourse on mental disability, 'competence' and 'independence' became code words for moral and racial conformity" (Carey 72).

Thus when we find the Dawes commissioners and others referring to "competence" and "incompetence" with regard to degree of Indian blood, a submerged context exists in which categories of competence were already established based on the naturalized category of mental disability. The idea of competence had been incorporated into U.S. law from its inception, through restrictions on "idiots," "incompetents," or "imbeciles" in a number of areas, including the right to make contracts (Carey 38–41).[13] As in the case of allotment, such restrictions were framed as a matter of protecting a class of people who were particularly vulnerable to exploitation because they lacked the ability to make informed, rational decisions about property (Trent 21, 64; Carey 40–41). By the nineteenth century incompetency in American jurisprudence was grounded, as legal historian Susanna Blumenthal has cogently argued, upon the supposition of a "default legal person" against whom the incompetent could be measured. Blumenthal demonstrates how this default figure, as materialized through "a steady stream of capacity suits across the nineteenth century . . . was cast in liberal humanist terms, as one who possessed the rational faculties of intelligence, moral sense, and free will" (1233, 1166). The default legal person functioned, in Rosemarie Garland Thomson's terms, as a normate, a "social figure through which people can represent themselves as definitive human beings" (*Extraordinary Bodies* 8). The legal normate is historically defined through the intersection of categories of disability with those of gender and race: "White men were assumed to have capacity, to be able, unless proven otherwise; for women and racialized others the beginning assumption was the reverse. Medical and legal scholars (by definition white and male) understood the incapacity or disability of women . . . and racialized others as marked on their minds and bodies as certainly as was that of the 'feebleminded,' the epileptic, the 'cripple,' and the 'idiot'" (Welke 8). Blumenthal particularizes this general description of legal capacity by explaining that early

American legal scholars, having rejected English law based on class hierarchy, "offered up a republican replacement—a scheme in which mental ability rather than social status would constitute the primary determinant of legal capacity and responsibility" (1158).

This early legal history illuminates the disability origins of the category of incompetency to which Indian people were assigned in the late nineteenth century. If we understand that the original function of blood quantum in American jurisprudence was to associate Indian blood with disability, then a variety of resulting policies, such as the conversion of shared land to individual holdings, encouraging intermarriage, the banning of Native languages, the removal of Indian children to boarding schools in the late nineteenth and early twentieth centuries, and the coerced urbanization of the 1954 Relocation Act, can be understood as a deliberate attempt to "rehabilitate" the Indian person into the normative white citizen defined by his able-mindedness.[14] Nowhere is this rehabilitative imperative more apparent than in the context of Hawai'i, where it was made explicit in the 1921 Hawai'ian Homes Commission Act, originally titled the Hawai'ian Rehabilitation Act.[15] Couched in concerns over the "disappearance" of the Native Hawai'ian population, this act proposed rehabilitation through individual homesteading, further enforcing the connection between blood quantum, competency, and private property: "Hawaiians would be rehabilitated through U.S. law, thus presupposing that some 'normal' state (whiteness) need be restored or at the very least compensated" (Halualani 156).[16] Examining the parallel rehabilitative discourses targeted at disabled people and Native people further demonstrates the mutual constitution of these categories and their accompanying fantasies.

The Road to Rehabilitation

Even on the mainland, where the language of rehabilitation was not made explicit, "Native Americans found their citizenship dependent on adopting 'civilized,' that is, white, living practices" (Welke 72). By incentivizing whiteness through the equation of white blood with competency, the state minimized its material and moral obligations toward the remaining "dependent" Indian nations, while comforting itself that it was embracing rehabilitative progressivism through the idea that Indians were improvable by the introduction of white and other "robust" bloodlines. Both these attitudes are epitomized in the words of Senator Higgins of Delaware in 1895:

This nation is generous, and means to be generous, to the Indians, but by that, I know, the people understand and mean the Indian aborigines, not the half-bloods, not the quarter-bloods, not the eighth-bloods, not those in whom you can not observe the physical admixture. . . . It seems to me one of the ways of getting rid of the Indian question is just this of intermarriage, and the gradual fading out of the Indian blood; the whole quality and character of the aborigine disappears, they lose all of the traditions of the race; there is no longer any occasion to maintain the tribal relations, and there is then every reason why they shall go and take their place as white people do everywhere. (53rd Congress Rec. S2614)

This passage epitomizes the dual violence of U.S. Indian policy at the turn of the century, in which rhetorics of charity were often overshadowed by the unabashed desire for the objects of that charity to disappear, or at least "gradually fade out." Getting rid of the Indian question, to many U.S. policymakers, meant getting rid of the Indian, and the most expedient means of doing so was to define *Indian* in the narrowest, most starkly biological terms possible. This drive toward assimilation emerged in tandem with the rehabilitative model of disability in the United States and Europe, as discussed in part I.[17] Both the philosophy and practice of rehabilitation invokes assimilation as its positive goal: "Rehabilitation marks the appearance of a culture that attempts to complete the act of identification, of making identical" (Stiker 128). Thus it is unsurprising that similar rhetorics were employed to define and regulate both Native and disabled people during this period, particularly during debates about whether social policy should focus on true rehabilitation or merely on containment of unruly populations.

One key component of such debates was the question of whether even supposedly inassimilable subjects, such as full-blooded Native people and so-called idiots, could be rehabilitated to some extent. Both in the case of Native Hawai'ians and in the treatment of the feebleminded, it was proposed that these populations could be partially rehabilitated through hard work, especially physical labor in the open air. Yet the charitable aura of these efforts was undercut by the accompanying assumption that opportunities for such work should either function quasi-punitively or—if perceived as a reward—be limited to those most incapacitated by their lack of non-Native blood or mental ability. In both cases the state interest in defining certain populations as incompetent and benefiting from their uncompensated labor was disguised under a veneer of benevolent concern.

By the 1920s the colonization of Hawai'i had impacted the Native residents such that it was feared that they were disappearing, or at least declining to an intolerable degree. Many Native Hawai'ians lived in poverty in the newly urbanized Honolulu area, and both U.S. policymakers and Native reformers sought to address what was seen as an economic and moral crisis (Gross 182–183; Kauanui 7). The result was the 1921 Hawaiian Homes Commission Act (HHCA), first titled the Hawaiian Rehabilitation Act to signal its purpose as not only rehabilitative but charitable. While the act set aside approximately 200,000 acres of land to be returned to Native Hawai'ians, its framers ultimately treated this apportionment of land not as a matter of justice or even compensation but as an act of charity toward a downtrodden race (Kauanui 139). In this regard, homesteading in Hawai'i went even further than allotment on the mainland toward redefining Native peoples as fundamentally disabled, while similarly recasting the United States as the generous benefactor of the disabled subject rather than the original source of the disability itself. Just as defining the feebleminded as a flexible and ever-increasing category allowed physicians, reformers, and eugenicists to assert increasing authority over such people's mobility and bodily autonomy, defining Native Hawai'ians as a fixed and ever-dwindling category also allowed legislators and powerful economic interests to disguise further attacks on Native self-determination as acts of pity and concern.

Fundamental to these policies was the enactment of distinctions between the good and bad subjects of such rehabilitative intervention. While early European and American settlers represented Native Hawai'ians as irredeemably "uncivilized" and "lazy" (Halualani 148), by the late nineteenth century this discourse of inferiority became nuanced by the perception of mixed-blood Hawai'ians as improvable subjects. In congressional hearings in 1920, while "pure" Hawai'ians were referred to as "unenterprising, apathetic, [and] thriftless," the "part Hawaiian, the part Caucasian, the part Chinese, the part Portuguese" were described as "a virile, prolific, and enterprising lot of people" (*Hawaiian Homes Commission Act* 15–16). This racialized distinction between unproductive and productive subjects was characterized in Hawai'i, as it was on the mainland, in terms of land management and capitalist property relations, for "the Hawaiians are not business men and have shown themselves unable to meet competitive conditions unaided" (Halualani 161). By ascribing the economic decline of the Native population to their inherent laziness and thriftlessness, the United States could justify a policy response that focused on a punitive regime of work: "We don't want to make the Hawaiians rich, we want to make them work" (Gross 195).[18] The Hawaiian Homes Commission repeatedly asserted that granting homesteads to Native Hawai'ians would enable them to "till the soil and become self-supporting and raise healthy, happy families and become homeowners" (Kauanui 7). This vision of the ideal American citizenry was also nuanced by assertions of a biologized racial particularity, as in a Hawai'ian congressional resolution which stated that "members of *the Hawaiian race or blood* should be encouraged to return to the status of independent and contented tillers of the soil, preserving to posterity the *valuable and sturdy traits of the race*" (*Journal of the House of Representatives* 734, my emphasis). As Ariela Gross observes, "The rhetoric of 'making them work' made quite explicit the gulf between the discourse of 'rehabilitation' and any idea of claims to land as a matter of justice; the Hawai'ians were understood not as a nation who deserved to have their land returned to them but as a labor force who should be allotted homesteads to turn them into good laborer-subjects of the United States" (196–197). Others echoed the rhetoric of rehabilitative labor: in 1921 Senator John H. Wise told the *Honolulu Star-Bulletin*, "The only way for rehabilitation to benefit the Hawaiian is through his own efforts—hard, honest work" (Kauanui 145). Even many Native Hawai'ians took up this argument, constructing work as a form of self-determination and empowerment. The Rev. Akaiko Akana, a founder of the Hawaiian Protective Association, in his 1918 pamphlet *Sinews for Racial Development*, urged his fellow Native people, "Back to the soil and work! Work! Work! Will be their future salvation in health and general welfare" (Gross 195). As the title of the pamphlet suggests, this rhetoric invoked a physiological basis for racial inequality and thus naturalized the proposed solution of manual labor to strengthen the "sinews" of the race.

It is striking, then, to see how similar rhetoric was employed just a few decades earlier with regard to the feebleminded, whose treatment had become increasingly custodial and even carceral by this point. Superintendants of institutions also called for their residents to work outside, tilling the soil, as a form of limited rehabilitation; as one superintendant told the Association of Medical Officers in 1892, "We are forcing the epileptic boys . . . to [do] this out-door work in fruit harvest with first-class moral as well as medical results. They take an interest in the work, do it quite well, and have fewer spasms while thus engaged" (qtd. in Trent 90–91). As in the case of Hawai'ians, such work is presented as therapeutic in itself, resulting in "moral as well as medical" improvements. However, there is no suggestion that this labor is or could be curative; the boys are not learning to harvest fruit with an eye toward eventual agricultural careers. Rather their labor functions merely to palliate their symptoms, rendering them more manageable within the institution, while simultaneously benefiting that institution with their uncompensated labor. Trent's *Inventing the Feeble Mind* comprehensively documents the extent to which such institutions relied on the labor of the residents, who performed menial tasks and also aided in the care of their fellows.

By contrast, in the case of Native Hawai'ians, the granting of homesteads to large numbers of claimants would not in fact have profited the state, much less the influential American economic interests invested in the rehabilitation process. Indeed there was the possibility that the hard work of Hawai'ians actually could lift their people out of poverty and into a position to contest the influence of the sugar companies in the state. In response, the sugar companies sent a powerful advocate to the congressional hearings on the HHCA who used the biological, racialized language of rehabilitative labor to undermine the initially benevolent intentions of the proposed act.

This advocate, Alexander G. M. Robertson, invoked the blood quantum competency framework to argue that only full-blooded Native Hawai'ians should be allowed to claim homesteads, since those with mixed blood should be able to manage on their own. In making this argument, he also emphasized that "these unenterprising, apathetic, thriftless natives of the pure blood" were in need of help due to their own incompetence rather than the effects of colonization, and thus called for "psychological rather than legislative" remedies (*Hawaiian Homes Commission Act* 15–16). Robertson then associated the "thriftless natives" with the category of the undeserving poor, asserting that nobody in Hawai'i was "indigent ... by reason of the lack of opportunity to work" (23–24). By contrast, he declared that part-Hawai'ians were "not the proper objects of public charity" since "they are able to stand on their own feet" (15–16). Thus part-Hawai'ians became defined by ability, while full-blooded Hawai'ians were defined as poor-yet-not-disabled, a category carefully constructed throughout the nineteenth century to ensure that the newly evolving welfare state would not encourage sloth among the able-bodied population.[19] By the time Robertson was finished arguing his case, it would seem that no Hawai'ians actually deserved the charitable assistance of the state.[20]

Thus rehabilitation, as in the case of the feebleminded, was transformed from a mechanism of assistance into one of discipline, whose purpose was no longer to uplift Native Hawai'ians but instead to make them pull their own weight. As the territorial governor Charles McCarthy insisted to Congress, "If the native Hawaiian would get out and work, and make a good living for himself and his family, by the sweat of his brow, the race would flourish. That is what the rehabilitation project aims at—not sitting on the fence and playing the ukulele" (qtd. in Kauanui 154). The denigration of Hawai'ians in these and other statements during the legislative hearings jibes oddly with their stated purpose of granting large tracts of valuable land to those same "lazy, ukulele-playing" Hawai'ians. Yet rather than quash the legislation, Congress yielded to Robertson's insistence that eligible homesteaders be defined by a one-half blood quantum, not the originally proposed one-thirty-second. As mentioned earlier, Senator Pittman wished to go further and limit homesteading eligibility to full-blood Hawai'ians, since "everybody knows that any part Hawaiian is capable of taking care of himself and does not need any rehabilitation" (*Hawaiian Homes Commission Act* 124). Because the original impetus for Hawai'ian rehabilitation was the decrease in the Native population, imposing a restrictive blood quantum encoded the rehabilitative paradox: while those who were improvable did not *need* help, those who were unimprovable did not *deserve* help, and thus legislation was passed that could help virtually no one.

This is a familiar story thus far; the history of U.S. imperialism is full of such oppressive acts and self-serving justifications that have been condemned both in general and in the particular case of the HHCA. My point is not merely to echo that condemnation but to note the peculiarity of this particular case. The legislative hearings reached a point where they had essentially defined all Native Hawai'ians out of the category of deserving assistance, *yet the parties involved did not abandon their task.* Instead they continued to debate in great detail the exact portion of Hawai'ian blood to be required under the act. It apparently no longer mattered that the act could help very few of the people whose plight had prompted its introduction. The question of identification became the new center of discussion, once more demonstrating the power of the fantasy to supersede its material origins.

It was inevitable that, once the HHCA was passed, its enforcement required the institution of a system of biocertification, requiring that applicants provide documentary evidence of their blood quantum: "These forms of evidence can amount to up to thirty notarized documents, along with an application more than thirty pages long to substantiate a claim of eligibility" (Kauanui 4). The current website for the Department of Hawaiian Homelands, like the BIA site, provides extensive instructions and explanations of the documents required to apply for a lease, including birth, death, and marriage certificates, family history charts, baptismal and military records, newspaper clippings, and affidavits. This documentary proliferation is even taken to the rather absurd degree of requiring "no-record" certifications when birth and death records are not available, underscoring the extent to which biocertification substitutes written documents for other forms of knowledge, such that even the lack of knowledge must be certified. This substitution is ironically enacted on the website through the hyperlinked word *biological* in the sentence "It is the responsibility of all applicants to trace and prove, through documentation, their biological line of Hawaiian ancestry." This hyperlink, rather than leading to the expected explanation of this biological requirement, takes the user to a list of documents required to establish eligibility, thus completing the tautological circle characteristic of biocertification.[21]

The tangible result of the narrow definition of eligible Hawai'ians, together with the extensive documentation required to prove eligibility, has been an abysmally low rate of distribution of the lands originally set aside in 1921. In 1991 an investigation revealed that, in the seventy years since the act was passed, fewer than six thousand Hawai'ians had been granted homesteads, an estimated thirty thousand applicants had died while waiting for grants, and twenty-two thousand were still on the waitlist (Kauanui 177). By 2006 only 42 percent of the 200,000 acres designated as Hawai'ian homelands had been granted as homesteads, and in 2011, the most recent year for which data are available, only 1,880 applications were processed while over twenty-five thousand people remained on the waitlist.[22] Like the backlog of an estimated two million applicants for Social Security Disability Insurance (SSDI), the backlog of Hawai'ian homelands applicants clearly testifies to a bureaucracy overwhelmed by its own investment in biocertification. Meanwhile, the argument that such intensive bureaucratic review is necessary to prevent fraud has been roundly disproved by the 2013 exposure of massive mishandling of Hawai'ian homelands grants, with two-thirds of leases going to non–Native Hawai'ian beneficiaries (Perez).[23] As I observed in chapter 6, the irony of this situation is that the supposed appeal of biocertification, the reason it appears to fulfill the fantasy of identification, is that it offers a simple, verifiable, and concrete solution to questions of identity. Yet in practice, biocertification invariably produces not straightforward answers but documentary sprawl, increased uncertainty, and bureaucratic stagnation.

It is certainly true that a number of people have benefited from the HHCA, receiving land grants, housing assistance, and other material aid. Whether this benefit outweighs its negative effects on the Hawai'ian community as a whole is debatable; however, it is simply undeniable that the use of blood quantum to regulate eligibility for homesteading has proved outrageously inefficient and that its elaborate structure of biocertification has been largely alienating and divisive. Why, then, is biocertification in Hawai'ian homesteading adhered to, and why was it instituted in the first place, rather than definitions based on culture, language, or other forms of identity? As in other examples of the fantasy explored in this book, the answer lies in the faith placed in science to reveal the truths of identity. In the Hawai'ian context, as in many others, the emerging field of anthropology played a key role, as anthropological studies of Native populations were adduced on both sides of the rehabilitation debate (Gross 193–194). Thus the early history of physical anthropology, and its development in relationship to normalizing concepts of race and disability, is an important context for understanding how biocertification came to play such a central role in twentieth-century negotiations of identification.

The (Pseudo)Science of Biocertification

Ironically, assimilationist arguments were once advanced as progressive alternatives to polygenesism, the belief that nonwhite races were separate and inferior species, epitomized by Josiah Nott's 1854 contention that "to one who has lived among American Indians, it is in vain to talk of civilizing them. You might as well attempt to change the nature of the buffalo" (Nott and Gliddon 69). A tension between polygenesism and assimilation can be found as early as 1805 in a letter by Return J. Meigs, federal agent to the Cherokee Nation, who wrote, "It seems as if the Graver of time had fixed the savage character so deeply in the native Indians . . . that it cannot be effaced," but then continued by observing, "Where the blood is mixed white . . . there is an apparent disposition leaning towards civilization" (qtd. in Sturm 56). The claim that mixed-blood Indians could in fact be improvable, thanks to the positive effects of white blood, was then advanced as evidence not only of the unfixed boundary between the races but also of the need for separate social policies targeting full- and mixed-blood Indians, and thus a need for biocertification of these targeted populations.

The division of Native people into categories of full-blood/unimprovable and mixed-blood/improvable was notably mirrored by developments in disability policy during the same period, particularly in the case of the feebleminded. Early approaches to the feebleminded in the United States centered on their "curability, or at least improvability," but shifted by the late nineteenth-century to a static model in which "no amount of education or good environment can change a feeble-minded individual into a normal one, any more than it can change a red-haired stock into a black-haired stock" (Carlson 138; Marks 83; see also Carey 49). This shift then directed individual and state resources away from temporary reformative models and toward permanent custodial ones (Trent 29–30). As discussed earlier, a similar tension between reformist and custodial impulses can be traced throughout U.S. policy toward Native peoples in the nineteenth and early twentieth centuries as well, in the practices of isolationism, relocation, allotment, and adoption.

The common philosophical ground of these two policy areas was their conflation of disability and Native blood with a presumed irrational animalism. In 1858, for example, a proponent of custodial approaches to feebleminded children declared, "Do all that we may, we cannot make out of the *real idiot* a reasoning and self-guiding man. We can arrest the downward tendency to brutishness which his infirmity entails. We can teach him even some elementary truths; and, what is more important still, we may draw out and strengthen his moral and social faculties, so as to make them lessen the activity of his animal nature; but, after all, he must ever [have] a child-like dependence upon others for guidance and support" (qtd. in Trent 29–30, my emphasis).[24] Such characterizations of the feebleminded person's "brutishness," "animal nature," and "child-like dependence" closely correspond to terms used to describe Native peoples throughout U.S. history, and, as mentioned earlier, are linked to that history through the concept of atavism, in which cognitively disabled people were thought to be throwbacks to earlier, more primitive "races." As we saw in chapter 5, this is the conceptual framework that underpinned Dr. John Langdon Down's labeling of a certain type of disabled people as "Mongolian idiots" in his 1866 "Observations on the Ethnic Classification of Idiots," connecting the shape of their eyes to those of another supposedly inferior racial type (Jackson 168–170; see also Carlson 139).

The merging of these approaches in research and policy was also crucially shaped by the emergence of racialist anthropology during this period, most influentially in the work of Samuel Morton. Morton's 1839 study, *Crania Americana*, is often credited with launching the field of physical anthropology in America (D. Thomas 40), largely through the "gathering of American Indian skulls and attempts at their description and comparison" (Beaulieu 293). In *Crania Americana*, Morton concluded that Native Americans (including "Esquimaux") were "crafty, sensual, ungrateful, obstinate and unfeeling" and that "the Indian brain was so deficient . . . that the race would be impossible to civilize" (54). By the end of the century Morton's followers had become institutionalized as experts who could be summoned to determine the identity of an ambiguously raced subject. One such expert, Albert E. Jenks, an anthropology professor at the University of Minnesota, testified in a 1915 land fraud case involving the White Earth Chippewa tribe that he could not only distinguish the hair of Indians from that of white people, but that he could tell full-bloods from mixed-bloods through cross-section analysis of a single hair (Beaulieu 294–297).[25] Yet by 1917 Jenks was forced to admit that his method might have its flaws, since upon further experimentation, he found that both he and his white associate Dr. Ales Hrdlicka had "hair of the most typical negro type," while Scandinavians had "hair more circular in cross-section than our pure-blood Pima Indians" (qtd. in Beaulieu 305). Nevertheless Jenks and Hrdlicka's expert testimony stood, legalizing "the largest possible number of land transfers [away from the Chippewa] and directly contribut[ing] to the codification of White Earth enrollment lists" (Meyer 240). Once again we see a fantasy of identification producing material and meaningful consequences, even as its scientific basis is questioned by the very "scientists" invoked to sustain it.

Jenks's associate, Dr. Hrdlicka, curator of the newly established Division of Physical Anthropology at the Smithsonian, preferred to use skin rather than hair for his racial determinations. In a fairly disturbing description of his skin reaction test, Hrdlicka wrote that he would "[draw] with some force the nail of the fore-finger over the chest, along the middle and also a few inches to each side. This creates a reaction consisting of reddening, or hyperaemia, along the lines drawn. In the full-bloods the reaction as a rule is quite slight to moderate, and evanescent, or of only moderate duration; in mixed-bloods, unless anaemic, it is more intense as well as lasting" (qtd. in Beaulieu 298). Historians have not documented the frequency or range of this test as actually applied. However, it is telling that in a 2004 chat room discussion of blood quantum on Powwows.com, a poster reported quite confidently that the official government determination of blood quantum once utilized a "scratch test" in which "they would scratch your arm and look to see what color the skin turned where it was scratched. This color was matched to a color chart that related color to blood quantum."[26] I have not found any historical verification of this exact version of the "scratch test," but it bears enough similarity to that described by Hrdlicka to suggest that his methods were influential and perhaps persistent into the mid-twentieth century. Certainly this comment demonstrates the *cultural* penetration of the scratch test, whatever its actual scientific or legal deployment may have been.

Although these examples of racialist anthropology have been broadly discussed and critiqued, their disability context has rarely been noted. For example, prior to his entrance to the field, Hrdlicka "worked at the Middletown State Hemopathic Hospital for the Insane where he attempted to determine the relationship between mental and physical characteristics" of the inmates (Beaulieu 292). Indeed the discourses of racial identification institutionalized by physical anthropologists developed in intimate connection with nineteenth-century efforts to measure and classify forms of physical and mental difference we would now understand through the rubric of disability. Physicians and anthropologists of the time did not in fact distinguish between characteristics ascribed to race and those ascribed to physical or mental ability as we do today. Thus when Morton originally opined that "the mental faculties [of American Indians] from infancy to old age, present a continued childhood" (54), he was not so much analogizing Indian minds to those of developmentally disabled individuals as merging the two into a flexible category of mental immaturity and incapacity. This merging, so different from our understanding of these categories today, is crucial for understanding how biocertification of Native and disabled people emerged in the early decades of the twentieth century, and why it persists so stubbornly today.

The Paradox of Commodification

Thus far we have seen how, throughout the nineteenth and into the early twentieth century, Native and disabled identities were made increasingly legible through the fantasy of identification, and how biocertification began to emerge as the mechanism by which to enforce and regulate these identities. Yet these early discourses of biocertification, predicated as they were upon the regulation of improvable and unimprovable subjects, are notably different from those that prevail today. As discussed in chapter 7, currently the biocertification of blood quantum is understood as a means to regulate access to the valuable commodity of Native identity rather than as a measure of competency. Similarly the biocertification of disability now primarily functions to limit access to resources and accommodations also figured as valuable and "special" rather than, as in the early legal cases, to justify the removal of rights and property (although certainly such removals still take place). In this section I will explore how the transformation of discourses of competency into those of commodity produced the current deployments of biocertification, demonstrating once more how the fantasy adapts itself over time to shifting and even contradictory purposes.

As the twentieth century progressed and the Boas school of cultural anthropology superseded physical anthropology, replacing its biological model of race-as-species with a cultural model of race-as-socially-constructed, claims that a certain percentage of white blood conferred mental and legal competency became no longer tenable. Instead by the 1930s blood quantum began to function primarily in the manner it is understood today, as a gatekeeping device to regulate which individuals would have access to certain rights, resources, and services. Thus rather than white blood being the valued commodity necessary to achieve full legal personhood, Indian blood is now perceived as a privileged commodity that confers special identification.

It is often pointed out that the usual racial logic of hypodescent is reversed in blood quantum policies, such that not only is one drop usually not enough to qualify the subject for racial recognition, but even more strikingly, the desirable racial identity being measured is not whiteness but "Indianness" (Kauanui 15; Sturm 105; TallBear, "DNA" 97). Such a move appears to reverse (though perhaps also confirms) critical race theorists' explanations of the property value of whiteness, articulated by Cheryl Harris and others.[27] If the CDIB functions as a "kind of currency" (Hamill 280), biocertification is reinscribed to serve a banking function in order to assure that only legitimate individuals receive credit, understood as both a material object and a state of belief.

Since a range of entitlements are linked to Indian status in the present-day United States, blood quantum requirements are often presented as a necessary gatekeeping device in order to prevent widespread fraud. Both the regulatory practices and the discursive negotiations of "Indian fraud" are strikingly similar to those used with regard to disability entitlements, invoking both a *model of scarcity*, in which resources must be reserved for those who truly deserve them, and a *distrust of self-identification*, in which statements of identity are automatically suspect unless and until validated by an outside authority, a validation that commonly takes the form of biocertification.[28] Garroute proffers both these arguments when she asserts that "there are simply too many tangible incentives motivating people to commit what is known as 'ethnic fraud.' When tribal affiliation carries with it access to limited material resources, their exploitation by illegitimate recipients occurs at the expense of legitimate ones. A policy of self-definition does not allow for regulating such access" (87). Garroute also quotes a woman who worked for an Indian service provider that followed a policy of accepting self-identification: "You really did have a lot of people showing up claiming that one of their ancestors, seven steps removed, had been some sort of 'Cherokee princess.' And we were obliged to accept that, and provide services. Hell, if all that was real, there are more Cherokees in the world than there are Chinese" (87). The expectation of a horde of claimants overwhelming the available resources is strikingly similar to that described by Welke at the turn of the century as "the idea that a tide of disability from without and within threatened to swamp the nation" (118–119), and to current concerns about increasing numbers of SSDI filings, Workers Compensation claims, and other demands on disability entitlements. Such concerns are voiced not only by the federal government but from within Indian communities, where the dilution of both blood and culture disturbingly produces "people with a minuscule blood quanta and no real articulation of tribal life [who] are eligible for tribal benefits such as scholarships" (Hamill 280). Thus many Indian writers and activists welcome legislation such as the Indian Arts and Crafts Act as "a means to flush out 'imposters' and make it impossible for them to represent themselves as indigenous against those who 'really are'" (qtd. in Barker 47).

Undeniably scarcity of resources is not merely a rhetorical tactic but also a material reality. Nevertheless it is striking that, in both disability and Indian contexts, cultural perceptions of the actual material gains connected to biocertified status are often quite exaggerated. Most nondisabled people in the United States are shocked to learn how small a percentage of their working income would be provided by SSDI or Workers Compensation, compared to how stringent the requirements are for qualifying for these benefits. Similarly some individuals "apply for tribal enrollment motivated only by the fallacious assumption that Indian status will end their tax responsibility and provide free educational benefits for their children" (Welburn 315–316). Garroute reports encountering non-Indians who operate under the false assumption that Indians receive all kinds of fantastic material benefits, such as free cars (169n13).

Nevertheless many Indians refuse to embrace the scarcity model's rejection of self-identification, insisting that biocertification must be questioned as the basis for identity:

> There are serious troubles in assuming that federal identification and recognition policies are the just means through which to "weed out the riff-raff," especially considering the historical and cultural processes of colonialism through which those policies have been developed. . . . Why is it that those who are performing consumer fraud are so easily and transparently collapsed with those who are mixed, unenrolled, and/or are members of unrecognized tribes and villages? What social factors contribute to the assumption that the unenrolled/unrecognized are fraudulent? (Barker 49)

The collapsing of categories between those individuals whose identities are ambiguous, uncertified, or "mixed" and those assumed to be perpetrating malicious fraud resonates with both historical and current discourses regarding disability certification and fakery.[29] In both cases, cultural assumptions regarding the "natural" status of bodily identity powerfully underpin identificatory fantasies that must equate ambiguity with fraud or risk undermining their own epistemological foundations.

The similarity of discourses of fraud in both disability and American Indian contexts is thus a necessary product of their shared status as biocertified identities in the twenty-first-century United States, as is the common misperception of these identities as lucrative commodities. In both cases a circular logic is at work, suggesting that something of great value must be at stake if so much effort is being put into policing its boundaries, even as the policing is figured as necessary due to exaggerated perceptions of value. While strikingly similar discourses may be found in nineteenth- and early twentieth-century court cases regarding racial identification of ambiguous black-white subjects during a period when biocertification of African American identity was still widely deployed, today it is extremely rare to encounter suspicions that a mixed-race individual is "claiming" African American identity for fraudulent purposes.[30] In contrast, as discussed in chapter 6, an entire industry exists today to monitor and investigate claims of disability, with a strong presumption of fraud underlying each step of the process and the burden of proof placed upon the disabled claimant. Similarly, as we have seen, federal requirements for Native status, such as the CDIB and the Hawai'ian homestead application, require extensive documentary evidence, any mistake or omission in which produces a presumption of ineligibility. Concern about fraud is also present within various Indian communities, as discussed below, again due to concerns about scarcity of resources and the unreliability of self-identification.[31]

When actual fraud takes place (as it undeniably does, though I would argue its real occurrence is far less common than the fantasy of fakery suggests), it seems not so much to prove the need for biocertification as to be evoked *by* the presence of biocertification:

> Certain Indian descendent recruitment organizations, for instance, have a disturbing habit of issuing documents "certified" by their own illegal copies of official seals belonging to federally recognized tribes and of making up "tribal enrollment cards" that may be indistinguishable from the real things. . . . A New Age magazine recently ran an advertisement headed by the remarkable announcement that "You can become a Native American . . . and how." The ad promises that "the Two Birds Society of Signal Hill, Calif., will give you your very own Indian name and authenticate it with a certificate stating that you are an honorary Native American." (All this for only $28.00). (Garroute 89, 91)

Like the counterfeiting of disabled parking permits, such counterfeit "Indian IDs" are meaningful only within a cultural and legal context that requires the validation of identity through official (bio)documentation.

One important difference between discourses of fraud in disability and Indian contexts is the attachment of nonmaterial value to the claimed identity. While the general stigmatization and denigration of disability identity means that it is rare to suspect someone of claiming disability for its symbolic value, white romanticization of Native culture since the 1970s has produced a growing number of people who claim Indian heritage or identity for symbolic rather than material purposes. As a result of these stereotyped perceptions of Indian people as "deeply spiritual, noble, indigenous environmentalists that worship Mother Earth" (Hamill 280), many tribes and individuals have to contend with (apparently) white claimants who suddenly discover that they have Indian ancestry—a phenomenon variously referred to as "Cherokee Grandmother Syndrome," "hobbyism," and the "tribe called Wanabi" (Fitzgerald 186; Hamill 280; Brownwell 217). Ironically such claims, while apparently placing value on Indianness—albeit a reductive, essentialized version—actually function to reinforce the power of whiteness, since claimants retain white privilege while absolving themselves of historical responsibility: "In claiming drops of 'Indian blood'—and especially in

tracing it to Pocahontas or another 'Indian princess'—the victors naturalize themselves and legitimize their occupation of the land" (Strong
and Van Winkle 552).

One pervasive effect of the stereotyping of Indian identity within a
context of suspicion of ambiguous subjects is that many Native people
find themselves implicitly or directly required to engage in what Rona
Halualani calls "performances of proving" (168), enacting stereotypical
aspects of Native culture to make their identity legible and acceptable to
a skeptical audience, a "public that cannot believe they are Indians unless
they dress in buckskin and feathers" (Rountree 45).[32] The relationship
between physical appearance, biocertification, and the need for performances of proving is captured by Becca Gercken-Hawkins, describing
her preparation to interview for jobs teaching Native literature: "Because
of my appearance and my lack of enrollment status, I expected questions
regarding my identity, but even so, I was surprised when a fellow graduate student advised me—in all seriousness—to straighten my hair and
work on a tan before any interviews. Thinking she was joking, I asked her
if I should put a feather in my hair, and she replied with a straight face
that a feather might be a bit much, but I should at least wear traditional
Native jewelry" (200). As Renee Ann Cramer observes, performances of
proving are expected not only from individuals but also from tribes, and
federal recognition policies, despite their ostensibly inclusive criteria,
reinforce such expectations: "By socially constructing a mythic Indian
and then measuring demands for recognition against it, federal recognition processes seem more often to depend on how many aboriginal traits
the petition tribe retains in common with the mythic notion of Indian
or tribe, than to truly understand the history and reality of the petition-
ing group. Because they are not constructed as authentic, unrecognized
tribes are rendered invisible to the federal gaze. They become . . . 'unseeable'" (60). The reductive notions of identity contained within both blood
quantum discourse and performances of proving render many individuals and tribes unseeable. Ironically biocertification may then emerge as a
source of positive identity for individuals who are able to use such documentary validation to deflect or override assumptions about their "inauthentic" appearance or behavior. Yet, more commonly, biocertification
and performances of proving operate interactionally, supplementing one
another in the construction of an imposed identity that supersedes the
individual's internal sense of self. The commodification of identity serves
as the claimed justification for this process and ironically produces far
more elaborate apparatuses of biocertification, in both disability and

Native contexts, than the competency model ever did. As biocertification continues to evolve and solidify into the twenty-first century, commodifications of bodily identity are proliferating both globally and at the cellular level. As we will see in the next chapter, the advent of modern genetics has provided a newly solid scientific underpinning for the deployment of fantasies of identification throughout the world.

9 / DNA and the Readable Self

> *At the same time that the science of genetics has moved from the labora-*
> *tory to the sphere of mass culture, from professional journals to television*
> *screens, the notion of the gene has undergone a transformation. Rather*
> *than being considered as one element of hereditary information, it has*
> *become the key to human relations and the basis of social cohesion.*
>
> —NELKIN AND LINDEE, *The DNA Mystique: The Gene as a Cultural Icon*

In her 1989 poem, "The Weakness," Toi Derricotte describes being
dragged out of a Saks department store by her grandmother as the eyes
of a hostile white crowd bore into them, seeing "through / her clothes,
under / her skin, all the way down / to the transparent / genes confess-
ing." The secret confessed by the grandmother's body, and by Derricotte's narrator as well, is racial, the trace of blackness that is no longer
discernible in hair or skin or any of those outward, obvious markers of
the previous century. Instead, by the close of the twentieth century, such
hidden bodily truths are found on the molecular level, in the genes that
are at once transparent and reflective, invisible yet easily seen once we
know how to look.[1]

It may be said that genes are the specters that haunt this book. Even as
we considered those fantasies of identification mediated through birthmarks, fingerprints, and blood, the idea that such outdated methods have
now been replaced by a truly objective and meaningful mark has hovered
at the margins of each example, begging the question: Is DNA, the truth
encoded in our very cells, the ultimate and satisfying realization of the
fantasy of identification? Certainly, unlike the pseudoscience of racialist medicine, or the fictional science of fingerprint expert Pudd'nhead
Wilson, or the nonscience of commonsense identification claims, DNA
analysis can be described as comparatively "real" science: it is research-
based, peer-reviewed, and accepted by a global scientific community.[2]
While scandals may occasionally arise regarding faulty DNA evidence

in courts, and any reputable geneticist will admit that there is still a great deal we don't know about how DNA functions, there is a much stronger argument to be made for its scientific validity than for that of any of the previous examples discussed in this book.

And yet fantasies of identification have never really been about science. They are about culture, about politics, about the rule of law and the unruliness of bodies. What DNA has to tell us about how our bodies work and how our identities are shaped is still largely unknown. But the power of DNA in the cultural imaginary, what Sarah Franklin and Jackie Stacey call "the genetic imaginary," has already formed the basis for twentieth- and twenty-first-century fantasies of identification that bear a striking resemblance to those preceding fantasies based on less-reputable scientific claims (Franklin 198; Stacey 9). Indeed the very fact that genetics is comparatively reliable science seems to provoke even more extreme and expansive fantasies about it. Genetic essentialism, the idea that DNA offers a master key to human identity, has already penetrated culture and politics to an astounding degree, considering the acknowledgment by geneticists that they have only scratched the surface of genomic knowledge.[3]

Stacey defines the genetic imaginary as a "fantasy landscape" in which "concerns about the destabilization of traditional markers of difference and privilege combine with those about the introduction of the unnatural and the inauthentic" (8). The language of fantasy is often used by those describing the social effects of genetics, for "the fantastical value of the gene has a considerable impact upon the way that difference, or even social relations in general, are understood" (Le Breton 14).[4] If we recall the wistful yearning for a definitive mark of identity in the nineteenth century and the search that led from birthmarks to fingerprints, we can understand why and how DNA began to be deployed for identification while it was still in the very earliest stages of being discovered, much less understood. Desire drives fantasy; fantasy demands realization; realization produces material effects. Science in these cases functions not as the basis for these effects but merely as their justification.

From Blood Quantum to Cheek Swabs

One immediate and telling example of this dynamic can be found in the burgeoning industry of home DNA testing, in which individuals mail biological samples directly to labs for genetic analysis. Such labs offer to screen for a variety of factors, ranging from the sex of a fetus to a predisposition to cancer. In the past decade this industry has grown at an exponential rate, far out of step with the pace of reliable science, a dynamic enabled in part by the lack of FDA regulations on home genetic testing. As a 2006 *New York Times* article reported, "once a scientific paper about the effect of a genetic variation is published, a test for the variation can usually be set up in months," without the need for clinical trials or other verification of the real significance or effects of the genetic variant (Pollack).

In this climate, and considering the tension surrounding questions of blood quantum and Indian identity, it is not surprising that labs claiming to test for Native American ancestry have proliferated both on the ground and in cyberspace. In 2005 Kimberly TallBear reported that at least fifteen companies were offering "Native American DNA" tests, in which a cheek swab could be tested for genetic markers commonly found in people with Native American ancestry, and that several were advertising regularly in publications such as *Indian Country Today* (TallBear, "Native" 235, 243). Such labs also commonly provide test takers with "a frameable document certifying their genetic ancestral affiliation," showing the near-seamless integration of biocertification into this new technology of identification (TallBear and Bolnick). Some companies market tests to entire tribes, offering "genetic identification systems" including "$320-per-person photo ID cards [that] sport computer chips and list specific DNA markers" (TallBear and Bolnick).

In 2012 countless testing sites for Native American DNA can be found online. These sites range from more modest offerings, which verify blood relationships in order to document a specific tie to an enrolled tribal member, to those that test for certain genetic markers, known as haplotypes or private polymorphisms, statistically associated with Native populations. These are the more disturbing and fantastical claims and are most likely to be aggressively marketed to both tribal and unenrolled Indian communities.[5] The science behind these claims is not so much falsified as highly exaggerated and often distorted. While it is true that such genetic markers exist, it is impossible to use them either to determine blood quantum or to identify someone as a member of a specific tribe. As Eric Beckenhauer explains, finding a private polymorphism "may prove an individual has some Indian ancestry, but its absence does not mean there is no Indian ancestry, and there is no way for it to indicate degree of Indian ancestry" (181–182). Furthermore because the tests look at only very specific and isolated markers, it is possible for someone to be 62/64 Indian and yet test negative, or to be only 1/64 Indian and yet test positive (183). The Indigenous Peoples Council on Biocolonialism has issued a briefing paper simply to explain the "scientific shortcomings" of using genetic markers to determine Native identity, highlighting in particular the likelihood of false negatives and positives that "readily misidentify non-Native people as Native, and misidentify Native people as non-Native" (Marks and Shelton). Meanwhile geneticists continue to reiterate that "there is no way known for genetics to establish ethnic groupings . . . no genetic test to perform in order to determine whether or not one is 'Caucasian,' 'Alpine,' or 'Hopi'" (Marks 165–167).[6]

The websites for DNA testing companies are careful to avoid claiming that their tests can actually prove degree of Indian ancestry or membership in a specific tribe. However, many of them employ extremely misleading rhetoric, such as "Whether your goal is to assist in validating your eligibility for government entitlements such as Native American Rights or just to satisfy your curiosity, our Ethnicity DNA testing is the only scientifically rigorous method available for this purpose in existence today" (Genelex); "Having a simple DNA saliva test to know your genetic background is an excellent way to overcome the lack of ancestry or immigration documents. You can definitely prove that you belong to a Native tribe by having a DNA test done" (Gene DNA Test); and "American Indian DNA testing has become the most reliable way to prove you are of native descent. . . . For the first time ever, one can check for conclusive evidence of all the stories and legends passed down through the family" (Mitochondrial DNA Testing).[7] Words and phrases such as *validating, scientifically rigorous, definitely prove,* and *conclusive evidence* not only serve to obscure the lack of actual scientific basis for such claims but also tellingly resonate with the language used in the Salomé Müller ruling, the Will West case, and many other examples discussed in this book. Clearly the power of the genetic imaginary has entirely overwhelmed the scientific facts and has combined with the desire for clear-cut boundaries of Indian identity to form a new—yet utterly familiar—twenty-first-century fantasy of identification.

The natural result of such misleading claims by DNA testing companies is that Indian tribes with financial assets now "regularly turn away DNA petitioners." Joyce Walker, an enrollment clerk for the Mashantucket Pequot, describes this new trend in a 2006 interview: "It used to be someone said 'my grandmother was an Indian.' Now it's 'my DNA says my grandmother was an Indian'" (Amy Harmon).[8] People of mixed African-Indian heritage have also sought to use DNA tests to support their claims for tribal citizenship (Koerner). In 2000 a non-Indian

Vermont state representative sponsored a bill to "establish standards and procedures for DNA testing to determine the identity of an individual as Native American at the request and expense of the individual" (TallBear, "DNA" 85). Rep. Fred Maslack apparently meant to support the Western Mohegan tribal government's efforts to regulate its membership but wrote the bill so broadly that it could be interpreted to mean that all people claiming Indian identity would be required to submit to DNA testing and could be excluded based on the findings.[9] Disturbingly Maslack did not seem to see a problem with this approach, commenting in various interviews that "[DNA] markers would be the last word on saying you're an Indian. You wouldn't be perpetrating fraud" (TallBear, "DNA" 85–86) and that "it makes sense to me that science should have the last word" (Beckenhauer 185). Maslack spoke wistfully of a future in which genetic testing "could be the definitive method" for determining Indian identity, echoing many earlier spokespeople for fantasies of identification based more on the social desire for definitive marks than the ability of science to provide them (Beckenhauer 185).

The Vermont bill was widely criticized and subsequently withdrawn. These criticisms tended to focus not on the fact that no genetic test that could conclusively prove descent from the Western Mohegan actually exists but rather on the problem with defining Indian identity as purely biological, and therefore racial. The Vermont Governor's Advisory Committee on Native American Affairs, for example, issued a statement opposing genetic testing for treating Indian identity as a "racial type" instead of a "spiritual identity" (Beckenhauer 186–187). TallBear explains the reasoning behind this choice: "The main problem is not the fact that the genetic technology cannot reveal all lines of biological descent. Even if advances in genetic science, or the use of additional genetic tests for additional markers, were to enable greater certainty in determining a person's descent from 'Native American' ancestors, the act of using science in that way is a technological manifestation of sociopolitical ideas of race. Such ideas assert that cultural identity can be conclusively established in an individual's biology" ("DNA" 84). This position makes sense on the level of strategy as well as principle, ensuring that continuing advances in genetics cannot be used to overcome all objections to DNA-based definitions of tribal identity. However, the rejection of the idea of Indian identity as racial or biological—and indeed the merging of the two categories—implies that the current standards used to define identity are primarily cultural or spiritual and that genetic testing will displace those preferable criteria. Yet, as discussed at length in chapter 7, current definitions of Indian identity on both the federal and tribal level combine cultural factors with an enduring and proliferative reliance upon blood quantum measurements that also claim a biological basis and are historically deeply racialized.[10] Thus genetic testing signals not a break from previous discourses and practices surrounding Indian identification but rather their logical continuation. This dynamic is reflected in law; as Beckenhauer points out in the case of the Federal Acknowledgement Act, since the law includes evidence that may identify "present members or ancestors of present members as being descendants of a historical tribe," it "implicitly invites the use of genetic studies as proof of Indian ancestry" (165). Thus it is likely that we will be seeing continuing efforts to implement genetic testing in addition to, or in place of, blood quantum criteria for validating Indian identity, as well as resistance from those who advocate cultural and kinship-based systems.

In the Indigenous People's Council on Biocolonialism briefing paper, after reviewing the faulty science of DNA testing for Indian identity, the authors conclude that "if these were medical diagnostic tests, they would never be approved or adopted" (Marks and Shelton). While appreciating the rhetorical power of this statement, I must also disagree with it. The advent of genetic testing has been marked by a lack of the usual standards for testing, confirmation, and regulation of medical practices in the modern United States: "With a few mouse clicks, consumers can order tests that promise to tell them if they are at risk for particular diseases, to trace their ancestry back to the time of Genghis Khan, to help choose which antidepressant would be best for them, to identify the sex of their fetus as few as five weeks into pregnancy and to give advice on diet or exercise" (Pollack). Here we can see that the prescient cultural promise of the fantasy of identification extends into and indeed merges the medical realm with questions of identity.

As noted earlier, tests are made available to the public within months of a laboratory's identification of a genetic marker, long before it is possible to know what the marker signifies for the carrier. Additionally, even if a particular genetic difference is known to be connected to a specific disease process, the actual expression of that difference in an individual can vary widely. This range of experiences despite the same genetic code—what geneticists refer to as the difference between phenotype and genotype—can be found in a number of conditions, from Down syndrome to the BRCA mutations linked to breast cancer (Bérubé, *Life* 79; Rothman 187–192). While genetic counselors are carefully trained to explain these differences to adults seeking genetic testing, prenatal genetic tests are routinely performed with little or no counseling and only the barest information about what test results mean before making decisions based on them.[11] In this sense many medical genetic tests actually resemble those offered for Indian DNA testing far more than one might like to think: "It turns out not to be so straightforward after all to draw a line that neatly divides 'medical' and 'other' grounds, that separates us with our good decisions from them with their bad ones" (Rothman 203).

Additionally the ability to detect genetic markers has far outstripped any possibility of developing effective treatments for the vast majority of medical conditions linked to those markers, particularly in the case of prenatal genetic testing. Thus bioethicists are increasingly raising concerns about the advisability of testing for many genetic conditions, considering that "only a very small proportion of genetic abnormalities that are detected can be controlled by medical intervention or the adoption of a particular lifestyle" (Le Breton 11). Yet the genetic imaginary persists in seeing genetics as the answer to any and all issues of bodily ambiguity, both in the medical realm and with regard to embodied social identities. Thus the distinction Marks and Shelton seek to draw between the real, reliable science of medicine and the faulty, biased science of ethnic DNA testing does not hold up when we look at the ways genetic testing is deployed in the current cultural realm. Rather than science being used to undermine fantasies of identification, the fantasies are increasingly taking over the realms of science, through an "ideology of reductive genetics" (Le Breton 14) that appears to promise, at last, a way to pinpoint the truth of bodies and keep them in their proper places: "With molecular genetics, and its ability to see differences not in the body or in the blood, but inside the cell, new hopes were raised—here we could locate race, locate the fundamental groupings of people" (Rothman 91). While this clearly is true in the case of race, as in the examples discussed earlier, I suggest that the most profound current example of this process can be found in the practice of genetic sex testing for female athletes, an example that also richly demonstrates the flexible expansion of the fantasy of identification from the realms of race and disability into that of sex/gender into the twenty-first century.

The Failures of Sex Testing

Clearly current science does not support claims of DNA testing in relation to Indian identity, but could a stronger case be made for the relevance of genetic testing for identifying biological sex? The discovery of sex-linked chromosomes in the mid-twentieth century opened up new possibilities for ascertaining the "true" identities of bodies previously mired in sexual ambiguity. Yet again, science has been overcome by fantasy, as what Anne Fausto-Sterling calls "the seductive nature of genetic explanations" (*Myths* 62) has led to the solidification of a powerful fantasy of sex identification that has ironically expanded the field of ambiguous bodies and created new categories of confusion and contested meaning.

In this second decade of the twenty-first century, two fantasies of sex identification are currently at work in both U.S. and globalized culture. The first, submerged fantasy is that biological sex is obvious and apparent, discovered simply by looking between someone's legs. This is the method used to identify newborns, producing the legal sex classification which then proliferates throughout a person's life in a variety of documents and settings. This is also the fantasy most operative in daily life, in which a person's genital status is implicitly and explicitly monitored in the locker room, the medical exam, the public restroom, and the sexual arena. Every modern individual is subject to this fantasy and thus can be said to participate in a form of biocertification, since birth certificates, passports, driver's licenses, and other forms of state identification documents must all list a biological sex.[12] Yet through this very universality, this version of biocertification is not the one used to designate a separate minority class of people—such as Native and disabled people—who are treated differently because of their membership in that class.

However, there is a second fantasy of sex identification at work, one that is focused only on people whose sex is ambiguous or contested and that, as in other examples discussed in this book, seeks to probe beneath the body's surface to find the elusive mark of true male- or femaleness (Fausto-Sterling, *Sexing* 54). The search for such a mark began in the mid-nineteenth century at the same time that attempts were being made to fix, delineate, and categorize differences based on race and disability. These attempts were largely unsuccessful, and the question of identifying sex remained for many decades either fixed within the sphere of commonsense inspection or debated and highly changeable in the medical and scientific realm (Holmes *Intersex* 41–47; Reis 54).[13] Then came the discovery of the structure of DNA in 1953 and sex-linked chromosomes in 1955. By the turn of the century the development of chromosomal testing and the proliferation of the genetic imaginary have produced a new fantasy of sex/gender identification that closely mirrors those regarding race and disability and that appears to be well on its way to becoming a globally dominant narrative. This is a profound testament to the flexibility and persistence of the master fantasy of identification, which attaches itself over time to different types of problematic bodies while retaining its core features largely unchanged.[14]

As Fausto-Sterling, Alice Domurat Dreger, Elizabeth Reis, and other historians have extensively documented, European and American physicians in the mid-nineteenth century began to search for definitive markers of sex in relation to the ambiguous bodies of people we would refer to today as intersex. The development of new medical techniques for visualizing and accessing the body's interior meant that the previous reliance upon external sex characteristics could be replaced by an emphasis on internal organs, particularly the gonads. Dreger describes the era of the 1870s–1915 as the "Age of Gonads," because a number of European medical men claimed that true sex could be determined only on the basis of ovaries or testes, both of which were often buried within the bodies of the intersex individuals in question (*Hermaphrodites* 146, 158).[15] Other historians, such as Ulrike Klöppel, however, have questioned this characterization, pointing out that there was still considerable disagreement about gonads, and many other factors were also taken into account to determine sex, such as genital appearance, pubertal development, and self-identification (172; Reis 85). Whether the idea of gonads as the determining marker of sex was dominant or merely one among competing claims during this period, it was clearly not a terribly successful claim and thus never reached the status of a fantasy of identification that spread beyond medicine into the wider cultural and political sphere.

It was not until the discovery of sex-linked chromosomes in the middle of the century that scientists and laypeople came together to agree upon an overmastering fantasy of sex identification. While gonads and genitals were still considered relevant, chromosomal sex gained a reputation for ultimate bodily truth with remarkable swiftness and tenacity, considering that the actual science involved—both in 1955 and today—is extremely complex and its results ambiguous. As in the case of fingerprints, we see how the yearning for a definitive mark produces its own realization by inserting new technologies of identification into a preexisting fantastic framework, which is then justified by the supposedly natural, unique, and objective information yielded by the technology. And even as both fantasies of sex identification circulate today, neither acknowledges that "visual evidence and genetic evidence are not . . . reliably transparent: both are open to manipulation and susceptible to the indeterminacies of interpretation" (Stacey 115).

This dynamic can be seen most clearly in the discourses and events of the past four decades of genetic sex testing in international sports competitions. Such testing was initiated at the 1968 Olympics, a mere thirteen years after the Barr body, a sex-linked chromosomal marker easily visible in a microscopic view of a cheek swab, was first described. Since the 1930s there had been isolated cases of suspicion or exposure of male athletes masquerading as women, and the Cold War focused these anxieties on competitors from the Soviet Bloc, especially those seen as unusually masculine in appearance (Elsas et al. 250; Heggie 158; Wonkam et al. 546).[16] Another, more subtle but likely contributing factor was the greater visibility and success of female athletes enabled in part by the gains of second-wave feminism; it is certainly striking that "just as opportunities for women in sport [began to expand], a panel of experts began scrutinizing female athletes' genitals, genes, and chromosomes" (Sullivan 416). Indeed the two main governing bodies of international sport, the International Amateur Athletic Federation (IAAF) and the International Olympic Committee (IOC), decided in the late 1960s that universal sex testing of female athletes was necessary to ensure fair play.

From 1966 to 1967 female athletes at several international competitions were required either to parade nude before a panel of physicians or to submit to gynecological examinations. Athletes complained that these tests were demeaning and invasive, and so in 1968 the IOC and IAAF turned to universal, laboratory-based screening for Barr bodies (inactive X-chromosomes) from a cheek smear (Puffer 1543; Sullivan 404). Such testing was described as "simpler, objective, and more dignified" (Elsas et al. 250), thus implying a concern for the rights and privacy of the athletes being tested. However, in practice, chromosomal testing functioned for the next three decades to shame and exclude female-identified athletes with intersex conditions without ever identifying a single male imposter. From the very first trial of universal chromosomal testing at the 1967 European Cup, which resulted in the disqualification of Polish sprinter Ewa Klobukowska, through its discontinuation in the 1990s, hundreds of athletes who had lived their entire lives as women were disqualified, their records erased, and their personal and professional lives devastated by the results of chromosomal sex testing (C. Cole 128–131; Puffer 1543). In 1988 the IOC's chief of testing, Dr. Eduardo Hayes, estimated that "one or two women have been banned at each Olympic Games, except for one, since 1968" (Elsas et al. 250). Researchers also posit "that significantly greater numbers of women have chosen to 'self-disqualify' out of fear . . . and that many more girls and women have withdrawn or been screened out during qualifying competitions" (Elsas et al. 250; see also Wonkam et al. 546). The response by the athletic governing bodies to a woman who "failed" the sex test was to suggest that she claim injury and quietly withdraw from athletic competitions.[17] This self-erasure was mirrored by a policy that began in 1967 with Klobukowska, whose "medals were revoked, her records voided, and her name erased from the record books" (C. Cole 130–131).

Due to intensifying critiques from both the scientific and athletic communities, the IAAF finally replaced universal chromosomal testing in 1992 with a policy of genital inspection during doping tests and the right to require medical examinations on a random or individual basis (Elsas et al. 251). The IOC, however, remained committed to universal genetic screening for another decade, replacing the controversial chromosomal test in 1991 with the more sophisticated PCR-SRY test (Elsas et al. 251; Puffer 1543). They did not abandon universal genetic screening until 2000, moving to a policy similar to that of the IAAF.[18] Sometimes described as the "I know it when I see it" policy (Camporesi and Maugeri 378), this new approach attempted to merge the two fantasies of sex identification—as obvious *and* hidden—and as a result tended to enforce the reductive potentials of both. Genetic screening continued to be performed, together with medical examinations, in cases where a female athlete was challenged or suspected, and athletes could still be disqualified on the bases of those tests. In 2006, for example, Santhi Soundarajan, a runner from India, was challenged due to her "masculine" appearance, and when she "failed" her genetic test, her silver medal in the 2006 Asian Games was taken away (Bhowmick and Thottam).

Does sex verification—or gender verification, as it has often been misleadingly named—constitute a fantasy of identification, or is it a valid instance of using available science to ensure fair play? I contend that the former is undeniably the case. Despite the greater validity of the science underlying genetic sex testing, its implementation has both exceeded and contradicted its scientific basis, and its broad cultural impact demonstrates the proliferation and persistence that characterize such fantasies. And, like many of the fantasies discussed in this book, it has had profound and often tragic material effects on those caught within its identificatory matrix.

I have already noted that implementation of chromosomal sex testing came fairly swiftly after the Barr body was first discovered. By 1967 scientists were already beginning to complicate the simple association of the Barr body with being female; in the words of one doctor, "Sex chromatin testing fell out of favor of most physicians and scientists shortly after the IOC introduced it" (Puffer 1543). This meant that, unlike in most other examples discussed in this book, criticism of the fantasy of genetic sex identification has proceeded most vocally from the realm of science itself. In 1994 laboratory technicians in Norway became the first to refuse to perform genetic sex screenings for the IOC, and "by 1996, virtually all major U.S. medical societies had passed resolutions calling for the elimination of gender verification at Olympic Games" (Elsas et al. 251). Beginning in the 1980s numerous articles appeared in major medical journals pointing out that "gender verification . . . is far more likely to bar unfairly from competition women with genetic abnormalities that confer no such advantage than safeguard fair competition" (Wonkam et al. 548) and that "a process designed to catch imposters has turned out to be a clumsy mechanism for detecting disorders of sexual development" (Hercher 551).[19] Yet officials (including medical officials) at the IOC continued to insist that genetic testing was absolutely essential in order to find male imposters—despite the fact that, in three decades, not a single male imposter had been detected by genetic screenings (Elsas et al. 251). Even the final abandonment of universal screening by the IOC in 2000 appeared to be driven more by concerns about cost than by any acknowledgment that genetic testing was a flawed means of determining sex, much less "gender" (Elsas et al. 252; Wonkam et al. 546).

Thus it becomes clear that "the issue organizing sex testing is not restricted to men impersonating women. Instead, the multiple categories that displace and replace one another imply a persistent and chronic passing that demands preventative measures—particularly measures that will render deviance visible" (C. Cole 137). As in other modern examples of rendering bodily deviance visible and thus governable, sex testing employed the fantastical technique of biocertification.[20] When chromosomal testing was widely initiated in 1968, it was accompanied by the institution of "femininity certificates," colloquially known as "Fem cards" (Sullivan 404).[21] So-called gender verification testing and the issuing of Fem cards were both overseen by a "femininity control head office" (Fausto-Sterling, *Sexing* 4). The substitution of the language of normative gender (femininity) for that of biological sex (femaleness) testifies to the merging of these categories which "displace and replace one another" to construct the fantasy of a clearly identifiable sex/gender that is at once social and biological, externally visible and internally verifiable. And as in other examples of biocertification, the body and text become interchangeable and metonymically linked, even as the number and types of certificates proliferate: "Once issued, the certificate, which is actually a wallet-size card signed by the president of the IOC Medical Commission, becomes the object inspected at those competitions requiring gender verification. Indeed . . . some competitors carry several certificates issued by various governance bodies because of the variability of screening procedures and qualifying criteria across competitions" (C. Cole 136). Biological sex is obvious, a matter of common sense—and if it is not, it can be easily determined by genetic testing. These two fantasies of sex identification collide and collapse in practice, when not only does the "obvious" require elaborate measurement and certification but one must carry several different certificates, all of which are supposed to validate the same, easily determined bodily truth.[22]

Examination of an actual femininity certificate, that of María José Martínez-Patiño, is telling in this regard. Martínez-Patiño gained notoriety in the 1980s when she became the first disqualified female athlete to publicly speak about her experiences and oppose sex verification. A champion hurdler, Martínez-Patiño forgot to bring her certificate of femininity to the World University Games in 1985, was genetically tested, and was found to have XY chromosomes. She was eventually determined to have androgen insensitivity syndrome (AIS), an intersex condition in which chromosomally male individuals are not sensitive to the masculinizing effects of testosterone and therefore develop as phenotypical women (Martínez-Patiño 538).[23] AIS is one of the conditions often cited to show the inappropriateness of genetic testing to ensure fair play, since the XY chromosomes confer no athletic advantage over other women. Disqualified and disgraced like so many before her, her sports scholarship revoked and her fiancé and friends abandoning her, Martínez-Patiño refused to quietly fade away. She vocally opposed sex testing, helping to bring about the policy changes of the 1990s, and published an essay in the leading British medical journal, Lancet, including a reproduction of her femininity certificate and asserting her identity as a woman despite her chromosomal status. "I have never cheated," she insisted (Martínez-Patiño 538).

Indeed if deception of any kind took place, it appears to have been by the IOC, not Martínez-Patiño. She explains that she had undergone sex testing in 1983 at the World Championships in Helsinki, resulting in the issuing of the certificate (538). Yet if she had undergone accurate chromosomal testing, her XY configuration would surely have been noted. Therefore the statement on her certificate that she "underwent an approved medical test, the result of which was sex-chromatin positive" is demonstrably false: either her certificate was simply issued based on her "obviously feminine" appearance—people with AIS generally have well-developed hips and breasts, since the feminizing effects of estrogen are not mitigated by testosterone as they are in XX women—or the testing process was remarkably sloppy. In either case, the femininity certificate, like other forms of biocertification, claims an absolute and rigid authority—here reinforced by various signatures, seals, and formal language—which has no solid scientific or biological basis. Indeed, what it certifies is merely a discursive "femininity," not femaleness, so perhaps its name is accurate after all.

Notably Martínez-Patiño herself, now a researcher and lecturer on women in sport, frames her resistance to sex testing by invoking the commonsense fantasy of sex identification: "I knew I was a woman. . . . I could hardly pretend to be a man; I have breasts and a vagina," as well as assertions of normative femininity: "Having had my womanliness tested—literally and figuratively—I suspect I have a surer sense of my femininity than other women" (538). Without discounting the tremendous courage shown by Martínez-Patiño in challenging the practice of sex testing, we may also note that this challenge did not incorporate a critique of notions of femininity and thus served to protect only the future interests of female athletes who, like Martínez-Patiño, appeared "womanly" and thus were unlikely to be challenged under the new policies of selective testing. Meanwhile female athletes who did not fit normative gender expectations, like Soundarajan in 2006, remained suspect targets for the ongoing fantasy of genetic sex identification.

Thus, selective testing has unsurprisingly functioned as a kind of "femininity test" in which athletes who combine exceptional achievement with a so-called masculine appearance are most likely to be required to undergo sex testing. The stigmatization and heteronormativity of this process came to world attention in 2009 with the case of Caster Semenya, a black South African champion runner. Close examination of the ongoing discourses of suspicion and hostility surrounding Semenya demonstrates the continuing power of the fantasy of sex identification, despite the scientific critiques and policy adjustments of the previous decades.

Caster Semenya and the Future of Sex

On August 19, 2009, the international press announced that the eighteen-year-old Semenya was undergoing sex verification testing, following her remarkable showing in the African Junior Championships and just before her world-record-setting victory in the 800-meter women's final in Berlin. Unlike in any previous cases of sex testing, the fact of testing was made public from the outset, and for the next year Semenya's story unfolded worldwide in excruciating detail, as the IAAF conducted its tests and deliberations, meanwhile banning Semenya from competition. Finally, on July 6, 2010, nearly a year after the tests were begun, the IAAF declared that Semenya was eligible to compete as a woman but did not release any details of its findings or of Semenya's test results. Semenya returned to competition and ran in two events in the 2012 Olympic Games. Her story brought the ongoing problems with sex testing in sports back into the public eye and continues to provoke debate and policy adjustments on a global level. In May 2011 the IAAF released an entirely new policy on sex testing, discussed further below, clearly in direct response to criticism of its handling of the Semenya case, and the IOC followed suit in June 2012, just before the London Olympic Games. A number of aspects of Semenya's story demonstrate the workings of the fantasy of identification, including the slippage between outer and inner bodily truths; the false claiming of scientific certainty; the conflation of racial, gendered, and medicalized identities; and the employment of the lay diagnostic gaze.

It was made quite clear from the outset that Semenya's "masculine" appearance was the main reason that she was challenged. Press coverage included many pictures of her at competitions, and her "deep voice and masculine physique," were widely discussed in the media and the blogosphere.[24] In the many online debates about Semenya, commenters frequently responded to her defenders by posting a link to a picture of Semenya with a statement along the lines of "How can you look at this and say this is not a man?" By contrast, interviews with Semenya's family and childhood acquaintances revealed that, while she had sometimes been teased for playing sports and wearing "boy's" clothes, in her hometown she had generally been accepted and seemed comfortable in her gender as a woman.[25] According to her former coaches, when Semenya began playing competitive sports, she "became accustomed to visiting the bathroom with a member of a competing team so that they could look at her private parts and then get on with the race" (Levy). Thus while Semenya had a nonnormative gender presentation up until the time of her sex testing, and sometimes had to prove her femaleness through "commonsense" inspections, her so-called masculinity became a truly vexed issue only when her athletic accomplishments made her visible to a global public.

The result of this shift was dramatic and far-reaching. Within weeks of the announcement that Semenya was being sex tested, she was featured in a cover story for the popular glossy South African magazine *You*, which was widely reported in the international press. The parts of the story most often reproduced were the cover picture of a garishly made-over Semenya and several quotations that served to perform a stereotypical femininity, such as "I'd like to dress up more often and wear dresses, but I never get the chance"; "I'd also like to learn to do my own makeup"; and "Now that I know what I can look like, I'd like to dress like this more often."[26] While some press outlets reported this story uncritically, many others questioned whether the article reflected Semenya's true feelings. This suspicion now appears more accurate, as in the years following the article's appearance, Semenya has invariably appeared in photos wearing baggy sports clothing, cornrows, and no makeup. The revelation that *You* paid a fee for the article, not to Semenya but to the national organization Athletics South Africa, added to its negative reception. South African LGBTI activist Funeka Soldaat called the makeover "a disaster," adding "To say that she enjoyed doing this, that's a lie! There is no way. There is no way!" (Levy). Perhaps due to such critiques, the article no longer appears on *You*'s website, but the made-over cover photo is widely disseminated in cyberspace.

If the *You* article was an ill-judged attempt to recuperate Semenya as a "real" woman, it appears to have been thoroughly unsuccessful. Instead, as the IAAF delayed releasing a decision on Semenya's eligibility, gossip and speculation continued to circulate until the Australian *Daily Telegraph* published a story on September 11, 2009, asserting that leaked medical results showed that Semenya had "male sex organs and no womb or ovaries" (Hurst). The story was quickly picked up and circulated globally, despite the refusal of the IAAF to confirm it. Indeed this claim has never been confirmed or denied by either the IAAF or Semenya herself but is nevertheless frequently repeated and assumed to be true. While the "male sex organs" in the headline of the *Telegraph* article refer to alleged internal testes, the terminology implies that Semenya has male genitalia, and thus has fueled furious voyeuristic speculation about her body. This speculation notably invokes and reinforces the tension between the two fantasies of sex identification outlined earlier.

For example, in response to the initial 2009 coverage in the *Guardian* about Semenya, one online commenter exclaimed, "Blimey. Since when has a sex test been 'an extremely complex procedure' involving medics, scientists, gynaecologists and psychologists, taking several weeks to complete? Assuming the, um, obvious method isn't appropriate, isn't it just a case of checking for XX or XY chromosomes?"[27] The "obvious" method, that of checking the genitalia, is juxtaposed with the "scientific" method, understood to be both simple and definitive. Another commenter quipped that "testing her gender ought to be as straightforward as the standard method of testing that of a chromosome: You pull its genes down."[28] (Dreger has also used this pun in her writings about intersex.) These comments are exemplary of hundreds that may be found online, demonstrating that the complexities and ambiguities of biological sex, asserted for decades by medical researchers and gender theorists alike, have failed to compete with the fantasy of genetic sex identification in the popular imagination.

As one commenter on the original *Guardian* story declared, "'She' looks like a bloke, sounds like a bloke, has more muscles than any female runner since the days of the East Germans and even seems to have a package swinging between her legs when 'she' runs."[29] The placing of *she* in quotation marks signals the writer's insistence that Semenya does not belong in the category of femaleness, an attitude taken further by the many commenters who refer to Semenya as "he" or even "it." The specifically invasive gaze "between her legs" was repeated by *Guardian* staff writer Mark Lawson the following day, though with a different conclusion: "Without being too indelicate about this, lycra running shorts and slow-mo HD television pictures show that if Semenya is a man, she is clearly no Linford Christie" (Lawson). Linford Christie, a Jamaican-born British sprinter, is now best known in British popular culture not for his running accomplishments but for the bulge in his running shorts, nicknamed "Linford's Lunchbox" by the *Sun* in 1998. (Christie sued the paper for defamation but could not prevent the term from being popularly adopted.) Lawson's invocation of racist sexual stereotypes about black men further solidifies the long-standing assumption that black bodies are available for white scrutiny and pseudoscientific dissection. And since Christie is also known for having been banned from sports for use of a performance-enhancing drug, the mention of his name in a supposed defense of Semenya, despite the claim that she is no Christie, works to subtly associate her name with the notion of unfair play.

Most reports state that the request for testing came after Semenya broke the record for the 800-meter dash, showing an "almost supernatural improvement" over her previous times for the event (Levy). Virtually no one in the IAAF or the international press seems to have questioned the complete illogic of associating sex testing with an unusually improved performance, since even *if* Semenya were a male imposter or had an intersex condition, these are not circumstances that would suddenly happen overnight to change her performance. Rather, as the IAAF itself acknowledged, this "sort of dramatic breakthrough . . . usually arouse[s] suspicion of drug use" (Smith, "Caster Semenya Row"). But Semenya had already been repeatedly tested for drugs. Somehow the natural—yet illogical—next step was to move to sex verification as the other primary form of screening for unfair advantage. The fantasy of identification seems to have provided the necessary metonymic link between two very different forms of testing, since "the optimism about the ability of science to reveal drug use lends confidence to scientific attempts to locate sex in the body" (C. Cole 145).

It is true that early reports about Semenya show an effort to distinguish between intersex conditions and other forms of presumed physical advantage. Nick Davies, a spokesman for the IAAF, told the *Guardian* on August 19, 2009, "If there's a problem and it turns out that there's been a fraud, that someone has changed sex, then obviously it would be much easier to strip results. However, if it's a natural thing and the athlete has always thought she's a woman or been a woman, it's not exactly cheating" (Kessel, "Gold"). The distinction between the fraudulent and the natural, however, was quickly subsumed in the general focus on Semenya's "unnatural" appearance, which evoked not only stereotypical ideas about masculinity and femininity but also a long tradition of scrutinizing black women's bodies to prove their abnormality. Many critics referred to this history, explicitly comparing the treatment of Semenya to that of Sarah Baartman, the so-called Hottentot Venus, who was taken to Europe from South Africa in the early 1800s and paraded before white audiences because of her supposedly freakish buttocks and genitals (Levy; Smith, "Caster Semenya Row").

At the same time that Semenya's body was being subjected to intensely public scrutiny and speculation, that scrutiny was also directed once more toward the practice of sex testing. The only detail about Semenya's body that was ever apparently confirmed was that she had a higher than "normal" level of testosterone ("Fresh Controversy"). Ironically these high testosterone levels had been noted months before the official gender verification ordeal began and had not apparently raised any eyebrows until Semenya's remarkable performance in Berlin. There are a number of reasons for higher testosterone levels in women, including intersex conditions such as Congenital Adrenal Hyperplasia, and non-intersex conditions such as Polycystic Ovarian Syndrome (PCOS). In both of these cases the person involved has XX chromosomes and would be certified as female by genetic testing. Indeed critics of genetic sex testing have long pointed out that hormone levels, not chromosomal sex, are more likely to account for the different abilities of male and female athletes, and some have gone so far as to suggest that testosterone levels should be used as the basis for future sex testing, or even as the new determinant of segregated levels in sport.[30]

Such calls have now been heeded, undoubtedly in response to the very public failure of the IAAF in the Semenya case not only to follow its own rather muddled protocols for sex verification but also to conform to "routinely accepted genetic test and genetic counseling principles" such as informed consent and patient confidentiality (Wonkam et al. 547; Hercher 552).[31] In May 2011 the IAAF published the new *IAAF Regulations Governing Eligibility of Females with Hyperandrogenism to Compete in Women's Competition*. These new guidelines make no mention of genetic sex but, as the title indicates, focus entirely on hormonal status, specifically the condition of hyperandrogenism, or an excess of male hormone (i.e., testosterone). In June 2012 the IOC issued its own *Regulations on Female Hyperandrogenism*, which went into force at the 2012 London Games. Rumors at once began to circulate that a number of female athletes were required to undergo hormonal treatment or gonadectomy prior to competing (Findlay); unsurprisingly this speculation largely centered on Semenya, who qualified to run in the 800-meter race in London (Long; Greenfield)

A close examination of the IAAF's published guidelines offers some indications of both the abandonment of the previous genetic fantasy of sex identification and the emergence of a new version. The new IAAF policy spells out the process of assessment for hyperandrogenism in meticulous detail, emphasizing confidentiality and professionalism at every step. It explicitly abandons the term *gender verification* and asserts that "if an athlete is recognized as a female in law, she is eligible to compete in women's competition in Athletics provided that she complies with IAAF Rules and Regulations" (*IAAF Regulations Explanatory Notes* 2). This would appear to be a significant advance over the reductive and inaccurate policies of the preceding decades. Yet the new policy also professes "a respect for the very essence of the male and female classifications in Athletics," a clear statement that the IAAF remains committed to the theory and practice of sex identification, despite using different terms and criteria (*IAAF Regulations* 3).

The new regulations consist of a twenty-nine-page document plus a five-page "Explanatory Note," more than twice the length of the previous version. Seven of these pages outline the new medical guidelines for examinations of athletes suspected to have hyperandrogenism, including illustrative diagrams for scoring the athlete's hirsutism and pubertal development according to standardized scales (*IAAF Regulations* 18–24). Yet the gist of the policy itself can be stated quite simply: if an athlete has testosterone levels in the male range, specified as greater or equal to 10 nmol/L, then she is ineligible to compete unless and until medical treatment lowers her levels to the female range (13). This supposedly objective and biological measurement has been adopted, ironically, in apparent response to those who had critiqued genetic sex testing by pointing out that hormones play a much larger role in physiological prowess than do chromosomes. Yet the choice of testosterone level as the sole determinant of eligibility merely substitutes one supposedly definitive biological measure of identity for another, and notably was determined in the absence of any scientific evidence proving that "athletes with higher testosterone perform better than athletes with lower levels" (Karkazis et al. 8) and with awareness that the IOC's own study in 2000 had found substantial overlap between the testosterone levels of male and female elite athletes (Jordan-Young and Karkazis). Here we can clearly see the flexible workings of a fantasy of identification, discarding one supposed biological marker of femaleness and adopting another, while remaining fully invested in the concept that such a marker *must* exist.

We can see the slippages in this rather hastily assembled version of the fantasy when we consider the remainder of the lengthy IAAF guidelines, which go into meticulous detail regarding the medical examinations required, far beyond a simple laboratory test for testosterone levels. Apparently these other examinations are to be used either to determine if there is a reason to test testosterone levels or to assess if the athlete's body is insensitive to testosterone. Yet subjecting athletes to a medical process that includes pelvic and rectal exams, scrutiny of the entire naked body to gage its hirsutism, and measuring the diameter of the breast and areola and the length and width of the clitoris, hardly appears to be a more respectful or appropriate solution than simply performing the blood and urine tests for testosterone levels. Rather the medical instructions read as if adopted wholesale from those developed for clinical screening for hyperandrogenism of patients in general (for example, a teenage girl who has not begun menstruating) rather than tailored to the specific circumstance of athletic testing. This impression is supported, for example, by a note that "vaginal examination may possibly require general anesthesia, especially if the patient is young," which appears to be applicable only to the screening of girls too young to be participating in elite international athletics (*IAAF Regulations* 20).[32] Overall the policy reads as a compromise between those who wished to abandon sex testing altogether and those who remained invested in the idea of regulable sex, and traces of both positions may be detected in its language.

Evidence of such debates may be found in earlier media coverage of the IOC's own deliberations regarding changes to sex testing policies. In January 2010, for example, a report on the panel of medical experts convened by the IOC reveals a diversity of viewpoints. Eric Vilain, a medical geneticist from UCLA, opposed the use of androgen levels to ensure fairness, questioning whether targeted athletes would have to lower their testosterone to the "average" level for women, which would disadvantage them in comparison to nontargeted athletes with levels on the high end for women.[33] Similarly Dr. Myron Genel of Yale declared that "there is no such thing" as a level playing field. However, others, such as Duke law professor Doriane Coleman, asserted that even lowering athletes' testosterone levels to acceptable female levels is not enough, since "the athlete has already reaped the benefits of a lifetime of heightened testosterone." Coleman apparently sought to exclude all athletes with current or past hyperandrogenism, while others took the position that all athletes with disorders of sexual development should be allowed to compete regardless of treatment (Kolata, "I.O.C. Panel"). The guidelines eventually issued by the IAAF, and the later regulations adopted by the IOC, seem to have attempted to strike a middle ground between these two viewpoints, and both emphasize the unique role of testosterone for assessing an athlete's eligibility.

In discussions about testosterone levels and the ideal of fairness, dis/ability is notably invoked both in contrast to and in connection with biological sex. Disability, as we have seen, serves to anchor the idea of the natural, here often figured in terms of genetic difference. For example, Laura Hercher argues that while "taking an excess of testosterone is cheating" and unquestionably wrong, "producing an excess of testosterone is a genetic advantage, and there is nothing inherently wrong with that. Genetic advantages are the norm and not the exception in competitive sports. High level competitive athletics are rife with individuals who are genetic outliers" (552). The example Hercher and others often cite to illustrate this viewpoint is Olympic swimmer Michael Phelps, whose unusually long limbs have prompted speculation about whether he has the genetic condition Marfan Syndrome, a connective tissue disorder that could give him certain advantages due to his bodily configuration and flexibility, while also conferring significant health risks (Griffin 107; Karkazis et al. 11). Hercher observes that "the question of whether or not Phelps has [Marfan Syndrome] has been as hotly debated in the blogosphere as the question of whether or not Caster Semenya is a hermaphrodite, but no one has suggested that having [Marfan] would disqualify him from competition" (552). Other critics have noted that many NBA players could be described as having acromegaly, a condition conferring unusual height and large hands, but again no one has suggested imposing "normal" height limits in basketball.[34] Rather it is taken for granted that successful basketball players are much taller than the average person. Thus some argue that, presuming that testosterone does boost athleticism, it should also be accepted that successful female athletes would have higher testosterone levels than the average woman. And as Dreger points out, some men have naturally higher levels of testosterone than others, likely conferring an athletic advantage, but no one suggests requiring male athletes to reduce their levels to those of average men ("Where's the Rulebook"). Vanessa Heggie observes that "there are probably hundred of genetic variations which lead to 'unfair' advantages in sport; only those associated with gender are used to exclude or disqualify athletes," and these variations are used only against female athletes, never to disqualify "super-masculine" males (158).

This inconsistency demonstrates that, in the case of female athletes, more is at stake than the concept of fairness. Clearly the category of femaleness itself is being defended against the epistemological threat of female masculinity, through a fantasy of sex identification that both invokes and reinforces femininity as a "regulatory ideal" (Butler, *Bodies* 1).[35] Despite its rejection of the term *gender verification*, the new

IAAF policy remains invested in this fantasy of femininity, particularly as revealed in the particulars of the medical exam mentioned earlier. Most striking are the two (out of seven) pages of the medical guidelines devoted to the Ferriman and Gallwey Hirsutism Scale, an assessment tool developed in 1961, which apparently remains the standard used by contemporary doctors to determine if a woman's body is too hairy or has hair in the "wrong" places (*IAAF Regulations* 23).

As Figure 9.1 indicates, the subject is given a score of zero to four for the hair on each part of her body, and a score above six is considered to signify clinical hirsutism, which should be medically investigated. Again, it is understandable that a scale like this could be useful for a physician initially diagnosing a patient, since hirsutism can be a sign of a medical condition that poses health risks, such as androgen-producing tumors, PCOS, and internal testes, which often become malignant. It is less clear, however, why the hirsutism scale plays such a large role in the guidelines for assessing elite female athletes. It is inconceivable that hair, or the lack thereof, would be cited as the reason for confirming or denying competitive eligibility; again, in the new IAAF and IOC regulations, serum testosterone levels are the *sole criterion* to determine eligibility. Thus the extensive attention to the Ferriman and Gallwey Scale in the medical guidelines seems less relevant to the new policy and more to be another version of the "femininity test" of previous policies.

In particular this scale functions to enfreak the bodies of subjects who present a troubling female masculinity, such as Caster Semenya. The pathologization of that masculinity is accomplished both through the imposition of a supposedly objective quantitative scale and through the visual depiction of category-confounding bodies in the illustration. The juxtaposition of "feminine" faces, breasts, and hips with "masculine" amounts of hair implies the freakish gender ambiguity of the pictured subject and calls for intervention to erase that ambiguity.[36] Presumably, in order to enable an accurate assessment, the subject must be told to abandon any usual practices of hair removal before the exam, thus potentially (and ironically) thwarting her own disciplinary rituals of femininity to ensure that she present as masculinized an appearance as possible. More disturbingly, although the IAAF guidelines are explicitly international in design and purpose, the hirsutism scale presents a normative white Euro-American version of the female body, with no acknowledgment of geographical, ethnic, or cultural diversity in hair growth or removal. Thus the medical guidelines appear to serve both

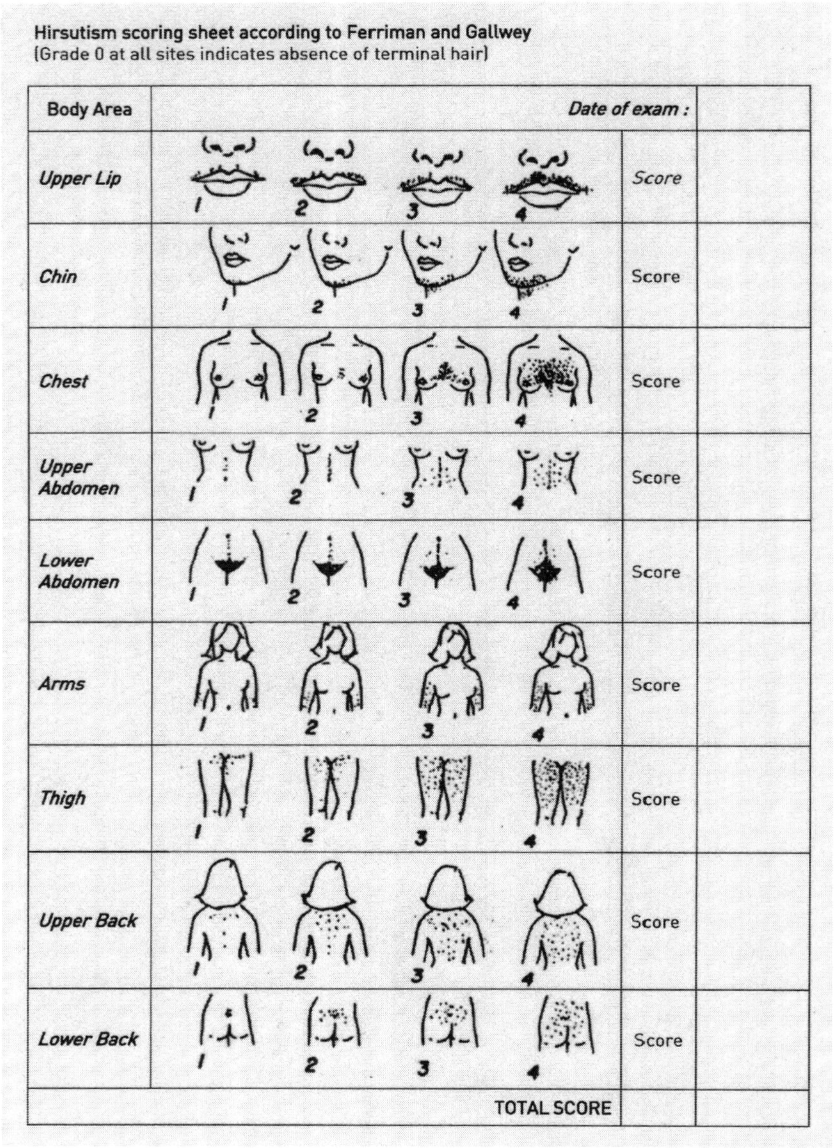

Hirsutism scoring sheet according to Ferriman and Gallwey
(Grade 0 at all sites indicates absence of terminal hair)

Body Area	Date of exam :		
Upper Lip	1 2 3 4	*Score*	
Chin	1 2 3 4	Score	
Chest	1 2 3 4	Score	
Upper Abdomen	1 2 3 4	Score	
Lower Abdomen	1 2 3 4	Score	
Arms	1 2 3 4	Score	
Thigh	1 2 3 4	Score	
Upper Back	1 2 3 4	Score	
Lower Back	1 2 3 4	Score	
	TOTAL SCORE		

FIGURE 9.1. Ferriman and Gallwey Hirsutism Scale Illustration, included in the 2011 *IAAF Regulations.*

their purported function, to diagnose and treat hyperandrogenism in female athletes, and a submerged, fantastical purpose of enforcing a normative white femininity upon those athletes, a point that again highlights the case of Semenya, a black African woman whose perception as freakishly masculine draws upon both gendered and racialized normative assumptions.

We may ironically note attempts by journalists covering the 2012 Olympics to support their speculations about Semenya's medical treatment through vehement claims that she "looks a lot more feminine than she did in 2009"—as one headline asserted—despite the fact that any observable changes in her appearance between 2009 and 2012 range from subtle to nonexistent: her body is still squarely muscular, her clothing and hair style androgynous, and her voice in televised interviews markedly deep in timbre (Greenfield; Findlay; Long). Semenya's appearance in 2012 would undoubtedly still evoke suspicion under the new IAAF and IOC guidelines, which call for active investigation of any female athlete who shows "deviation in sex characteristics" (*IOC Regulations* 2), such as "deep voice," "breast atrophy," "increased muscle mass," and "body hair of male type" (*IAAF Regulations* 20), criteria that are "entangled with deeply subjective and stereotypical Western definitions of femininity" (Karkazis et al. 13).

The enfreakment of "masculine" female athletes provides another semantic link to disability in discussions of sex testing. The other athlete often compared to Semenya is Oscar Pistorius, the runner whose prosthetic legs first caused controversy in 2008, leading to a battle over his eligibility to compete in the Olympics (Camporesi and Maugeri 378; Richard Williams). This conceptual parallel was visually enacted at the 2012 Games, when Semenya was chosen to bear South Africa's flag at the opening ceremonies and Pistorius did the same at the closing ceremonies. While Phelps is compared to Semenya to demonstrate that athletes with natural advantages are inherent in, not exterior to elite competitions, Pistorius is cited to raise questions about the "natural" itself. As Dreger wrote in the *New York Times*, "Restrictions on testosterone, on prosthetic limbs, and on men competing in women's sports are meant to protect . . . against unnatural advantages . . . but athletes left the realm of the natural a long time ago" ("Science"). Whereas Phelps's uncontested insider status implies that Semenya deserves the same inclusion, Pistorius's position outside of the natural conditions of humanity presents a more vexed context. While his comparison to Semenya invokes absolute physical difference through disability, the threat he poses to fantasies of a level playing field is that of super-ability, as the controversy surrounding his eligibility focuses on the question of whether his prosthetic "cheetah" legs provide an unfair advantage, much like Semenya's higher levels of testosterone (Richard Williams). Pistorius's qualification for the 2012 Games reignited the controversy in the media, but his overall poor showing meant that debates over his eligibility became subsumed in stereotyped discourses about his role as inspiration rather than rival to his fellow runners.

Semenya, however, approached the Games as a heavy favorite to win the 800-meter race, and she continues to be the target of suspicion, hostility, and doubt more than two years after she was officially declared to be female. Following her original record-setting victory in Berlin in 2009, some of her opponents voiced their anger to the press, such as Italian runner Elisa Cusma, who declared, "For me, she is not a woman. She's a man" (Camporesi and Maugeri 378). A year later, when Semenya returned to international competitions, such sentiments appeared unchanged, despite the IAAF's decision. After losing to Semenya in August 2010, Canadian runner Diane Cummins insisted, "Even if she is a female, she's on the very fringe of the normal athlete female biological composition from what I understand of hormone testing. So, from that perspective, most of us just feel that we are literally running against a man" (Callow). And while South Africans remained mostly supportive, a gaff by Athletics South Africa hinted of prejudices remaining within the organization. In April 2011 it was reported that the ASA website listed Semenya as a man and then failed to correct the error. The president of the ASA apologized and stated that "there was never any intention to embarrass Caster Semenya," but it seems unlikely that this was an innocent error. Meanwhile, at the South African Athletics Championships in Durban, runner Lebogang Phalula, who came in second, tried to make an announcement over the public system about her frustration at competing against Semenya.[37]

Some ascribe this continuing hostility to the fact that the IAAF did not release Semenya's test results, as seen in British runner Jemma Simpson's comments to the press: "No one really knows what the outcome is. . . . She's just been allowed to come back on the scene and we're expected just to get on with it. . . . It would be nice to just—I know it's really none of our business—but it would just be nice to be reassured more than anything" (Kessel, "Caster"). That desire for reassurance drives the continuing fantasy of identification based on a definite, incontrovertible measure of sex. As Dreger said in an interview about Semenya, "People always press me: 'Isn't there one marker we can use?' No. . . . Science is making it more difficult and not less" (Levy). Despite ongoing media speculation about Semenya's intersex status and what treatment she may have undergone during her eleven-month hiatus from competition, she has kept what little privacy is left to her after the testing debacle and refused to confirm or deny the rumors. Yet more is at issue here than privacy. Even if full medical details were provided, they would not contain that definitive, single marker of femaleness the fantasy demands because such a marker simply does not exist.[38]

Meanwhile, as the 2012 Games approached, media coverage continued to repeat as fact the rumors of Semenya's intersex condition and to speculate about her treatment, for example diagramming "before and after" pictures of her body in 2009 and 2012 to highlight her supposedly feminized features (Greenfield). Semenya herself continued to refuse to discuss her medical treatment, but Dane Cornelius, a track and field manager at the University of Pretoria, where Semenya lives and trains, told the *Toronto Star*, "I know she gets treatment. What the treatment entails, I can't give the details" (Findlay). Again the usual standards of confidentiality appear to be set aside when Semenya comes under discussion by both sports professionals and the media. In this context, as one commentator observed just before the Games began, "If Semenya wins the gold, she is likely to be accused of having an unfair advantage. If she runs poorly, she is likely to be accused of sandbagging the race so as not to be accused of having an unfair advantage" (D. Epstein).

That comment proved prescient, as Semenya's second-place finish in the 800-meter provoked an immediate flurry of speculation that she held back on purpose.[39] Semenya vehemently denied this claim, and it will likely remain a topic of speculation and uncertainty; what is certain, however, is that gold medalist Mariya Savinova—who bitterly remarked, "Just look at her!" after finishing fifth to Semenya at the 2009 World Championships—hugged Semenya and told her she did "a good job" after beating her at both the 2011 World Championships and the 2012 Olympics (D. Epstein; "Caster Semenya Denies"). Here we see once more the power of a fantasy to constrain a subject within its identificatory matrix, and the material consequences of that power.

The story of Caster Semenya raises the question of the future of fantasies of identification and of the possibilities for resistance or revision of them. As we have seen, the new IAAF policy, while abandoning the genetic model of sex, nevertheless perpetuates the fantasy of sex identification through both the designation of a single biological measure for eligibility and the continued enfreakment of nonnormative female bodies. It is discouraging that this new policy, while certainly superior in many ways to previous ones, is still so deeply invested in notions of biological identity. Is the answer, then, to abandon scientific approaches to identification altogether? Or should we simply seek to modify these approaches to reflect more accurate science? While these questions are not easily answerable, it is imperative that we begin to form answers to them, both conceptually and in the realms of policy and law. Such answers should not be confined to the issue of sex/gender in sports, or even sex/gender more widely, but must address the globally expanding institutional power of fantasies of identification in the modern world. As genetic science and biotechnology advance, further structures of bio-certification are likely to be deployed in multiple realms and along multiple axes of identity and power. Our exploration of what happened in the case of sex testing and Caster Semenya offers chilling evidence of how new advances in science will be (mis)used to justify these deployments unless interventions can be made on the levels of culture, representation, and policy.

Conclusion: Future Identifications

Fantasies of identification inevitably fail to accomplish their primary claim of neatly categorizing all bodies and identities. Yet, as we have seen, merely the insistent *attempt* to fulfill that claim has material and often devastating effects on lives and communities. The question we are left with, then, is: What alternative systems of identification are possible? If my critique of current fantastical modes of identification—such as blood quantum, disability certification, and genetic testing—has demonstrated their many inadequacies, does it follow that these modes should be abandoned altogether? How would we respond to the undeniable challenges of limited resources, vast populations, and false identity claims?

As a study primarily centered on the workings of culture, this book does not pretend to offer specific policy solutions. However, culture is the realm that allows us to draw broad and pertinent connections between policy, representation, and lived experience, and thus to indicate similarly broad and interconnective directions for the future. In this conclusion I gesture in several such directions in the hopes of steering discourse, and eventually policy, away from some of the worst errors of the fantasy thus far.

The first and perhaps most obvious course of action is to challenge the fantasy of identification wherever it may be encountered. My goal throughout this project has been to expose and denaturalize the workings of a deeply embedded and generally unquestioned fantasy, and thus to provide the tools for further exposures and critiques. Through such critiques it is possible to form new coalitional politics between different groups targeted by these fantasies. Most crucially such a politics must displace disability as the anchor of physical "truth," developing new claims of justice and self-determination for racial, ethnic, and gender politics that do not rely on a methodological or symbolic distancing from disability. Without such a transformation, I contend, disability will always be lurking at the margins of discourse, ready to be invoked to justify a range of oppressive and reductive identifications.

In connection with this move, we must explore alternatives to scientific knowledge models for authenticating identities. As we have seen, such alternatives are already robustly circulated in Native contexts, drawing upon cultural and kinship-based traditions of self-making. Yet these alternatives exist in frustrated tension with the state's insistence upon biocertification, and recent trends toward DNA-based identification indicate further penetrance of the fantasy into tribal and individual models of Native identity. I suggest that the events discussed in chapter 9, and their correspondence to previous forms of the fantasy, indicate that we must approach the age of genetics with caution, closely interrogating the scientific claims underpinning the genetic imaginary and delinking them from policy whenever possible.

On the other hand, a wholesale replacement of biocertification and other fantastical means of identification with a system based purely on self-identification appears neither possible nor practical. None of us is so naïve as to think that such a system would not lend itself to a certain amount of fraud and misidentification. However, I do contend that current understandings of identity can and should be modified to give greater authority to the expert knowledge that individuals have about their own bodies—and by extension, that communities have about their members. Such a model already functions in practice, if not in policy, in the case of disability certification, as disabled people often compose the elaborate letters of authentication that their physicians officially sign. A culture that acknowledges this form of expertise, I believe, is less likely to impose reductive or inaccurate identities and more likely to distribute resources appropriately.

How may such changes be made? This book has demonstrated a long-standing and ongoing interactional relationship between cultural representation, law, and policy. Representation is not the only step toward material change, but neither is it a passive reflector of such change. The resistant and counteridentificatory strands woven through the history of fantasies of identification signal the possibility and importance of change, and it is to these we must look if we seek to create a future based more on justice than fantasy.

Notes

Introduction

1. *Oxford English Dictionary* 3rd edition. See L. Davis, *Enforcing Normalcy* 24.

2. Braddock and Parish 35; Martin 129; Welke 118. Braddock and Parish note that "the 1840 census reflected pervasive racism. All black residents in some towns were classified as insane" (35). See also Goldberg 38; Chinn 3–5.

3. On the emergence of disability institutions and the rise of rehabilitation in the United States, see Albrecht; Braddock and Parish; Byrom; Carey; Trent.

4. On the effects of urbanization and expansion on the stability and knowability of identities, see Braddock and Parish 34; Halttunen 1–7; Lenz 22; Lindberg 5. On geographic mobility and racial anxiety, see Gross 30.

5. The archival title of this pamphlet is *The Identification Division of the FBI: A Brief Outline of the History, Services, and Operating Techniques of the World's Largest Repository of Fingerprints*. The image reproduced here as Figure I.1 appears on page 7 of the pamphlet.

6. Katherine Rowe's account of viewing this display about the West case at FBI headquarters, in her *Dead Hands: Fictions of Agency, Renaissance to Modern*, was published in 1999 (163–164). As of this writing, in 2012, there is no mention of the West case on the FBI's official website.

7. For example, Fort Lauderdale Police Department (http://www.flpd.org/index.aspx?page=63), Crime Scene Forensics (http://www.crimescene-forensics.com/History_of_Fingerprints.html), Triplett's Fingerprint Dictionary (http://www.fprints.nwlean.net/w.htm), Iowa Department of Public Safety (http://www.dps.state.ia.us/DCI/supportoperations/Information/records/fingerprint_procedures_manual_section_2.pdf). All accessed May 27, 2011.

8. See S. Cole 144; Rowe 176–178.

9. See S. Cole 124–126; Rowe 168–169; Chinn 47.

10. See Chinn 43–45; S. Cole 77, 99; Gillman 91; Rowe 180; Rogin 78–80; R. Thomas 667, 679; Sundquist, "Mark Twain" 63.

11. Caplan is quoting historian Beatrice Fraenkel.

12. See chapter 5 for details and sources on these events.

13. Mitchell and Snyder also "argue that imaginative literature takes up its narrative project as a counter to scientific or truth-telling discourses. It is productively parasitic upon other disciplinary systems that define disability in more deterministic ways" (*Narrative Prosthesis* 1–2). In the works I examine, however, I see the relationship between imaginative, scientific, and historical discourses as more complex and multidirectional than the counterpoint envisioned here.

14. Samira Kawash describes a similar dynamic in the "substitution of cultural representations of passing for the actual occurrence of passing, a happening that proved in any event inaccessible to the scientific gaze," observing that "while the eclipse of empirical data by cultural accounts might be viewed with deep suspicion in most scientific inquiries, here it happens almost unthinkingly. Further, that both literary critics *and social scientists* would align passing research with novelists rather than with actual people who might be passing suggests that the importance of passing in the early twentieth century was less as a sociological phenomenon than as part of a cultural imaginary of racial difference and racial division" (128). Similarly Michael Bérubé notes that "our society's representations of disability are intricately tied to, and sometimes the very basis for, our public policies for 'administering' disability" ("Citizenship" 56). My analysis of identification similarly ascribes the blurring of literature and science to a deep investment in the cultural imaginary that I call the fantasy of identification.

15. See Martin 54; Keetley 3; Baynton 38; Bankole 124; Fett 4, 170–171.

16. I should acknowledge that I place a greater emphasis on the role of these medical experts than does Gross, whose excellent history of racial identity trials in the United States argues that evidence of common sense, community, association, and performance played a larger role in such trials than medical or scientific evidence. Without discounting the importance of these other forms of identification, I believe there are also significant moments in which an overwhelming importance was placed upon signs of racial identity marked on the body, as becomes clear in my discussion of the Salomé Müller trial in chapter 4. I agree with Gross, however, that many trials of racial identity involved a complex negotiation between these different forms of identity-making and that adherence to the fantasy of identification was far from solidified during the antebellum period:

> Scientific experts were invoked at a time when doctors, lawyers, and other professionals were beginning to stake their claims to expert knowledge. The result was a tug of war between judge and jury, expert and lay witnesses, creating bitter arguments among those claiming to know racial identity scientifically and those claiming to know it experientially. So-called expert knowledge was countered with "common sense" arguments. That is, while medical experts relied on racial "science," juries used common sense to make visual inspections and hear testimony about reputation. Sometimes, however, lay witnesses spoke in the language of science and expertise, and often doctors resorted to notions of common sense. Scientific and "performance" evidence could work together, as they did for Abby Guy; or they could be opposed to each other, as in the trial of Alexina Morrison (Gross 38–39). Gross cites the 1857 freedom suit of Alexina Morrison as an example of a racial identity trial in which Morrison's "white" behavior was given as much credence as was the expert testimony on her physical "marks" (1–3).

17. As I discuss in chapter 4, Robyn Wiegman places this shift a bit earlier, in the "late seventeenth century" (24). However, Guillaumin and Wiegman concur on the effects of this dynamic in the nineteenth and twentieth centuries, so their difference on the earlier period does not affect the usefulness of both their analyses for my argument.

18. See also Jordan, who discusses the naturalization of racial difference in the context of the general "secularization of Western society" (217).

19. "In fact, the very concept of normalcy by which most people (by definition) shape their existence is in fact tied inexorably to the concept of disability, or rather, the concept of disability is a function of a concept of normalcy. Normalcy and disability are part of the same system" (L. Davis, *Enforcing Normalcy* 2).

20. To further clarify the equation of racial inferiority with disability, Van Evrie also writes that the only circumstance in which an African American person might be equal to a white person would be if the white person were "idiotic, insane, or otherwise incapable" (qtd. in Baynton 38).

21. I differ somewhat from Baynton's claim that "by the late nineteenth and early twentieth centuries ... the concept of the natural was to a great extent displaced or subsumed by the concept of normality" (35). While I certainly acknowledge the growing ascendancy of normality throughout the past two centuries, in the mid-nineteenth- to early twentieth-century texts I discuss, I find the two concepts deployed in overlapping and mutually supportive ways.

22. For some representative works addressing the relationship of disability to gender and sexuality, see Clare; Garland Thomson *Extraordinary Bodies*; Hall; Kafer; McRuer and Wilkerson. On disability in relationship to race and ethnicity, see Bell, *Blackness and Disability*; Boster; James; Quayson; Wu.

23. "Including disability in the discourses that constitute race, gender, ethnicity, sexuality, and class complicates the body's cultural construction and acknowledges that all physical existence is inflected by multiple narratives of identity, felt or attributed, denigrated or privileged" (Garland Thomson, *Extraordinary Bodies* 135–136).

24. "Two contradictory notions—race as clear-cut identity (with the ever-present possibility of deception) versus race as ever-shifting category (with the ever-present possibility of confusion)—together make up our contemporary 'common sense' of race: what we know without being aware we know it" (Gross 16).

25. The emergence of the literary detective genre during the same period as the consolidation of medical authority in England and the United States does not appear coincidental. The most famous of those detectives, Sherlock Holmes, was modeled after one of Sir Arthur Conan Doyle's medical professors (Accardo 30), and then provided the inspiration for Twain's Pudd'nhead Wilson, the fingerprinting lawyer discussed in chapter 5, who embodies the intersection of medicine and the law as the primary social mechanisms for determining identity. "Like the flood of scientific writing on criminology that appeared in England during the 1890s, these fictions of criminality [Sherlock Holmes stories] link questions of personal identity and physiology with questions of national identity and security in ways that redefine the relation of an individual's body with the body politic" (R. Thomas 655).

26. For recent critiques, see Shakespeare; Mitchell and Snyder, *Cultural Locations of Disability*.

27. See Koenig et al. for rebuttals to recent challenges to this understanding of genetics and race.

28. As I discuss in chapter 9, attempts to determine sex from gonadal status were inconsistent and did not take hold. See Dreger, *Hermaphrodites*; Fausto-Sterling, *Sexing*; Holmes, *Critical Intersex*; Reis.

29. Butler directly addresses intersexuality in her later book, *Undoing Gender*, but her earlier work, *Bodies That Matter*, provides a richer source for my purposes because of its focus on the materialization of "sex."

1 / Ellen Craft's Masquerade

1. For discussion of these shifts in race and gender anxieties, see Wiegman; Sanchez-Eppler; Sorisio. See Reis for discussion of the relationship between fears of racial instability, gender fraud, and bodily ambiguity in the nineteenth century.

2. Although William is the narrator of *Running a Thousand Miles for Freedom*, there appears to be no critical consensus on the authorship of the narrative. While William is generally listed as the sole author, Barbara McCaskill's 1999 edition credits both William and Ellen as authors, apparently in recognition of the presumably collaborative nature of both their escape and their subsequent story-making on the abolitionist circuit. Blassingame (83) and Keetley (13, 18n15, citing Jean Yellin) attribute the narrative to a collaboration between Ellen, William, and a (presumably white) amanuensis. Browder expresses disbelief that the illiterate William could have learned to write such an erudite and allusive text and thus refuses to see the narrative as "authentic in any sense," apparently attributing authorship to a white abolitionist (25). Charles Heglar and Sarah Brusky make separate and convincing cases that there must have been considerable collaboration between William and Ellen in the production of the narrative since portions describe Ellen's experiences at which William was not present. Feminist critics, such as McCaskill, Weinauer, and Garber, examine the ways nineteenth-century notions of femininity restricted Ellen's ability to take on an equal role in authorship with her husband but also explore historical evidence suggesting that Ellen could be both articulate and outspoken on occasion. Among these many possible approaches, I have chosen to align myself with McCaskill by treating the narrative as a collaborative effort and referring to both Crafts as the authors.

3. Andrews; Bland *Voices of the Fugitives*; De Grave; Brusky; Keetley; McCaskill; and Weinauer discuss the Crafts' narrative in terms of both race and gender. Barrett discusses the narrative primarily in relation to race, while Garber addresses its gender dynamics. Sterling's often-quoted biographical account, like Blackett's definitive biographical essay, is largely concerned with the Crafts' travels with the abolitionist movement.

4. Jerrold Hirsch and Karen Hirsch's 1997 observation largely holds true today: "Flip through the pages of the numerous books on African American slavery and you will find almost nothing about disability. Disability is not yet a category of analysis in studies of slavery or in most other historical inquiry" (1). The Hirsches' unpublished article on disability in the FWP slave narratives offers tantalizing hints of the rich insights such an analysis might offer, as does Boster; Barclay. It is also important to note that many texts of African American history, such as those by Bankole, Fett, and White, document the enslaved African American

experience of disability without naming it as such. Similarly historians of disability in America have barely touched on the issue of slavery. For example, Longmore and Umansky's otherwise excellent 2001 collection *The New Disability History: American Perspectives* includes only two contributions that even mention slavery, one of which (the Baynton essay cited below) considers how metaphors of disability were used to both justify and oppose slavery, and the other of which examines the personal papers of a Southern white family which occasionally mention slavery approvingly.

5. See Bankole 30–31; Fett 170–188; Savitt 163; White 79–87. It is crucial to note that this strategy is deeply gendered, as White observes: slave women employed feigned illness more frequently and more successfully than did men (79–81).

6. Brusky, for example, is concerned with how the narrative "highlights the importance of gender to constructions of race," especially white race (189–190). Weinauer similarly discusses the narrative as demonstrating the unfixed boundaries of race, gender, and class through Ellen's transgression of those boundaries, but she suggests that gender ultimately emerges as more fixed than either race or class (38). Browder claims that the narrative demonstrates "what happens when people apply the logic of class to a construct of race" based on American beliefs in the fluidity of class and the fixity of racial identity (7). Garber is concerned to show how the figure of Ellen Craft as transvestite displaces "social anxiety from one category to another (race, class, gender)" (283).

7. See Baynton for a thorough analysis of this dynamic in nineteenth- and early twentieth-century discourse.

8. The enduring opposition of African American liberation and the disabled body is notably signified in the title of Morton's 1991 book, *Disfigured Images: The Historical Assault on Afro-American Women.*

9. Unlike Ellen Craft, some light-skinned fugitive slaves such as Moses Roper had to wear wigs to pass as white (Roper 59, 81).

10. Armistead's *Five Hundred Thousand Strokes of Freedom*, a compilation of the Leeds Anti- Slavery pamphlets published in 1853, is not paginated except within a few individual pamphlets. Instead it is organized by the numerical order of the pamphlets, and so I cite it here by pamphlet number, as LAS (pamphlet number).

11. In their own narrative the Crafts also make clear the intimate violence of Ellen's whiteness, stating directly that she is the daughter of her master (3).

12. Browder sums up the paradox: "Much as we may like to think that race and ethnicity are not essential qualities, they are certainly treated as such in the United States. Race may be a construction, but color remains a visual cue; and most Americans use visual, physiological cues to make their judgments about a person's racial identity" (9).

13. See C. Davis and Gates's introduction to *The Slave's Narrative* for further discussion of the importance of literacy in relation to slave narratives and African American liberation.

14. In Brown's 1864 revision of his novel as *Clotelle: A Tale of the Southern States*, he makes this connection more apparent in his phrasing, rewriting the speech as a single sentence: "I have often been told that I would make a better looking man than woman, and if I had the money I might avail myself of it to bid farewell to this place" (46).

15. This is the same account Sterling reproduces in her biography of Ellen Craft and to which I refer later in this chapter. This anonymous account appeared in the Newark, New Jersey, *Daily Mercury* on January 19, 1849 (Brown, *Clotel* 269).

16. Brown published four versions of his novel: *Clotel; or, The President's Daughter. A Narrative of Slave Life in the United States*, published in London in 1853 and usually treated as the standard text; a serialization as *Miralda; or the Beautiful Quadroon. A Romance of American Slavery* in the *Weekly Anglo-African*, December 1, 1860–March 16, 1861; an 1864 revision in book form as *Clotelle: A Tale of the Southern States*; and a final version with additional material in 1867, *Clotelle; or, the Colored Heroine. A Tale of the Southern States*. For a comparison of the four versions, see Fabi.

17. Child is referring to the notorious proponent of racist medicine Dr. Samuel A. Cartwright, known for inventing not only the diagnosis of drapetomania but its related "affliction," Dysaesthesia Aethiopios, or "rascality" (Bankole 239).

18. Most notably Gilbert and Gubar.

19. In a further demonstration of the key role of literacy, the Crafts waited to publish an account of their escape until they (or, by most accounts, William) had sufficiently mastered reading and writing to author an original narrative. See Blackett ix.

20. Blackett, 66; McCaskill, "Yours" 523; Weinauer 55n11. Sterling acknowledges this dynamic but also asserts that Ellen "had decided opinions of her own and was willing to express them" (47).

21. I certainly empathize with those contemporary feminist critics who appear to prefer Brown's account, such as Brusky (79), but remain wary of taking her account as the "real" version, as Garber appears to do (283).

22. After Andrews's initially dismissive description of Josephine Brown's work, he notes her "explicit feminist statements" against rape of slave women and suggests that "it is significant that when Josephine allowed herself as a biographer to speak out in this highly personal way, it was to call attention to the special plight of women of color" (Andrews, introduction xxxviii).

23. Baynton is one of the few who have analyzed this dynamic with attention to the construction of disability equal to that of gender. He observes that, "as with disabled people today, women's social position was treated as a medical problem that necessitated separate and special care" (42–43). Garland Thomson suggests that femininity and abnormality have been connected in Western culture since Aristotle, but she focuses on nineteenth-century America as a particular site of such attitudes (*Extraordinary Bodies* 28).

24. According to Andrews, *Biography of an American Bondsman* was a "precedent-setting book" that "launched the tradition of biographies authored by black American women" (introduction xxxiii).

25. In keeping with the objectification of William as a mobility aid, he must ride in the baggage car while Ellen travels first class.

26. For the source of this account, see note 15. According to the *Oxford English Dictionary, gingerly* with regard to walking could mean either "elegantly" or "cautiously"; context here suggests that the first, now obsolete definition is meant.

27. I am drawing on Herndl's apt characterization of the (white) nineteenth-century invalid woman.

28. Ellen's whiteness likely reinforced her perception as an invalid, particularly as racialist views of the time virtually equated African blood with physical hardiness,

especially for women (McCaskill, "Yours" 517). While Southern slave owners might have accused Ellen of "playing the lady," white Northern and especially British abolitionists saw her as *being* that lady. Lady Byron, we recall, was deeply impressed by Ellen's whiteness and described her as having "the appearance of a well-bred and educated lady" (J. Brown 80–81). McCaskill observes that "Ellen had become by 1851, with notice of her disembarkation on Liverpool's shore, as white and womanly as Millard Fillmore was Presidential" and that on the abolitionist stage, Ellen's "silence and bashfulness enhanced the abolitionists' tactics of transmuting her identity racially and sexually from sullied quadroon slave to civilized, authentic 'white' lady" ("Yours" 521, 523). In such descriptions, race, class, and gender clearly cannot be separated from their mutually constitutive and reinforcing relationships, and neither can disability—for where the genteel, idealized white lady is, the invalid will not be far behind. See Herndl.

2 / Confidence in the Nineteenth Century

1. The name stemmed from his trademark request to his victims to "have confidence" enough to entrust him with their property—which of course they never saw again. Essential to Thompson's success was his ability, through his genteel appearance and glib tongue, to convince perfect strangers that he was actually an old acquaintance momentarily forgotten (Melville 227).

2. See especially Halttunen; Lindberg. Lindberg writes, "I do not wish to argue that the con man is a unique American institution.... What I am suggesting is that the confidence man appears with surprising frequency and emphasis in American literature and popular culture, that this American trickster is peculiarly identified with the themes of promise and confidence, and that he reveals certain popular ambivalences of judgment" (9).

3. In this chapter I use the term "con *man*" deliberately, since the representations discussed here are notably male. In the previous chapter I explored how Ellen Craft, a female and gender-transgressive figure, also enacted the disability con. On confidence artists and fears of gender deception, see Reis 30.

4. See the March 2006 special issue of *Leviathan: A Journal of Melville Studies*, which includes two essays on disability in *The Confidence Man*, including an earlier version of this chapter. Mitchell and Snyder's essay in that volume also appears as a chapter in their *Cultural Locations of Disability*.

5. For specific political and historical contexts for the novel, see Trimpi; Cook.

6. See Albrecht; Braddock and Parish; Byrom; Stiker; Stone.

7. Most Melville critics, even those who specifically focus on the body, have tended to ignore disability altogether. Those who do address it usually treat it as a metaphor, as in the Trimpi example discussed in this chapter. Cameron, for example, discusses the theme of dismemberment in Melville as a sign of philosophical alienation from the body and its boundaries rather than in terms of actual physical disability (5).

8. As Pimple notes, there is much critical debate over whether the mute is the first incarnation of the confidence man (34). Interpretations of the mute's significance are equally diverse: Van Cromphout sees the mute as a theatricalized victim who represents absolute otherness to the passengers (40), while Lenz sees the mute as an ambivalent, mysterious, and eccentric figure (120), Cook reads the mute as "a displaced image of Melville in late adolescence" (85), and Trimpi suggests that the mute represents an

"evangelical preacher or missionary," perhaps based on the abolitionist writer and editor Benjamin Lundy (1789–1839) (39). See also Bryant for an overview of critical approaches to the character of the mute.

9. See Mitchell and Snyder, *Cultural Locations of Disability*, ch. 1, for a discussion of *The Confidence Man*, disability, and charity in nineteenth-century America.

10. In contrast to this stereotype, an 1859 letter written to the *American Annals of the Deaf and Dumb* excoriates mutes who travel as vagrants and offers an example whom Melville's confidence man would have welcomed as a brother: a hotelkeeper complains of "a mute, who assumed the air of a rich gentlemen, after having been with him for some days, [who] left for another hotel, and so on, till he had been at each hotel, when he took his departure for parts unknown without paying a cent!" (Chamberlayne 237–238).

11. "Although postrevolutionary Americans might feel humor, sympathy, benevolence, and even admiration for the familiar *local idiot*, after the panic of 1819 they began to view *idiocy* with a mixture of curiosity, anxiety, and after the Civil War, fear. This change of perspective—from particular individuals to a general type—began with a major shift in the way Americans dealt with a host of so-called worthy dependents (widows, orphans, and disabled people) and unworthy dependents (the unemployed and criminals)" (Trent 10). See also Byrom 133; Mitchell and Snyder, *Narrative Prosthesis* 121; Garland Thomson, *Extraordinary Bodies* 47.

12. For a full discussion of the roots and functions of this symbolic association, see Garland Thomson, *Extraordinary Bodies*; Norden; Cassuto. Mitchell and Snyder address this association in detail with regard to Ahab: "His incapacities—physical, sexual, and psychological—are all eventually chalked up to complications associated with his original dismemberment. . . . Disability conjures up a ubiquitous series of associations between corrupted exterior and contaminated interior" (*Narrative Prosthesis* 123, 139). One of several instances of such metaphors in *The Confidence Man* is the Methodist's comment on the wooden-legged man: "There he shambles off on his one lone leg, emblematic of his one-sided view of humanity" (12).

13. Stone explores the historical roots of this dynamic, noting that, while other traditional categories of social dependency—childhood, old age, and widowhood—are fairly easy to obtain information about, "disability . . . has always been more problematic, both because no single condition of 'disability' is universally recognized, and because physical and mental incapacity are conditions that can be feigned for secondary gain. Hence, the concept of disability has always been based on the perceived need to detect deception" (23).

14. Mitchell and Snyder are drawing on Samuel Otter's foundational discussion of these surface sciences in his 1999 *Melville's Anatomies*.

15. Parker's comment is found in the Norton edition of *The Confidence Man* which he edited (126n1).

16. Garland Thomson expands this point in her discussion of freak shows: "The American produces and acts, but the onstage freak is idle and passive. The American looks and names, but the freak is looked at and named. The American is mobile, entering and exiting the show at will and ranging around the social order, but the freak is fixed, confined by the material structures and the conventions of the staging and socially immobilized by a deviant body. The American is rational and controlled but

the freak is carnal and contingent" (*Extraordinary Bodies* 65). This analysis is also relevant to my discussion of Twain's "freakish" twins in chapter 5.

17. New York City Police Chief Peter Conlin, who led the 1896 crackdown on sham disabled beggars and soon thereafter authorized the arrest of beggars who truly were disabled, saw little distinction, since, in his words, "a number of beggars who are really afflicted and deformed" were "persistent," "impudent," and "a source of annoyance," and disgusted the ladies (qtd. in Norden 16).

3 / The Disability Con Onscreen

1. See Siebers; Samuels.

2. "Mr. Monk and the Red-Headed Stranger," season 12, episode 1, original air date October 11, 2002.

3. See www.transabled.org.

4. See Niver, for example.

5. Made in 1973, before the 1980s backlash against disability benefits, *The Sting*— unquestionably the classic con man movie of the late twentieth century—does not employ the disability con in any significant way, unlike its 1980s and 1990s analogues, discussed below.

6. See Gordon.

4 / The Trials of Salomé Müller

1. Qtd. in S. Cole, 12, my emphasis.

2. "Blood," *Law and Order*, season 8, original air date November 13, 1997.

3. *The Hidden Hand* was serialized by the *New York Ledger* three separate times between 1859 and 1883 before its publication as a book in 1888 (Ings 131; Southworth xlvi). What do we make of the fact that so many hand-shaped marks appeared in the time immediately preceding the introduction of fingerprints? I suggest that the idea that hands somehow carried clues to identity preceded the formal study of finger-prints and was already present in the cultural imaginary from which these authors drew their ideas. In doing so, of course, their works reinforced the cultural investment in locating identity in the hands, what Twain calls the "natal signature" written there, just as hands were used for writing (*Pudd'nhead Wilson* 109). See Rowe for further discussion of this association.

4. For evidence of how widely such notions were still held at the time, see W.G.

5. "By the late seventeenth century, however, color had become the primary orga-nizing principle around which the natural historian classified human differences, and a century later, it functioned as the visible precondition for anatomical investigations into the newly emergent object of knowledge, 'man'" (Wiegman 24).

6. Wiegman further argues:

> In tattooing, for instance, the sign of lowly status takes its form from an exterior branding, imposed at a precise point in time and performed by a disciplinary sys-tem readily available to the slave's immediate (however disempowered) return gaze. But in the application of disciplinary power to the entire surface of the body, in the manufacturing of a discourse of natural inferiority that resides, without physical imposition, on the skin—that application is the product of a different technology, one in which the processes of organization are similarly imposed but wholly veiled.

In this dispersion of the locus of power, the body is made the productive agent, a sign wrapped in the visibility it cannot help but wear. This does not mean that the public branding will no longer occur, but that from now on it plays a secondary role to the primacy of the bodily mark, reinforcing that mark through the seeming natural relation between visible body and auction block, plantation whipping, or later, lynch scene. (213n13)

7. The first quotation is taken from the work of historian Douglas Baynton (40), while the second is by the eighteenth-century racial scientist Samuel Stanhope Smith (qtd. in Martin 38).

8. See, for example, Henderson 4–7; Mitchell and Snyder, *Narrative Prosthesis* ix–x.

9. See Hartman for an extended discussion of how such exhibits and subsequent descriptions of violently marked bodies reinscribe such violations in the viewer and reader.

10. One contemporary literary example of scars functioning on this multivalenced level is Sethe's "chokecherry tree" of scars in Toni Morrison's *Beloved*.

11. Salomé Müller was known by several other names during her lifetime and in historical and literary documents, including Sally Miller, Salome Miller, Mary Miller, and Bridget Wilson. "Miller" is not a slurring of Müller, but the surname of her original master, John Fitz Miller. Preferring to err on the side of self-determination, I have chosen to call her Salomé Müller based on the apparent, though scanty, historical evidence that in freedom she claimed this name as her own. Scholars relying primarily on legal records, such as Keetley and Bailey, use the name "Sally Miller," which is recorded in the original lawsuit, *Miller v. Belmonti*.

12. I differ here from the interpretation offered by Gross, which emphasizes the extent to which Müller performed white womanhood (58–63). While this was undeniably a factor, the trial transcripts clearly declare the birthmarks to be the deciding factor in granting Müller her freedom.

13. See also Gross.

14. Haney López further notes that, by the 1920s, "in the Court's opinion, science had failed as an arbiter of human difference; common knowledge succeeded it as the touchstone of racial division. In elevating common knowledge, the Court no doubt remained convinced that racial divisions followed real, natural, physical differences. This explains the Court's frustration with science, which to the Court's mind was curiously and suspiciously unable to identify and quantify those racial differences so readily apparent to it" ("White by Law" 630). As I argue in the next chapter, however, the courts did not entirely abandon the quantifying power of science but reinvested its faith into the new science of identification, fingerprinting.

15. See *Miller v. Belmonti*; Cable 166, 178; "The Case of Salomé Müller" 197–198; Bailey 8, 139, 147, 176. William Wells Brown's account does not mention the birthmarks, while William and Ellen Craft declare that the midwife herself testified to the marks at the trial (Craft and Craft 5).

16. Examples of similar accounts include the following from the Boston law journal, the *Law Reporter*, published in 1845:

Among the other Germans who were called into the house of Mrs. Schubert, was the *accoucheuse* who assisted at the birth of the child Salomé Müller, in the village of Langensoultsback, on the Lower Rhine. Having identified her, she called Mrs. Schubert into an adjoining room, and asked her if she had a recollection of two very peculiar marks upon the person of the child, resembling moles, and about the size of coffee grains, upon the inner part of each thigh. Mrs. Schubert had a distinct recollection of the marks. . . . The plaintiff was then called into the room, and upon examination of her person the marks were perceived precisely as they were remembered by her godmother and the midwife. ("The Case of Salomé Müller" 197–198)

17. Petry ascribes to this concern the "oddly flat" and "dull" proliferation of names, dates, places, and other meticulously researched historical details with which Cable overwhelms the dramatic potential of his tale, for "Cable's decision to write a story that tells nothing but the truth in order to argue that (1) what we understand by the term 'truth' is at best unreliable and that (2) its unreliability is due largely to the words used to record and convey it, does not make for particularly satisfying reading: as with many experiments in writing, it pleases intellectually more than aesthetically" (22, 29–30).

18. "Knowability of racial categories is one of the myths of race" (Espinoza and Harris 445).

5 / Of Fiction and Fingerprints

1. In using the short titles *Pudd'nhead Wilson* and *Those Extraordinary Twins* I am following the format of the 1980 Norton critical edition because I find editor Sidney E. Berger's explanation of this choice convincing. Berger writes, "In most editions of this novel the title is given as *The Tragedy of Pudd'nhead Wilson*. But on the first page of the Morgan manuscript, in Clemens' own hand, the title is simply *Pudd'nhead Wilson, A Tale*." Berger's explanation for using "the simple title *Those Extraordinary Twins*," because on the title page of the first printed edition (American Publishing Company, 1894) "the words 'The Tragedy of' and 'And the Comedy' are printed in very small type, and seems to be more descriptive than titular," carries somewhat less authority than the preceding reference to Twain's original manuscript, but I am following his example here as well for consistency. It is certainly true, as Berger notes, that Twain's novel being a tragedy and his story a comedy remain "topics of debate among scholars" (*Pudd'nhead Wilson* xiv). See note 4 for more on the textual history of these works.

2. Wigger 518. See also Chinn 46–49; Gillman 88–89, 91; Cox 19; Rowe 180; Rogin 78–80; Sundquist, "Mark Twain" 63.

3. On Wilson as a scientist, see Gillman 90; Fredricks 495n13. Twain establishes Wilson as an all-knowing expert when Wilson declares during the trial, "There is hardly a person in this room, white or black, whose natal signature I cannot produce, and not one of them can so disguise himself that I cannot pick him out from a multitude of his fellow creatures and unerringly identify him by his hands. And if he and I should live to be a hundred I could still do it!" (*Pudd'nhead Wilson* 109).

4. The complete textual history of the work(s) is quite complicated. The two original 1892 manuscripts, the Berg manuscript, which is titled "Those Extraordinary Twins," and the longer Morgan manuscript, titled "Pudd'nhead Wilson," both precede Twain's decision to split the twins' story from the longer tale. After the "Caesarean operation," the *Pudd'nhead Wilson* section was serialized in the *Century Magazine* beginning in December 1893 and was published in book form in 1894 in the United States (by the American Publishing Company) and simultaneously in England (by Chatto & Windus). The American edition also included the excised twins material,

which Twain sold for an additional $1,500. The 1980 Norton critical edition referenced in this chapter uses the Morgan manuscript for most of its copy-text but takes the order of chapters and incidents from the *Century*. The other versions have also been critically incorporated where judged relevant by editor Sidney E. Berger (*Pudd'nhead Wilson* 173–181).

5. Hershel Parker is the best known of the critics of *Pudd'nhead Wilson* who see it as hopelessly flawed by the revision process and Twain's careless editing. See Russell's discussion (56–57). For another perspective, see Gillman and Robinson's introduction to *Pudd'nhead Wilson: Race, Conflict, and Culture*: "We read the incoherence in Twain's narrative not as aesthetic failure but as political symptom, the irruption into this narrative about mistaken racial identity of materials from the nineteenth-century political unconscious" (vii).

6. On gender in the novel, see Jehlen; Morris; Gillman.

7. See Gillman 82–83; Sundquist, "Mark Twain" 66.

8. Wu cogently argues that "the rendering of the Bunkers' anatomy . . . into a metaphor" and the "invocation of readily recognizable racial stereotypes about the Asian mind" are used by Twain in "Personal Habits" to depict "the seeming paradox of national unity with which many white Americans struggled during the latter part of the nineteenth century" (39).

9. Twain inconsistently describes this process as conferring control of the twins' "body" (*Those Extraordinary Twins* 127, 138, 139) or of their "legs" (139, 140, 143, 149–153, 155, 158, 167). However, the twins are consistently portrayed as having individual control of their upper bodies, so that it becomes clear that only the legs are meant, even when Twain refers to the "body."

10. Lennard Davis incorporates Galton's development of fingerprinting into his valuable discussion of the emergence of normalcy in the nineteenth century but does not address the role of disability in Galton's actual studies of fingerprinting (*Enforcing Normalcy* 32).

11. "I took a large number of prints from the worst idiots in the London district, through the obliging assistance of Dr. Fletcher Beech, of the Darenth Asylum" (Galton, *Finger Prints* 197). While I can find no exact record of when Galton visited the asylum, it was presumably between his first indication of interest in fingerprinting, in 1888, and the publication of these results in 1892.

6 / Proving Disability

1. In addition to Sandahl's brief discussion of *The Reciprocal Gaze* in her article "Ahh, Freak Out," she can also be seen performing it in the 1996 documentary film *Vital Signs: Crip Culture Talks Back*.

2. Formerly the ICIDH (International Classification of Impairment, Disability, and Handicap), which was revised in 2001 in part in response to criticism by disability rights advocates. See Wendell, ch. 1, for an insightful overview of different disability definitions. See Mitchell and Snyder, *Cultural Locations*, for discussion of the revision of the ICIDH.

3. For another illustrative example, see Longmore, *Why I Burned My Book*, in which he describes burning his biography of George Washington to protest Social Security rules which meant that earning any royalties from the book would cut off his access to the ventilator he needed to stay alive. The ventilator, like

the attendant services needed by Panzarino, cost far more than either individual could earn by working, but by making such services contingent on zero income, the system functions to push many disabled people who could earn a living into enforced poverty and total dependency on the state. This situation has somewhat improved through new Social Security programs such as the Plan to Achieve Self Support, largely due to the activism of Panzarino, Longmore, and others in the disability rights movement, but is still far from enabling the majority of disabled Americans to work and live independently. Currently the rate of unemployment for disabled people in the United States is 26 percent, and 25 percent of noninstitutionalized disabled Americans live below the poverty line (National Center for Disability Statistics, http://www.ilr.cornell.edu/edi/disabilitystatistics/index.cfm, accessed May 28, 2011).

4. All discussion of state disabled parking permit applications in this chapter draws on the application forms and guidelines accessible online for each state in 2012.

5. Canada's provinces all require a uniform 50 meters, about 150 feet, or, as Manitoba's application helpfully explains, "roughly the distance from a mall's parking lot to its entrance." Apparently Canadians do not need to walk quite as far as do people in the United States, and disabled people who cross the national border may again find themselves redefined by these subjective statutes.

6. The Social Security Administration uses a completely different definition of "severely disabled," meaning those who are unable to work altogether or are unable to work regularly (Haber 324). Panzarino, in the example cited earlier, would be considered quite severely disabled in terms of parking, but not disabled at all in terms of employability.

7. I do not mean to suggest that disabled people whose impairments stay the same or worsen should be ungrateful or miserable but rather to point out that for those of us who live with various levels of pain and debilitation, the reduction of pain or increase of strength often brings a sense of joy and satisfaction, of rediscovering aspects of our physical selves. I bring up this issue to highlight the ugliness of a medico-administrative attitude that implies that we might not want to feel better or be more independent because we might lose our precious parking places.

8. Their website is www.handicappedfraud.org.

9. See http://www.handicappedfraud.org/gfx/stateletters_florida.jpg; http://www.handicappedfraud.org/gfx/stateletters_hawaii.jpg.

10. As of September 2012. New postings appear every week.

11. The site prescribes the following steps: "1) Don't confront the person. These people may be handicapped, and we don't want to create any hassle for them. Or, they may be law breakers, and could become very agitated at being pointed out. 2) Record their license plate number. 3) Record their placard number (on the placard itself). 4) Leave a post-it note on their car that says they've been reported at HandicappedFraud.org."

12. While one might argue for a more logical relationship between high heels and mobility, the fact is that many mobility-disabled women are able to wear heels exactly because they can walk only very short distances and so do not feel the effects as do nondisabled women who walk and stand on heels all day. I would also assert that a disabled woman with a valid permit should be able to choose whatever footwear she desires without being subject to perpetual challenges by strangers and society at large.

13. In the following chapter I discuss Halualani on "performances of proving" in the Native context.

14. Walking on a treadmill is an extremely common form of physical therapy strengthening for people with mobility disabilities.

7 / Revising Blood Quantum

1. Throughout this book I use *American Indian* and *Indian* to refer to Native peoples of the mainland United States, and *Native* as an inclusive term for indigenous peoples of the Americas, including Native Alaskans, Native Hawai'ians, and Native and Métis people living in Canada.

2. "Many BIA regulations governing the administration of federal Indian benefit programs also rely on a one-half or one-quarter blood quantum requirement. Examples of such regulations include the Indian Hiring Preference, Employment Assistance for Adult Indians, Vocation Training for Adult Indians, Educational Loans and Grants, and Land Acquisition. In addition, the BIA's Indian Education policies define an eligible Indian or Alaska Native student as one who is 'recognized by the Secretary of the Interior as eligible for Federal Services, because of their status as Indians or Alaska Natives, whose Indian blood quantum is ¼ degree or more'" (Brownwell 280–281).

3. For examples of Indian perspectives against the use of blood quantum, see Balu; Barker; Brownwell; Cramer; Nagel; Strong and Van Winkle; Tallbear, "DNA." For those who feel it has value when administered by tribal authorities, see Garroute; Miller. For discussions of tribal or individual endorsement of blood quantum, see Lawrence; Sturm; Meyer; Fitzgerald.

4. In March 1999 Indians in Denver marched in protest over the use of blood quantum, demonstrating the urgency felt in particular by urban Indian communities toward identificatory policies that often exclude them (Brownwell 309).

5. For a discussion of recent efforts to use DNA to determine blood quantum, see chapter 9.

6. See Barker 31, 42; Brownwell 280; Fitzgerald 69; Gross 153–160; Meyer 232–233; Welburn 300.

7. This document is now officially titled "Certificate of Degree of Indian or Native Alaskan Blood" but is still commonly referred to as the CDIB.

8. On the importance of culture and kinship, see Sturm; Meyer; Garroute.

9. "You're frowned on if you're not identifiable. The stigma is that you're *yonega* [white]. Some people have a lot of problems, especially younger kids, if you're not identifiable. That's sad" (Cherokee elder qtd. in Sturm 114). See also T. Wilson 109, 122; Fitzgerald 171–185.

10. See Nagel 91; Brownwell 317.

11. "Bureau of Indian Affairs Certificate of Degree of Indian or Alaska Native Blood Instructions," OMB Control #1076–0153, expiration date October 31, 2014. Downloaded from www.bia.gov.

12. See Cramer 18–21; Brownwell 288; Nagel 242.

13. "Even the most restrictive of these federal rules may seem lax when compared to the specific enrollment rules of particular recognized tribes, which can specify amount or type of ancestry or impose residency requirements for membership" (Nagel 242). While ultimate decision making about tribal membership rests with the

tribal governments, and their deployments of blood quantum play a crucial role in determinations of Indian status, I focus in this chapter on federal uses of blood quantum in order to illuminate its relationship to the national investment in the fantasy of identification.

14. "White officials used the terms 'half blood' and 'mixed blood' to stand for 'politically progressive'—that is, assimilationist, in favor of U.S. citizenship and adoption of American land use practices—whereas 'full blood' meant to them 'conservative' or 'traditionalist' as much as it referred to any actual designation of ancestry. But these distinctions first took on legal and economic significance only after enrollment and allotment, when federal legislation passed in 1904 and 1908 lifted restrictions on the right to sell or transfer one's land allotment according to blood quantum" (Gross 160).

15. See Cramer; Spruhan, "The Origins"; TallBear, "DNA"; Meyer 241. Tom Jones's 2013 exhibit, *Identity Genocide* explicitly responds to the impact of casino revenues on definitions of Ho Chunk identity within his tribe. On the controversial changes that have excluded Cherokee freedmen and Black Seminoles, see Brooks; Gross 169–176.

16. In 1986 President Reagan proposed reinstating a one-quarter blood quantum requirement for IHS, but tribal opposition quashed the attempt (LaValle 16).

17. See http://www.ihs.gov/IHM/.

18. Table is reproduced from the *IHS Standard Code Book*, "Blood Quantum," www.ihs.gov/scb.

19. See http://www.ihs.gov/NDW/documents/Data_TC/W_DataQualityMart_UG _V1.0.pdf.

20. This current (as of 2013) policy may well be one of the "hidden regulations" regarding blood quantum for which the BIA was reprimanded by the Department of the Interior in 1986, according to Brownwell (289).

21. For example, the demand "Show me your CDIB" to prove Cherokee identity in Oklahoma exists in paradoxical combination with a view of "the whole idea of blood quantum as one of the mechanisms that White society uses to divide Indians from one another" (Hamill 281).

22. On this controversy, see Allen; Strong and Van Winkle.

23. Tom Jones, "Artist's Statement for Identity Genocide," 2012, personal communication.

24. See http://tomjoneshochunk.com/.

25. Based on the pictures I have been able to find, this appears to be true of the installation at the Eiteljorg Museum of American Indian and Western Art in Indianapolis in 2005, not of the original 2002 installation at the Sacred Circle Gallery in Seattle. See S'eiltin; Nottage.

26. Muñoz uses this quotation from Butler in his explication of disidentification (12).

27. For discussion and critiques of the social model of disability, see Shakespeare; Wendell.

28. "'Blood' is, by now, thoroughly embedded, one way or another, in the construction of Native American identity. . . . Dismantling the intricate edifice of racism embodied in 'Indian blood' is not simply a matter of exposing its essentialism and discarding its associated policies, but a more delicate and complicated task: that is, acknowledging 'Indian blood' as a discourse of conquest with manifold and contradictory effects, but without invalidating rights and resistances that have been couched in terms of that very discourse" (Strong and Van Winkle 563, 565).

29. See Teuton.

8 / Realms of Biocertification

1. On the uniqueness of certification for American Indians compared to other U.S. ethnic and racial groups, see Brownwell 309; Fitzgerald 159. On the deployment of biocertification in relation to sex/gender, see chapter 9.

2. As in the previous chapter, I use *American Indian* and *Indian* to refer to Native peoples of the mainland United States, and *Native* as an inclusive term for indigenous peoples of the Americas, including Native Alaskans, Native Hawai'ians, and Native and Métis people living in Canada.

3. On the inverse relationship between "looking Indian" and needing to provide certification of Indian identity, see Sturm 114; Allen 97; Cramer 60; Fitzgerald 166–185; Meyer 239. "According to BIA internal documents, persons either capable of establishing their Indian ancestry or 'exhibiting sufficient "Indian" physical characteristics to be equated with possession of one-half or more degree of Indian blood' were told they were entitled to benefits established by the IRA" (Brownwell 288). On disability biocertification and assumptions about "looking disabled," see chapter 6.

4. See Schweik, "Disability": "These histories of exclusion, removal, dependence, interdependence, and independence are not in any way separate stories" (420). On the pitfalls and potentialities of analogies between identity categories, see Samuels.

5. I do not mean to imply that "Native people" and "disabled people" are two discrete groups; of course, many Native people have disabilities, and vice versa. However, political critiques and movements centering on each identity have largely operated in isolation from one another, and it is that separation—of bodies of knowledge and social movements—which this chapter seeks to bridge. For more on the racial isolation of disability studies, see Bell. For intersections between American Indian and disability identities, see Schweik, "Disability"; forthcoming work by Susan Burch on the institutionalization of American Indians labeled mentally ill.

6. See Spruhan, "A Legal History" 4–8, on previous, sporadic deployments of blood quantum on the state level.

7. "Between 1887 and 1905, Allotment reduced tribal lands from 138 million acres to 52 million acres. A full 86 million acres of tribal land, or two-thirds of all tribal territory, went into white hands as a result of the Dawes Act" (Cramer 17).

8. See Cramer 7; Gross 177. See also sources discussed in chapter 7.

9. As Sturm observes in the case of Oklahoma Cherokees, "the justification for this division between fuller bloods and lesser bloods was based on the eugenic notion that 'competency,' the ability to understand the complex and shifting system of land tenure in Oklahoma, somehow correlated with degree of race mixture" (79).

10. "The key players in the HHCA [Hawaiian Homes Commission Act] hearings redefined 'need' in racial terms by using blood quantum as an indicator of social competency, where those defined by the 50-percent rule were deemed incapable of looking out for themselves" (Kauanui 8).

11. For extended discussions of these events, see Trent; Carey; Carlson.

12. Similarly Mitchell and Snyder, in their study of American eugenic discourses, explain, "Unlike other critical studies of this period, which regard disability as a slander upon otherwise *able* populations, our argument positions disabled people as unjustly mired within their own dehumanizing classifications. In taking this

approach, we situate disability not as a marker of inferiority, but rather as representing an array of maligned differences akin to other socially denigrated communities" (*Cultural Locations* 74). See also Baynton.

13. "The underlying principle for such restrictions was summarized by U.S. Supreme Court Justice William Strong in *Dexter v. Hall* (1872) when he stated that a contract required 'the assent of two minds. But a lunatic, or a person non compos mentis, has nothing which the law recognizes as a mind, and it would seem, therefore, upon principle, that he cannot make a contract which may have any efficacy as such'" (Carey 38–39).

14. Thanks to Tom Jones for pointing me to the Indian Relocation Act in relation to this dynamic, particularly the practice of buying Indians one-way bus tickets to urban areas. This practice continued the fracturing dynamic described by Cramer as beginning at the time of allotment: "With the Dawes Act, U.S. Indian policy changed from forced removal of Indian tribes onto consolidated reservation lands to one of assimilation, population shifting, and detribalization. . . . American Indians were meant to lose their separate ethnic identities and become *citizens*" (17).

15. See Gross 201; Halualani 155; Kauanui 2.

16. Here we also see the double bind of defining eligibility to receive land by Native blood quantum and competency by white blood quantum:

> Thus, as the legal discourse goes, the more "pure" a Hawai'ian is (100 percent), the less she or he is a self-determined, independent American citizen with rights and privileges; the more "mixed" a Hawai'ian is (30 and 50 percent, respectively, and below), the less she or he is entitled to make a cultural claim to Hawai'ian land, artifacts, and practice (for the amount of "Hawai'ianness" is practically nothing); and the more she or he (as an assimilable citizen) absolves the political state from recognizing its own colonial shadow. (Halualani 163–164)

17. See sources cited in chapter 2: Albrecht; Braddock and Parish; Byrom; Stiker. On the development of rehabilitation for the "feeble-minded," see Carlson; Trent.

18. Schweik similarly observes that at, the turn of the century, "like 'disability' and 'work,' 'Indian' and 'ability and willingness to work' were, apparently, a near contradiction in terms" ("Disability" 428).

19. See chapters 1, 2, and 3 for discussions of the construction and enforcement of the distinction between deserving and undeserving poor through categories of real and feigned disability. On the history of welfare in the United States, see Gordon.

20. "Once participants shifted away from an entitlement framework for rehabilitation, in terms of Hawaiians' right to the lands in question, the blood racialization of Hawaiians was able to take hold because they were then basing eligibility for the proposal on a welfare framework and understanding of who was most deserving" (Kauanui 138–139).

21. See http://hawaii.gov/dhhl/.

22. *Hawaiian Data Book* 2006, 39, http://www.oha.org/pdf/databook/2006/Data-Book2006LandHoldings.pdf; Department of Hawaiian Home Lands *2011 Annual Report*, http://dhhl.hawaii.gov/icro/annual-reports/.

23. Summaries of the *Honolulu Star Advertiser*'s three-part series exposing mismanagement of Hawai'ian homelands grants, published in May of 2013, can be found at http://www.

oiwi.tv/channels/news/star-advertiser-3-part-expose-on-the-department-of-hawaiian-homelands/, accessed September 3, 2013.

24. Pennsylvania Training School for Feeble-Minded Children, 1858, qtd. in Trent 29–30.

25. Such "hair tests" were employed again in 1936, in the case of the Lumbee Indians of Robeson County, North Carolina. Harvard anthropologist Carl Selzer "measured their features and put a pencil in each Indian's hair, noting 'Indian' blood if the pencil slipped through and 'Negroid' if it did not. The 'diagnoses' were based solely on physical characteristics. The absurd results of his study listed children as Indian while omitting their parents and placed brothers and sisters on opposite sides of the half-blood line. Of the 209 Indians Selzer 'diagnosed,' he concluded that only twenty-two were Indians" (Brownwell 288–289).

26. See http://forums.powwows.com/f26/blood-quantum-what-does-being-indian-actually-mean-22821/, accessed August 20, 2013.

27. See Haney López, "White by Law"; Goldberg.

28. On self-identification, see Barker; Brownwell. On the scarcity model, see Beckenhauer.

29. See chapters 2, 3, and 6.

30. For examples of biocertification in nineteenth-century court cases regarding mixed black-white individuals, see chapter 4. For an excellent discussion of an early twentieth-century case, see Chinn's discussion of the Rhinelander trial. For an atypical example of a contemporary mixed-race person accused of claiming to be black for personal advantage, see Piper.

31. For instance, "the Association of American Indian and Alaska Native Professors has developed a formal Statement on Ethnic Fraud that . . . warns educational institutions about applicants who inappropriately claim a tribal identity" (Garroute 87).

32. See also Miller 7; Lawrence 23.

9 / DNA and the Readable Self

1. Yet it is also true that "genetic avisuality troubles an imaginary driven by the fantasy of a revelatory science. The gap between the precision of reading someone's genes technically (of being able to prove someone's presence at a crime scene from a fragment of skin, for example) and the elusiveness of the visual evidence of genetic artifice produces both the desire for certainty and the fear of its impossibility" (Stacey 265). The tension between this desire and fear, I suggest, is one of the driving forces behind our insistent fantasies of genetic identification.

2. By naming genetics as comparatively real science, I do not mean to reify it, or any realm of science, as purely objective or absolute. The work of many scholars has amply demonstrated the constructed nature of scientific knowledge, as well as the ways supposedly objective models encode racial and gendered assumption. (See, for example, Gould; Magnet; Schiebinger). However, I do contend that within the constructed realm of science, it is possible to distinguish between more or less reliable inquiries and methodologies, and genetics does differ significantly from the other forms of "science" discussed in this book since it is research-based, peer-reviewed, and otherwise developed in accordance with the scientific method—unlike, for example, racialist anthropology or Galton's work on fingerprinting.

3. See Beckenhauer 175.

4. On the film *Gattaca*, Stacey writes, "The promise of genetic screening is to give a scientific certainty to the fantasy of authorship and autonomy that governs conventional masculinity. The film systematically presents but then undoes the foundations of such a fantasy, through its exposure of the illusions of the predictive certainty of genetic codes" (126).

5. For further discussion of the difference between these two forms of testing, and their marketing to tribal communities, see TallBear, "Native."

6. See also the discussions of race and genetics in Koenig et al.

7. The Genelex statements come from an advertisement they placed in the *Indian Country Today* newsweekly on September 22, 2004 (Tallbear, "Native" 243). Text from Gene DNA Test was found on their now defunct website on April 24, 2011. Text from Mitochondrial DNA Test was found on their website on April 24, 2011. In 2013 Genelex has removed all reference to "Native American DNA testing" from their website, but other sites have appeared offering similar services and making similar claims, such as FamilyTreeDNA and Accumetrics. Given the rapidly evolving medium of the Internet and swiftly changing landscape of home genetic testing, new websites and testing services will likely continue to emerge and vanish over the coming years.

8. The Mashantucket Pequot have reportedly considered actually using DNA tests for enrollment purposes. However, because no tribe has been isolated throughout its history, "in all likelihood genetic markers found in the Pequot also exist in many other tribes. Consequently, adoption of a DNA-based enrollment policy might actually expand the number of individuals qualifying for tribal enrollment" (TallBear and Bolnick).

9. "The chief of the Western Mohegan and Representative Fred Maslack both referred to 'identity' as being a matter of either having the appropriate paperwork or having done conclusive DNA testing, and the proposed legislation was concerned with proving biological authenticity of the Mohegan" (TallBear, "DNA" 86). See also Beckenhauer 184–186.

10. "Insofar as genetic testing is criticized for attempting to define a social identity using biological characteristics, it differs remarkably little from the use of blood quantum standards: both are undeniably biological measures" (Beckenhauer 187).

11. See Rothman 187–192; Le Breton 5–10.

12. Fausto-Sterling quotes Leslie Feinberg as calling for an end to the biocertification of sex/gender: "Sex categories should be removed from all basic identification papers—from driver's licenses to passports—and since the right of each person to define their own sex is so basic, it should be eliminated from birth certificates as well." Fausto-Sterling goes on to ask, "Indeed, why are physical genitals necessary for identification? Surely attributes both more visible (such as height, build, and eye color) and less visible (fingerprints and DNA profiles) would be of greater use" (*Sexing* 111). Here she invokes forms of bodily identification that are supposedly less value-laden and oppressive than those based on sex. Yet, as I have argued throughout this book, all such forms of bio-identification are embedded within power relationships and inevitably become charged with meanings related to bodily aspects such as sex, gender, race, and dis/ability.

13. See also Dreger, *Hermaphrodites*; Fausto-Sterling, *Sexing*.

14. The tension between these two fantasies is captured in Le Breton's description of the effect of genetic science on bodily normativity: "Previously, there was a norm that operated in relation to appearances and forms of behavior, leaving a certain room

for manoeuvre, but today the norm penetrates the invisible interior of the body: the gene" (11).

15. See also Fausto-Sterling, *Sexing* 40.

16. Heggie offers a correction to the dominant narrative regarding sex testing when she notes that there were attempts at systematic sex testing as early as the 1940s, and also that historical narratives of "gender fraud" have tended to exaggerate tales of individuals with Nazi or communist affiliations while ignoring their British or American counterparts (158–159, 161).

17. This is an important and corrective context to Heggie's claim that no one *officially* failed the Barr body test after 1968, which she could be due to athletes being prescreened in their home countries (160).

18. An excellent capsule summary of the history of sex testing in international sports can be found in Wonkam et al. 546.

19. See also Puffer 1543.

20. Biocertification has also been deployed in the arena of LGBT sports: "During the 2002 Sydney Gay Games, all competitors had to choose one of the two categories to compete in, for those events organized under male or female divisions. Legal documentation was required to verify one's chosen division. . . . Interestingly, and similar in many respects to 'Fem Cards,' the Gay Games administrators would provide an Accreditation Pass to registered participants" (Sullivan 411).

21. Heggie notes that medical certificates of femininity began to be required by the IAAF in 1946 and the IOC in 1948, but "although certificates were required, these were not evidence of a standardized, internationally recognized gender test" (159). The discovery of the Barr body provided the necessary scientific underpinning for this nascent form of biocertification to become fully institutionalized.

22. At the 1996 Atlanta Olympics, 3,387 female athletes were issued gender verification cards. All but 296 had genetic testing at this time (those had certificates from previous Olympics; Elsas et al. 252).

23. For a discussion of Martínez-Patiño's story, see Elsas et al. 250; Hercher 552; Fausto-Sterling, *Sexing* 1–2; Kolata, "Gender Testing"; Sullivan 405–406.

24. See, for example, Smith, "Athlete Caster Semenya."

25. See "Caster Semenya's Mother Hits Out at Gender Dispute"; Smith, "Gender Row" and "Caster Semenya Row."

26. See Smith, "Caster Is a Cover Girl"; "Makeover for SA Gender-Row Runner." See also Chase.

27. Online commenter on Kessel, "Gold."

28. Online commenter on G. Turner.

29. Online commenter on Kessel, "Gold."

30. See Camporesi and Maugeri 379; Dreger, "The Sex of Athletes"; Levy.

31. Many reports indicate that Semenya thought she was simply going for another urinary drug test and instead was subjected to invasive gynecological exams and blood work. Additionally details about the testing procedure and purported results were often reported in the media before they were communicated to Semenya herself. Wilfrid Daniels, an Athletics South Africa official who resigned over the handling of Semenya, has described finding Semenya on the day before the Berlin championship, glued to the television's coverage about the announced sex tests: "And they're talking about her and she's trying to understand what they're saying. Because nobody has

spoken to her, to tell her, look, this is what these tests might mean. I felt so ashamed" (qtd. in Levy).

32. We may also note here the inclusion of some odd language in the *IAAF Regulations* that suggests both translation difficulties and a rush to get the new guidelines into print, but nevertheless jibes oddly with their presentation as medically precise and legally binding documents. The most notable of these is the listing of a Ferriman and Gallwey hirsutism score high enough to provoke suspicions of hyperandrogenism as: ">6 / ! minimized by the beauty" (IAAF *Regulations* 20). One can only imagine what was possibly meant by this exclamatory addendum, but it certainly does not provoke confidence in the authors of the guidelines as trustworthy regulators of "authentic" femaleness or femininity.

33. Dr. Vilain apparently changed his mind and became a vocal defender of the use of testosterone levels to determine eligibility in the 2012 IOC guidelines (Jordan-Young and Karkazis).

34. See Camporesi and Maugeri 379; Dreger, "Where's the Rulebook"; Karkazis et al. 11.

35. On female masculinity as social threat and transgressive positionality, see Halberstam.

36. A similar effect is described by Garland Thomson in responses to Julia Pastrana, a nineteenth-century hirsute Mexican woman displayed in both freak shows and medical settings: "Pastrana's deviance is in her body's combination of male and female markers, in the troubling coincidence of 'a beard' and 'moustache and whiskers' with 'remarkably full' breasts and menstruation" (*Extraordinary Bodies* 73).

37. "Website Makes Caster Boob." The ill-phrased headline of this article drew many witticisms from online commenters.

38. As June Thomas wrote on Slate.com, "Even if [Semenya] started every press conference by reciting her estrogen level that day, she'd still be suspect."

39. Ornstein; J. Thomas; "Caster Semenya Denies."

Bibliography

Accardo, Pasquale J. *Diagnosis and Detection: The Medical Iconography of Sherlock Holmes.* Rutherford, NJ: Fairleigh Dickinson University Press, 1987. Print.

Albrecht, Gary L. *The Disability Business: Rehabilitation in America.* Newbury Park, CA: Sage, 1992. Print.

Allen, Chadwick. "Blood (and) Memory." *American Literature* 71.1 (1999): 93–116. Print.

Althusser, Louis. "Ideology and Ideological State Apparatuses: Notes toward an Investigation." *Lenin and Philosophy and Other Essays.* New York: Monthly Review Press, 1971. 127–186. Print.

Anderson, Benedict. *Imagined Communities: Reflections on the Origin and Spread of Nationalism.* 1983. New York: Verso, 1996. Print.

Andrews, William L. Introduction. *Two Biographies by African-American Women.* Ed. Henry Louis Gates Jr. Oxford: Oxford University Press, 1991. xxxiii–xliii. Print.

———. *To Tell a Free Story.* Chicago: University of Illinois Press, 1986. Print.

Armistead, Wilson. *Five Hundred Thousand Strokes of Freedom.* 1853. Miami: Mnemosyne, 1969. Print.

Bailey, John. *The Lost German Slave Girl: The Extraordinary True Story of Sally Miller and Her Fight for Freedom in Old New Orleans.* New York: Atlantic Monthly Press, 2003. Print.

Baker, Houston. *Workings of the Spirit: The Poetics of Afro-American Women's Writing.* Chicago: University of Chicago Press, 1991. Print.

Balu, Rekha. "Indian Identity: Who's Drawing the Boundaries?" *American Bar Association.* Web. http://www.nativeweb.org/pages/legal/identity.html.

Bankole, Katherine. *Slavery and Medicine: Enslavement and Medical Practices in Antebellum Louisiana.* New York: Garland, 1998. Print.

Barclay, Jenifer L. "Health, Disability, and Soundness." *Enslaved Women in America: An Encyclopedia.* Ed. Daina R. Berry. Greenwood Press/ABC-CLIO, 2012. Google Ebook.

Barker, Joanne. "Indian USA." *Wicazo Sa Review* 18.1 (2003): 25–79. Print.

Barrett, Lindon. "Hand-Writing: Legibility and the White Body in *Running a Thousand Miles for Freedom.*" *American Literature* 69.2 (1997): 315–336. Print.

Baudrillard, Jean. "The Precession of Simulacra." 1976. *Media and Cultural Studies: Keyworks.* Ed. Douglas M. Kellner and Meenakshi Gigi Durham. Oxford: Blackwell, 2001. 521–549. Print.

Baynton, Douglas. "Disability and the Justification of Inequality in American History." *The New Disability History: American Perspectives.* Ed. Paul K. Longmore and Lauri Umansky. New York: New York University Press, 2001. 33–57. Print.

Beaulieu, David. "Curly Hair and Big Feet: Physical Anthropology and the Implementation of Land Allotment on the White Earth Chippewa Reservation." *American Indian Quarterly* 7 (1984): 281–314. Print.

Beavan, Colin. *Fingerprints: The Origins of Crime Detection and the Murder Case That Launched Forensic Science.* New York: Hyperion, 2001. Print.

Beckenhauer, Eric. "Redefining Race: Can Genetic Testing Provide Biological Proof of Indian Ethnicity?" *Stanford Law Review* 56.1 (2003): 161–190. Print.

Bell, Christopher, ed. *Blackness and Disability: Critical Examinations and Cultural Interventions.* East Lansing: Michigan State University Press, 2012.

———. "Is Disability Studies Actually White Disability Studies?" *The Disability Studies Reader.* Ed. Lennard J. Davis. 3rd ed. New York: Routledge. 2005. 374–382. Print.

Bellis, Peter J. *No Mysteries Out of Ourselves: Identity and Textual Form in the Novels of Herman Melville.* Philadelphia: University of Pennsylvania Press, 1990. Print.

Berkson, Dorothy. "Mark Twain's Two-Headed Novel: Racial Symbolism and Social Realism in Pudd'nhead Wilson." *Studies in American Humor* 3.4 (1984): 309–320. Print.

Berlant, Lauren. *The Anatomy of National Fantasy: Hawthorne, Utopia, and Everyday Life.* Chicago: University of Chicago Press, 1991. Print.

Bérubé, Michael. "Citizenship and Disability." *Dissent* 50.2 (2003): 52–57.

———. *Life As We Know It: A Father, a Family, and an Exceptional Child.* New York: Random House, 1996. Print.

Bhabha, Homi K. *The Location of Culture.* New York: Routledge, 1994. Print.

Bhowmick, Nilanjana, and Jyoti Thottam. "Gender and Athletics: India's Own Caster Semenya." *Time* 1 Sept. 2009. Web.

Bieder, Robert E. *Science Encounters the Indian, 1920–1880: The Early Years of American Ethnology.* Norman: University of Oklahoma Press, 1986. Print.

Blackett, R. J. M. "The Odyssey of William and Ellen Craft." *Running a Thousand Miles for Freedom: The Escape of William and Ellen Craft from Slavery.* 1860. Baton Rouge: Louisiana State University Press, 1999. Print.

Bland, Sterling Lecater, Jr., ed. *African-American Slave Narratives: An Anthology.* 3 vols. Westport, CT: Greenwood Press, 2001. Print.

———. *Voices of the Fugitives: Runaway Slave Stories and Their Fictions of Self Creation.* Westport, CT: Greenwood Press, 2000. Print.

Blassingame, John W. "Using the Testimony of Ex-Slaves." *The Slave's Narrative.* Ed. Charles T. Davis and Henry Louis Gates Jr. New York: Oxford University Press, 1985. 81–92. Print.

Blumenthal, Susanna. "The Default Legal Person." *UCLA Law Review* 54.5 (2007): 1135–1265. Print.

Boster, Dea Hadley. *African American Slavery and Disability: Bodies, Property and Power in the Antebellum South, 1800–1860.* New York: Routledge, 2012. Print.

Braddock, David L., and Susan L. Parish. "An Institutional History of Disability." *Handbook of Disability Studies.* Ed. Gary L. Albrecht et al. Thousand Oaks, CA: Sage, 2001. 23–31. Print.

Brookes, Martin. *Extreme Measures: The Dark Visions and Bright Ideas of Francis Galton.* New York: Bloomsbury, 2004. Print.

Brooks, James F., ed. *Confounding the Color Line: The Indian-Black Experience in North America.* Lincoln: University of Nebraska Press, 2002. Print.

Browder, Laura. *Slippery Characters: Ethnic Impersonators and American Identities.* Chapel Hill: University of North Carolina Press, 2000. Print.

Brown, Josephine. *Biography of an American Bondsman.* 1856. *Two Biographies by African-American Women.* Ed. Henry Louis Gates Jr. Oxford: Oxford University Press, 1991. 3–104. Print.

Brown, Steven E. "What Is Disability Culture?" *Disability Studies Quarterly* 22.2 (2002): 34–50. Print.

Brown, William Wells. *Clotel; or, The President's Daughter.* 1853. Ed. M. Giulia Fabi. New York: Penguin, 2004. Print.

———. *Clotelle: A Tale of the Southern States.* 1864. *William Wells Brown and Clotelle: A Portrait of the Artist in the First Negro Novel.* Ed. J. Noel Heermance. North Haven, CT: Archon Books, 1969. 1–104. Print.

Brownell, Margo. "Who Is an Indian? Searching for an Answer to the Question at the Core of Federal Indian Law." *University of Michigan Journal of Law Reform* 34.1 (2001): 275–320. Print.

Brusky, Sarah. "The Travels of William and Ellen Craft." *Prospects: An Annual of American Cultural Studies* 25 (2000): 177–192. Print.

Bryant, John. "The Confidence-Man: Melville's Problem Novel." *A Companion to Melville Studies.* Ed. John Bryant. New York: Greenwood Press, 1986. 315–350. Print.

Burch, Susan. "Dislocated Pasts: Removals, Asylums, and Community in

American History." Unpublished talk. University of Wisconsin, Madison. 16 Apr. 2012.

Butler, Judith. *Bodies That Matter: On the Discursive Limits of "Sex."* New York: Routledge, 1993. Print.

———. *Undoing Gender.* New York: Routledge, 2004. Print.

Byerman, Keith. "We Wear the Mask: Deceit as Theme and Style in Slave Narratives." *The Art of Slave Narrative: Original Essays in Criticism and Theory.* Ed. John Sekora and Darwin T. Turner. Macomb: Western Illinois University Press, 1982. 70–82. Print.

Byrom, Brad. "A Pupil and a Patient: Hospital-Schools in Progressive America." *The New Disability History: American Perspectives.* Ed. Paul K. Longmore and Lauri Umansky. New York: New York University Press, 2001. 133–156. Print.

Cable, George Washington. "Salome Müller, the White Slave." *Strange True Stories of Louisiana.* Boston: Berwick and Smith, 1889. Print.

Callow, James. "Caster Semenya Faces Growing Backlash after Competitors Have Their Say." *Guardian.* 23 Aug. 2010. Web..

Cameron, Sharon. *The Corporeal Self: Allegories of the Body in Melville and Hawthorne.* Baltimore: Johns Hopkins University Press, 1981. Print.

Campbell, Fiona Kumari. "Legislating Disability: Negative Ontologies and the Government of Legal Identities." *Foucault and the Government of Disability.* Ed. Shelley Tremain. Ann Arbor: University of Michigan Press, 2005. 108–130. Print.

Camporesi, Silvia, and Paolo Maugeri. "Caster Semenya: Sport, Categories, and the Creative Role of Ethics." *Journal of Medical Ethics* 36 (2010): 378–379. Print.

Caplan, Jane. "'This or That Particular Person': Protocols of Identification in Nineteenth-Century Europe." *Documenting Individual Identity: The Development of State Practices in the Modern World.* Ed. Jane Caplan and John Torpey. Princeton: Princeton University Press, 2001. 49–66. Print.

Caplan, Jane, and John Torpey, eds. *Documenting Individual Identity: The Development of State Practices in the Modern World.* Princeton: Princeton University Press, 2001. Print.

Cardinal-Schubert, Joane. "Artist's Statement on *Preservation of a Species: DECONSTRUCTIVISTS (This is the house that Joe built)." Indigena: Contemporary Native Perspectives.* Ed. Gerald McMaster and Lee-Ann Martin. Hull, Quebec: Canadian Museum of Civilization, 1992. 132–135. Print.

Carey, Allison C. *On the Margins of Citizenship: Intellectual Disability and Civil Rights in Twentieth-Century America.* Philadelphia: Temple University Press, 2009. Print.

Carlson, Licia. "Docile Bodies, Docile Minds: Foucauldian Reflections on Mental Retardation." *Foucault and the Government of Disability.* Ed. Shelley Tremain. Ann Arbor: University of Michigan Press, 2005. 133–152. Print.

"The Case of Salomé Müller." *Law Reporter* (September 1845): 194–205. Print.

Cassuto, Leonard. "'What an Object He Would Have Made of Me!' Tattooing and the Racial Freak in Melville's *Typee*." *Freakery: Cultural Spectacles of the Extraordinary Body*. Ed. Rosemarie Garland Thomson. New York: New York University Press, 1996. 234–247. Print.

"Caster Semenya Denies Accusations That She Did Not Want to Win Olympic 800m Gold." *Telegraph* 12 Aug. 2012. Web.

"Caster Semenya's Mother Hits Out at Gender Dispute." *Guardian* 20 Aug. 2009. Web.

Castile, George Pierre. "The Commodification of Indian Identity." *American Anthropologist* 98.4 (1996): 743–749. Print.

Chamberlayne, H. M. "Vagrancy among Deaf-Mutes." 1859. *Deaf World: A Historical Reader and Primary Sourcebook*. Ed. Lois Braddock. New York: New York University Press, 2001. 237–238. Print.

Chapel, Charles Edward. *Fingerprinting: A Manual of Identification*. New York: Coward-McCann, 1941. Print.

Chase, Chris. "Embattled Track Star Caster Semenya Gets New Coach, New Look." *Yahoo Sports* 8 Sept. 2009. Web.

Child, Lydia Maria. *The Stars and Stripes: A Melo-Drama. The Liberty Bell.* Boston: Prentiss, Sawyer, 1858. 122–185. Print.

Chinn, Sarah E. *Technology and the Logic of American Racism: A Cultural History of the Body as Evidence*. London: Continuum, 2000. Print.

Clare, Eli. *Exile and Pride: Disability, Queerness, and Liberation*. Cambridge, MA: South End Press, 1999. Print.

Clarke, Lewis, and Milton Clarke. "Narratives of the Sufferings of Lewis and Milton Clarke, Sons of a Soldier of the Revolution, During a Captivity of More Than Twenty Years Among Slaveholders of Kentucky, One of the So Called Christian States of North America. Dictated by Themselves." 1846. *African-American Slave Narratives: An Anthology*. Ed. Sterling Lecater Bland Jr. 3 vols. Westport, CT: Greenwood Press, 2001. 119–196. Print.

Cole, Cheryl L. "One Chromosome Too Many?" *The Olympics at the Millennium: Power, Politics, and the Games*. Ed. Kay Schaffer and Sidonie Smith. New Brunswick, NJ: Rutgers University Press, 2000. 128–145. Print.

Cole, Simon A. *Suspect Identities: A History of Fingerprinting and Criminal Identification*. Cambridge, MA: Harvard University Press, 2001. Print.

"Convicted by the Baby." *New York Times* 14 Feb. 1887. Print.

Cook, Jonathan. *Satirical Apocalypse: An Anatomy of Melville's* The Confidence Man. Westport, CT: Greenwood Press, 1996. Print.

Cox, James. "*Pudd'nhead Wilson* Revisited." *Mark Twain's Pudd'nhead Wilson: Race, Conflict, and Culture*. Ed. Susan K. Gillman and Forrest G. Robinson. Durham, NC: Duke University Press, 1990. 1–21. Print.

Craft, William, and Ellen Craft. *Running a Thousand Miles for Freedom: The*

Escape of William and Ellen Craft from Slavery. 1860. Ed. Barbara McCaskill. Athens: University of Georgia Press, 1999. Print.

Cramer, Renee Ann. *Cash, Color, and Colonialism: The Politics of Tribal Acknowledgment.* Norman: University of Oklahoma Press, 2005. Print.

Daniel v. Guy. 23 Ark. 50. Supreme Court of Ark. Jan. 1861. Print.

Davis, Adrienne D. "Identity Notes, Part One: Playing in the Light." *Critical White Studies: Looking behind the Mirror.* Ed. Richard Delgado and Jean Stefanic. Philadelphia: Temple University Press, 1997. 231–238. Print.

Davis, Charles T., and Henry Louis Gates Jr., ed. *The Slave's Narrative.* New York: Oxford University Press, 1985. Print.

Davis, Lennard J., ed. *The Disability Studies Reader.* 3rd ed. New York: Routledge. 2005. Print.

———. *Enforcing Normalcy: Disability, Deafness, and the Body.* New York: Verso, 1995. Print.

De Grave, Kathleen. *Swindler, Spy, Rebel: The Confidence Woman in Nineteenth-Century America.* Columbia: University of Missouri Press, 1995. Print.

Delgado, Richard, and Jean Stefanic. *Critical Race Theory: The Cutting Edge.* 2nd ed. Philadelphia: Temple University Press, 2000. Print.

———. *Critical White Studies: Looking behind the Mirror.* Philadelphia: Temple University Press, 1997. Print.

Derricotte, Toi. "The Weakness." *Captivity.* Pittsburgh: University of Pittsburgh Press, 1989. 13–14. Print.

Derrida, Jacques. *Of Grammatology.* 1976. Trans. Gayatri Chakravorty Spivak. Baltimore: Johns Hopkins University Press, 1997. Print.

Desjarlait, Robert. "Blood Quantum vs. Lineal Descent: How Much Indian Are You? The Debate over How to Define Who Is Indian." *Circle* 22.11 (2001): 1–5. Print.

Dirty Rotten Scoundrels. Dir. Frank Oz. MGM, 1988. Film.

Douglass, Frederick. *The Narrative of the Life of Frederick Douglass, An American Slave.* 1845. Ed. Houston A. Baker Jr. New York: Penguin, 1986. Print.

Dreger, Alice Domurat. *Hermaphrodites and the Medical Invention of Sex.* Cambridge, MA: Harvard University Press, 1998. Print.

———. *One of Us: Conjoined Twins and the Future of Normal.* Cambridge, MA: Harvard University Press, 2004. Print.

———. "Science Is Forcing Sports to Re-examine Their Core Principles." *New York Times* 13 Sept. 2009. Web.

———. "The Sex of Athletes: One Issue, Many Variables." *New York Times* 24 Oct. 2009. Web.

———. "Where's the Rulebook for Sex Verification?" *New York Times.* 22 Aug. 2009. Web.

Elliott, Carl, and Paul Brodwin. "Identity and Genetic Ancestry Testing." *BMJ: British Medical Journal* 325.7378 (2002): 1469–1471. Print.

Elsas, Louis J., et al. "Gender Verification of Female Athletes." *Genetics in Medicine* 2.4 (2000): 249–254. Print.

Epstein, David. "Inside Track and Field." *Sports Illustrated* 9 Aug. 2012. Web.

Epstein, Julia. *Altered Conditions: Disease, Medicine, and Storytelling.* New York, Routledge, 1995. Print.

Espinoza, Leslie, and Angela P. Harris. "Embracing the Tar-Baby: LatCrit Theory and the Sticky Mess of Race." *Critical Race Theory: The Cutting Edge.* Ed. Richard Delgado and Jean Stefanic. 2nd ed. Philadelphia: Temple University Press, 2000. 440–447. Print.

The Ex. Dir. Jesse Peretz. Weinstein Company, 2007. Film.

Fabi, M. Giulia. Introduction. William Wells Brown, *Clotel; or, The President's Daughter.* 1853. Ed. M. Giulia Fabi. New York: Penguin, 2004. vii–xxviii. Print.

The Fake Beggar. Dir. Thomas Edison. Edison, 1898. Film.

Fausto-Sterling, Anne. *Myths of Gender: Biological Theories about Women and Men.* New York: Basic Books, 1985. Print.

———. *Sexing the Body: Gender Politics and the Construction of Sexuality.* New York: Basic Books, 2000. Print.

Fett, Sharla M. *Working Cures: Healing, Health, and Power on Southern Slave Plantations.* Chapel Hill: University of North Carolina Press, 2002. Print.

Findlay, Stephanie. "Olympics Struggle with 'Policing Femininity.'" *Toronto Star* 8 June 2012. Web.

Fitzgerald, Kathleen J. *Beyond White Ethnicity: Developing a Sociological Understanding of Native American Identity Reclamation.* New York: Lexington Books, 2007. Print.

Fjellman, Stephen M. *Vinyl Leaves: Walt Disney World and America.* Boulder, CO: Westview Press, 1992. Print.

Forbes, Jack D. "The Manipulation of Race, Caste, and Identity: Classifying AfroAmericans, Native Americans and Red-Black People." *Journal of Ethnic Studies* 17.4 (1990): 1–51. Print.

Foucault, Michel. *Abnormal: Lectures at the Collège de France, 1974–1975.* Trans. Graham Burchell. Ed. Calerio Marchetti and Antonella Salomoni. New York: Picador, 2003. Print.

———. *The Birth of the Clinic: An Archaeology of Medical Perception.* 1963. Trans. A. M. Sheridan Smith. New York: Vintage, 1994. Print.

———. *Discipline and Punish: The Birth of the Prison.* 1975. Trans. Alan Sheridan. New York: Vintage, 1995. Print.

———. *History of Sexuality. Vol. 1: An Introduction.* 1978. Trans. Robert Hurley. New York: Vintage, 1990. Print.

———. *Power/Knowledge: Selected Interviews and Other Writings, 1972–1977.* 1980. Trans. Colin Gordon. Ed. Colin Gordon et al. New York: Pantheon Books, 1980. Print.

Franklin, Sarah. "Life Itself: Global Nature and the Genetic Imaginary." *Global*

Nature, Global Culture. Ed. Sarah Franklin et al. London: Sage, 2000. 188–227. Print.

Fredricks, Nancy. "Twain's Indelible Twins." *Nineteenth-Century Literature* 43.4 (1989): 484–499. Print.

"Fresh Controversy for Caster Semenya as Tests Reveal High Testosterone Levels." *Guardian* 25 Aug. 2009. Web.

Fullerton, Thomas. "The Birth-Mark." *Atlantic Monthly* 2.11 (1858): 412–413. Print.

Galloway, Terry. *Mean Little Deaf Queer: A Memoir*. Boston: Beacon Press, 2009. Print.

Galton, Francis. *Finger Prints*. London: Macmillan, 1892. Print.

———. "Identification by Finger-Tips." *Nineteenth Century* 30 (August 1891): 303–311. Print.

Garber, Marjorie. *Vested Interests*. New York: Routledge, 1992. Print.

Garland Thomson, Rosemarie. *Extraordinary Bodies: Figuring Physical Disability in American Culture and Literature*. New York: Columbia University Press, 1997. Print.

———. Introduction. *Freakery: Cultural Spectacles of the Extraordinary Body*. New York: New York University Press, 1996. 1–19. Print.

Garroute, Eva Marie. *Real Indians: Identity and the Survival of Native America*. Berkeley: University of California Press, 2003. Print.

Gates, Henry Louis, Jr. Introduction. *"Race," Writing, and Difference*. Chicago: University of Chicago Press, 1986. 1–20. Print.

Gercken-Hawkins, Becca. "'Maybe You Only Look White': Ethnic Authority and Indian Authenticity in Academia." *American Indian Quarterly* 27.1–2 (2003): 200–202. Print.

Gilbert, Sandra M., and Susan Gubar. *The Madwoman in the Attic: The Woman Writer and the Nineteenth-Century Literary Imagination*. 1979. New Haven, CT: Yale University Press, 1984. Print.

Gillham, Nicholas. *A Life of Sir Francis Galton: From African Exploration to the Birth of Eugenics*. Oxford: Oxford University Press, 2001. Print.

Gillman, Susan K. *Dark Twins: Imposture and Identity in Mark Twain's America*. Chicago: University of Chicago Press, 1989. Print.

Gillman, Susan K., and Forrest G. Robinson, eds. *Mark Twain's Pudd'nhead Wilson: Race, Conflict, and Culture*. Durham, NC: Duke University Press, 1990. Print.

Ginsberg, Elaine K., ed. *Passing and the Fictions of Identity*. Durham, NC: Duke University Press, 1996. Print.

Goldberg, David Theo. *Racial Subjects: Writing on Race in America*. New York: Routledge, 1997. Print.

Gonzales, Angela. "The (Re)articulation of American Indian Identity: Maintaining Boundaries and Regulating Access to Ethnically Tied Resources." *American Indian Culture and Research Journal* 22.4 (1998): 199–225. Print.

Gordon, Linda. *Pitied but Not Entitled: Single Mothers and the History of Welfare.* New York: Free Press, 1994. Print.

Gossett, Thomas F. *Race: The History of an Idea in America.* Dallas: Southern Methodist University Press, 1963. Print.

Gould, Stephen Jay. *The Mismeasure of Man.* New York: Norton, 1981. Print.

Grammond, Sebastien. *Identity Captured by Law: Membership in Canada's Indigenous Peoples and Linguistic Minorities.* Montreal: McGill-Queen's University Press, 2009. Print.

Graves, Joseph L. *The Emperor's New Clothes: Biological Theories of Race at the New Millennium.* New Brunswick, NJ: Rutgers University Press, 2001. Print.

Greenblatt, Stephen. "Towards a Poetics of Culture." *The New Historicism.* Ed. H. Aram Veeser. New York: Routledge, 1989. 1–14. Print.

Greenfield, Rebecca. "Runner Caster Semenya Looks a Lot More Feminine Than She Did in 2009." *Atlantic Wire* 12 June 2012. Web.

Griffin, Pat. "'Ain't I a Woman?' Transgender and Intersex Student Athletes in Women's Collegiate Sports." *Transfeminism: Perspectives in and beyond Transgender and Gender Studies.* Ed. Anne Enke. Philadelphia: Temple University Press, 2012. 98–111. Print.

Gross, Ariela J. *What Blood Won't Tell: A History of Race on Trial in America.* Cambridge, MA: Harvard University Press, 2006. Print.

Guillaumin, Colette. "Race and Nature: The System of Marks." *Feminist Issues* 8.2 (1988): 25–43. Print.

Haber, Lawrence D. "Some Parameters for Social Policy in Disability: A Cross-National Comparison." *Milbank Memorial Fund Quarterly: Health and Society* 51.3 (1973): 319–340. Print.

Hagan, William T. "Full Blood, Mixed Blood, Generic, and Ersatz: The Problem of Indian Identity." *Arizona and the West* 27.1 (1985): 309–326. Print.

Halberstam, Judith. *Female Masculinity.* Durham, NC: Duke University Press, 1998. Print.

Hall, Kim Q., ed. *Feminist Disability Studies.* Bloomington: Indiana University Press, 2011. Print.

Halttunen, Karen. *Confidence Men and Painted Women: A Study of Middle-Class Culture in America, 1830–1870.* New Haven, CT: Yale University Press, 1982. Print.

Halualani, Rona Tamiko. "Purifying the State: State Discourses, Blood Quantum, and the Legal Mis/Recognition of Hawaiians." *Between Law and Culture: Relocating Legal Studies.* Ed. David Theo Goldberg, Michael Musheno, and Lisa C. Bower. Minneapolis: University of Minnesota Press, 2001. 145–173. Print.

Hamill, James. "Show Me Your CDIB: Blood Quantum and Indian Identity among Indian People of Oklahoma." *American Behavioral Scientist* 47.3 (2003): 267–282. Print.

Handley, Meg. "The IOC Grapples with Olympic Sex Testing." *Time* 11 Feb. 2010. Web.

Haney López, Ian F. "The Social Construction of Race." *Critical Race Theory: The Cutting Edge.* Ed. Richard Delgado and Jean Stefanic. 2nd ed. Philadelphia: Temple University Press, 2000. 163–175. Print.

———. "White by Law." *Critical Race Theory: The Cutting Edge.* Ed. Richard Delgado and Jean Stefanic. 2nd ed. Philadelphia: Temple University Press, 2000. 626–634. Print.

Harmon, Alexandra. "Tribal Enrollment Councils: Lessons on Law and Indian Identity." *Western Historical Quarterly* 32.2 (2001): 175–200. Print.

Harmon, Amy. "Seeking Ancestry in DNA Ties Uncovered by Tests." *New York Times* 12 Apr. 2006. Web.

Harris, Cheryl I. "Whiteness as Property." *Harvard Law Review* 106.8 (1993): 1707–1791. Print.

Hartman, Saidiya. *Scenes of Subjection: Terror, Slavery, and Self-Making in Nineteenth-Century America.* New York: Oxford University Press, 1997. Print.

Hawaiian Homes Commission Act, 1920. Hearings before the Committee on Territories, United States Senate, Sixty-sixth Congress, Third Session on H.R. 13500. Washington, DC: Government Printing Office, 1921. Print.

Hawthorne, Nathaniel. "The Birthmark." 1843. *Nathaniel Hawthorne's Tales.* Ed. James McIntosh. New York: Norton, 1987. 118–131. Print.

Heermance, J. Noel. *William Wells Brown and Clotelle: A Portrait of the Artist in the First Negro Novel.* North Haven, CT: Archon Books, 1969. Print.

Heggie, Vanessa. "Testing Sex and Gender in Sport: Reinventing, Reimagining, and Reconstructing Histories." *Endeavour* 34.4 (2010): 157–163. Print.

Heglar, Charles J. *Rethinking the Slave Narrative: Slave Marriage and the Narratives of Henry Bibb and William and Ellen Craft.* Westport, CT: Greenwood Press, 2001. Print.

Henderson, Carol E. *Scarring the Black Body: Race and Representation in African American Literature.* Columbia: University of Missouri Press, 2002. Print.

Hercher, Laura. "Gender Verification: A Term Whose Time Has Come and Gone." *Journal of Genetic Counseling* 19 (8 Sept. 2010): 551–553. Print.

Herndl, Diane Price. *Invalid Women: Figuring Feminine Illness in American Fiction and Culture, 1840–1940.* Chapel Hill: University of North Carolina Press, 1993. Print.

Hevey, David. "The Enfreakment of Photography." *The Disability Studies Reader.* Ed. Lennard J. Davis. 3rd ed. New York: Routledge. 2005. 507–521. Print.

Hirsch, Jerrold, and Karen Hirsch. "'I Worked as Long as I Was Able': Slavery, Freedom, and Disability in the FWP Slave Narratives." Society for Disability Studies Annual Meeting. 24 May 1997. Print.

Holmes, Morgan, ed. *Critical Intersex.* London: Ashgate, 2010. Print.

———. *Intersex: A Perilous Difference.* Selinsgrove, PA: Susquehanna University Press, 2008. Print.

Hopkinson, J. "The Case of 'Isaac' or 'William Stansbury': Claimed as a Fugitive from the Service of Ruth Williams, of Prince George County, in the State of Maryland." *Law Reporter* 2 (1840?): 104–113. Print.

Horkheimer, Max, and Theodor W. Adorno. *Dialectic of Enlightenment.* 1972. New York: Continuum, 1988. Print.

Hudgins v. Wright. 11 Va. 134. Supreme Court of Virginia. 1806. Print.

Hurst, Mike. "Caster Semenya Has Male Sex Organs and No Womb or Ovaries." *Daily Telegraph Australia* 11 Sept. 2009. Web.

IAAF Hyperandrogenism Regulations: Explanatory Notes. International Association of Athletics Federations. 1 May 2011. Web. www.iaaf.org.

IAAF Regulations Governing Eligibility of Females with Hyperandrogenism to Compete in Women's Competitions. International Association of Athletics Federations. 1 May 2011. Web. www.iaaf.org.

The Identification Division of the FBI: A Brief Outline of the History, Services, and Operating Techniques of the World's Largest Repository of Fingerprints. [*Fingerprint Identification*]. Washington, DC: Federal Bureau of Investigation, U.S. Dept. of Justice, 1991. Print.

Ignatieff, Michael. "State, Civil Society and Total Institutions: A Critique of Recent Social Histories of Punishment." *Social Control and the State.* Ed. Stanley Cohen and Andrew Scull. New York: St. Martin's Press, 1983. 75–105. Print.

Ings, Katharine Nicholson. "Blackness and the Literary Imagination: Uncovering *The Hidden Hand*." *Passing and the Fictions of Identity.* Ed. Elaine K. Ginsberg. Durham, NC: Duke University Press, 1996. 131–150. Print.

IOC Regulations on Female Hyperandrogenism. International Olympic Committee. 2012. Web. www.olympic.org.

Jackson, Mark. "Changing Depictions of Disease: Race, Representation, and the History of 'Mongolism.'" *Race, Science, and Medicine, 1700–1960.* Ed. Waltraud Ernst and Bernard Harris. New York: Routledge, 1999. 167–188. Print.

Jacobs, Harriet. *Incidents in the Life of a Slave Girl.* 1861. Ed. Jane Fagan Yellin. Cambridge, MA: Harvard University Press, 2000. Print.

James, Jennifer C. *A Freedom Bought with Blood: African-American War Literature from the Civil War to World War II.* Chapel Hill: University of North Carolina Press, 2007. Print.

Jameson, Fredric. *The Political Unconscious: Narrative as a Socially Symbolic Act.* Ithaca, NY: Cornell University Press, 1981. Print.

Jehlen, Myra. "The Ties That Bind: Race and Sex in *Pudd'nhead Wilson*." *Mark Twain's Pudd'nhead Wilson: Race, Conflict, and Culture.* Ed. Susan K. Gillman and Forrest G. Robinson. Durham, NC: Duke University Press, 1990. 105–120. Print.

Johnson, Georgia Douglas. *William and Ellen Craft. Negro History in Thirteen*

Plays. Ed. Willis Richardson and May Miller. Washington, DC: Associated Publishers, 1935. 164–186. Print.

Jones, Dale. "The Grotesque in Melville's *The Confidence-Man.*" *Colby Library Quarterly* 19.4 (1983). 194–205. Print.

Jones, Megan. "Why I Use a White Cane to Let People Know I Am Deaf." *Ragged Edge* July/Aug. 1997. Web.

Jordan, Winthrop D. *White over Black: American Attitudes toward the Negro, 1550–1812.* Baltimore: Penguin, 1968. Print.

Jordan-Young, Rebecca, and Katrina Karkazis. "The IOC's Superwoman Complex: How Flawed Sex-Testing Discriminates." *Guardian* 2 July 2012. Web.

Joseph, Anne M. "Anthropometry, the Police Expert, and the Deptford Murders: The Contested Introduction of Fingerprinting for the Identification of Criminals in Late Victorian and Edwardian Britain." *Documenting Individual Identity: The Development of State Practices in the Modern World.* Ed. Jane Caplan and John Torpey. Princeton: Princeton University Press, 2001. 164–183. Print.

Journal of the House of Representatives of the Tenth Legislature of the Territory of Hawaii. Regular Session. Honolulu. 1919. Print.

Kafer, Alison. "Compulsory Bodies: Reflections on Heterosexuality and Able-bodiedness." *Journal of Women's History* 15.3 (2003): 77–89. Print.

Kangas, Matthew. "Oil, Blood, and Money Make Slippery Subjects in Sacred Circle Exhibit." *Seattle Times* 10 May 2002. Web.

Karkazis, Katrina, Rebecca Jordan-Young, Georgiann Davis, and Silvia Camporesi. "Out of Bounds? A Critique of the New Policies on Hyperandrogenism in Elite Female Athletes." *American Journal of Bioethics* 12.7 (2012): 3–16. Print.

Kauanui, J. Kēhaulani. *Hawaiian Blood: Colonialism and the Politics of Sovereignty and Indigeneity.* Durham, NC: Duke University Press, 2008. Print.

Kawash, Samira. *Dislocating the Color Line: Identity, Hybridity, and Singularity in African-American Narrative.* Stanford: Stanford University Press, 1997. Print.

Keetley, Dawn. "Racial Conviction, Racial Confusion: Indeterminate Identities in Women's Slave Narratives and Southern Courts." *a/b: Auto/Biography Studies* 10.2 (1995): 1–20. Print.

Kessel, Anna. "Caster Semenya Third in Brussels 800m as Gender Debate Rages On." *Guardian* 28 Aug. 2010. Web.

———. "Gold Medal Athlete Caster Semenya Told to Prove She Is a Woman." *Guardian* 19 Aug. 2009. Web.

Klages, Mary. *Woeful Afflictions: Disability and Sentimentality in Victorian America.* Philadelphia: University of Pennsylvania Press, 1999. Print.

Klöppel, Ulrike. "Who Has the Right to Change Gender Status? Drawing Boundaries between Inter- and Transsexuality." *Critical Intersex.* Ed. Morgan Holmes. London: Ashgate, 2010. 171–187. Print.

Koenig, Barbara A., Sandra Soo-Jin Lee, and Sarah S. Richardson, eds. *Revisiting Race in a Genomic Age*. New Brunswick, NJ: Rutgers University Press, 2008. Print.

Koerner, Brendan I. "Blood Feud." *Wired* 13.9 (2005). Web.

Kohrman, Matthew. "Why Am I Not Disabled? Making State Subjects, Making Statistics in Post-Mao China." *Disability in Local and Global Worlds*. Ed. Benedicte Ingstad and Susan Reynolds Whyte. Berkeley: University of California Press, 2007. 212–236. Print.

Kolata, Gina. "Gender Testing Hangs before the Games as a Muddled and Vexing Mess." *New York Times* 16 Jan. 2010. Web.

———. "I.O.C. Panel Calls for Treatment in Sex Ambiguity Cases." *New York Times* 21 Jan. 2010. Web.

Ladd, Barbara. *Nationalism and the Color Line in George W. Cable, Mark Twain, and William Faulkner*. Baton Rouge: Louisiana State University Press, 1996. Print.

LaValle, John P. "The General Allotment Act 'Eligibility' Hoax: Distortions of Law, Policy, and History in Derogation of Indian Tribes." *Wicazo Sa Review* 14.1 (1999): 251–302. Print.

Lawrence, Bonita. "Gender, Race, and the Regulation of Native Identity in Canada and the United States: An Overview." *Hypatia* 18.2 (2003): 3–31. Print.

Lawson, Mark. "Unsporting Behavior." *Guardian* 20 Aug. 2009. Web.

Le Breton, David. "Genetic Fundamentalism or the Cult of the Gene." *Body and Society* 10.4 (2004): 1–20. Print.

Lenz, William. *Fast Talk and Flush Times: The Confidence-Man as a Literary Convention*. Columbia: University of Missouri Press, 1985. Print.

Levy, Ariel. "Either/Or: Sports, Sex, and the Case of Caster Semenya." *New Yorker* 30 Nov. 2009. Web.

Lindberg, Gary. *The Confidence-Man in American Literature*. New York: Oxford University Press, 1982. Print.

Linton, Simi. *Claiming Disability: Knowledge and Identity*. New York: New York University Press, 1998. Print.

Long, Jackie. "Athlete Caster Semenya Unbowed by Gender Row." *BBC Newsnight, South Africa* 25 Jan. 2011. Web. www.bbc.co.uk.

Longmore, Paul K. *Why I Burned My Book and Other Essays on Disability*. Philadelphia: Temple University Press, 2003. Print.

Longmore, Paul K., and Lauri Umansky, eds. *The New Disability History: American Perspectives*. New York: New York University Press, 2001. Print.

Lott, Eric. *Love and Theft: Blackface Minstrelsy and the American Working Class*. New York: Oxford University Press, 1995. Print.

Lovett, Laura L. "African and Cherokee by Choice: Race and Resistance under Legalized Segregation." *Confounding the Color Line: The Indian-Black Experience in North America*. Ed. James F. Brooks. Lincoln: University of Nebraska Press, 2002. 192–222. Print.

Luckenbach, Rodney. "The Street Beggar: Victim or Con Artist?" *Police Chief* 60.10 (1998): 126. Print.

Magnet, Shoshana Amielle. *When Biometrics Fail: Gender, Race, and the Technology of Identity.* Durham, NC: Duke University Press, 2012. Print.

"Makeover for SA Gender-Row Runner." *BBC News* 8 Sept. 2009. Web.

Marks, Jonathan. *Human Biodiversity: Genes, Race, and History.* New York: Aldine de Gruyter, 1995. Print.

Marks, Jonathan, and Brett Lee Shelton. "Genetic 'Markers'—Not a Valid Test of Native Identity." Indigenous Peoples Council on Biocolonialism. 8 July 2010. Web.

Martin, Charles D. *The White African American Body: A Cultural and Literary Exploration.* New Brunswick, NJ: Rutgers University Press, 2002. Print.

Martínez-Patiño, María José. "Personal Account: A Woman Tried and Tested." *Lancet* 366 (Dec. 2005): 538. Print.

McBride, Donald F. "Disease Inheritance and Race Determination by Fingerprints." *Identification News,* August 1987. Web. http://www.scafo.org/library/110203.html.

McCaskill, Barbara. "Introduction: William and Ellen Craft in Transatlantic Literature and Life." William Craft and Ellen Craft, *Running a Thousand Miles for Freedom: The Escape of William and Ellen Craft from Slavery.* 1860. Ed. Barbara McCaskill. Athens: University of Georgia Press, 1999. vii–xxv. Print.

———. "'Yours Very Truly': Ellen Craft—The Fugitive as Text and Artifact." *African-American Review* 28.4 (1994): 509–529. Print.

McMaster, Gerald, and Lee-Ann Martin, eds. *Indigena: Contemporary Native Perspectives.* Hull, Quebec: Canadian Museum of Civilization, 1992. Print.

McRuer, Robert. *Crip Theory: Cultural Signs of Queerness and Disability.* New York: New York University Press, 2006. Print.

McRuer, Robert, and Abby Wilkerson, eds. *Desiring Disability: Queer Theory Meets Disability Studies.* GLQ 9.1–2 (2003). Print.

Melville, Herman. *The Confidence Man: His Masquerade.* 1857. Ed. Hershel Parker. New York: Norton, 1971. Print.

Meyer, Melissa L. "American Indian Blood Quantum Requirements: Blood Is Thicker than Family." *Over the Edge: Remapping the American West.* Ed. Valerie J. Matsumoto and Blake Allmendinger. Berkeley: University of California Press, 1998. 231–249. Print.

Michaels, Lloyd. "The Confidence Man in Modern Film." *University of Toronto Quarterly* 62.3 (1993): 375–387. Print.

Miller v. Belmonti. 11 Rob. 339. Supreme Court of Louisiana, Eastern District. 1845. Print.

Miller, Mark Edwin. *Forgotten Tribes: Unrecognized Indians and the Federal*

Acknowledgement Process. Lincoln: University of Nebraska Press, 2004. Print.

Mitchell, David T., and Sharon L. Snyder, eds. *The Body and Physical Difference: Discourses of Disability*. Ann Arbor: University of Michigan Press, 1997. Print.

———. *Cultural Locations of Disability*. Chicago: University of Chicago Press, 2006. Print.

———. "Masquerades of Impairment: Charity as a Confidence Game." *Leviathan* 8.1 (2006): 35–60. Print.

———. *Narrative Prosthesis: Disability and the Dependencies of Discourse*. Ann Arbor: University of Michigan Press, 2000. Print.

Mollow, Anna. "Identity Politics and Disability Studies: A Critique of Recent Theory." *Michigan Quarterly Review* 43.2 (2004): 269–296. Print.

Momaday, N. Scott. *The Names*. New York: Harper & Row, 1976. Print.

Montgomery, Cal. "A Hard Look at Invisible Disability." *Ragged Edge Online*, no. 2 (2001). Web. www.ragged-edge-mag.com.

Morris, Linda A. "Beneath the Veil: Clothing, Race, and Gender in Twain's *Pudd'nhead Wilson*." *Studies in American Fiction* 27.1 (1999): 37–52. Print.

Morrison, Toni. *Beloved*. New York: Knopf, 1987. Print.

———. *Playing in the Dark: Whiteness and Literary Imagination*. New York: Random House, 1992. Print.

Morton, Patricia. *Disfigured Images: The Historical Assault on Afro-American Women*. New York: Greenwood Press, 1991. Print.

Morton, Samuel George. *Crania Americana: A Comparative View of the Skulls of Various Aboriginal Natives of North and South America*. Philadelphia: John Penington, 1839. Print.

Moss, Robert. "Tracing Mark Twain's Intentions: The Retreat from Issues of Race in *Pudd'nhead Wilson*." *American Literary History* 30.2 (1998): 43–55. Print.

Muñoz, José Esteban. *Disidentifications: Queers of Color and the Performance of Politics*. Minneapolis: University of Minnesota Press, 1999. Print.

Nagel, Joane. *American Indian Ethnic Renewal: Red Power and the Resurgence of Identity and Culture*. New York: Oxford University Press, 1996. Print.

Nelkin, Dorothy, and M. Susan Lindee. *The DNA Mystique: The Gene as a Cultural Icon*. New York: W. H. Freeman, 1995. Print.

Nemiroff, Diana, Robert Houle, and Charlotte Townsend-Gault, eds. *Land Spirit Power: First Nations at the National Gallery of Canada*. Ottawa: National Gallery of Canada, 1992. Print.

Niver, Kemp R. *Motion Pictures from the Library of Congress Paper Print Collection 1894–1912*. Ed. Bebe Bergstein. Berkeley: University of California Press, 1967. Print.

Norden, Martin F. *The Cinema of Isolation: A History of Physical Disability in the Movies*. New Brunswick, NJ: Rutgers University Press, 1994. Print.

Nott, Josiah C., and George R. Gliddon. *Types of Mankind, or, Ethnological Researches*. Philadelphia: Lippincott, Grambo, 1855. Print.

Nottage, James H., ed. *Into the Fray: The Eiteljorg Fellowship for Native American Fine Art, 2005*. Seattle: University of Washington Press, 2005. Print.

Olsen, Robert D., Sr. "A Fingerprint Fable: The Will and William West Case." *Identification News* 37.1 (1987). Web. http://www.scafo.org/library/110105.html.

Ornstein, David. "Caster Semenya Loses Out on 800m Gold to Maria Savinova. *BBC Sport* 11 Aug. 2012. Web.

Otten, Thomas J. "Pauline Hopkins and the Hidden Self of Race." *English Literary History* 59.1 (1992): 227–256. Print.

Otter, Samuel. "Melville and Disability." *Leviathan* 8.1 (2006): 7–16. Print.

———. *Melville's Anatomies*. Berkeley: University of California Press, 1999. Print.

Panzarino, Connie. *The Me in the Mirror*. Seattle: Seal Press, 1994. Print.

Passalacqua, Veronica. "Tanis Maria S'eiltin: Coming Full Circle." *Into the Fray: The Eiteljorg Fellowship for Native American Fine Art, 2005*. Ed. James H. Nottage. Seattle: University of Washington Press, 2005. 97–109. Print.

Pennington, James W. C. "The Fugitive Blacksmith." 1849. *African-American Slave Narratives: An Anthology*. Ed. Sterling Lecater Bland Jr. 3 vols. Westport, CT: Greenwood Press, 2001. 541–598. Print.

Perez, Rob. "DHHL Mismanagement: Still Standing." *Honolulu Star Advertiser* 5 May, 2013. Web.

Peters, Susan. "Is There a Disability Culture? A Syncretisation of Three Possible World Views." *Disability & Society* 15.4 (2000): 583–601. Print.

Petry, Alice Hall. "The Limits of Truth in Cable's 'Salome Müller.'" *PLL: Papers on Language & Literature* 27.1 (1991): 20–31. Print.

Pimple, Kenneth D. "Personal Narrative, Melville's *The Confidence-Man*, and the Problem of Deception." *Western Folklore* 51.1 (1992): 33–50. Print.

Piper, Adrian. "Passing for White, Passing for Black." *Passing and the Fictions of Identity*. Ed. Elaine K. Ginsberg. Durham, NC: Duke University Press, 1996. 234–269. Print.

Pollack, Andrew. "The Wide, Wild World of Genetic Testing." *New York Times* 22 Aug. 2009. Web.

Porter, Carolyn. "Roxana's Plot." *Mark Twain's Pudd'nhead Wilson: Race, Conflict, and Culture*. Ed. Susan K. Gillman and Forrest G. Robinson. Durham, NC: Duke University Press, 1990. 121–136. Print.

Porter, James I. Foreword. *The Body and Physical Difference: Discourses of Disability*. Ed. David T. Mitchell and Sharon L. Snyder. Ann Arbor: University of Michigan Press, 1997. xiii–xiv. Print.

Puffer, James C. "Gender Verification of Female Olympic Athletes." *Medicine and Science in Sports and Exercise* 34.10 (2002): 1543. Print.

Quayson, Ato. *Aesthetic Nervousness: Disability and the Crisis of Representation*. New York: Columbia University Press, 2007. Print.

Ray. Dir. Taylor Hackford. Universal, 2004. Film.

Reis, Elizabeth. *Bodies in Doubt: An American History of Intersex*. Baltimore: Johns Hopkins University Press, 2009. Print.

Reports of the Department of the Interior. Vol. II. Washington, DC: Government Printing Office, 1908. Print.

Roberts, Dorothy E. "The Genetic Tie." *Critical White Studies: Looking behind the Mirror*. Ed. Richard Delgado and Jean Stefanic. Philadelphia: Temple University Press, 1997. 186–189. Print.

Robinson, Forrest G. *In Bad Faith: The Dynamics of Deception in Mark Twain's America*. Cambridge, MA: Harvard University Press, 1986. Print.

———. "The Sense of Disorder in *Pudd'nhead Wilson*." *Mark Twain's Pudd'nhead Wilson: Race, Conflict, and Culture*. Ed. Susan K. Gillman and Forrest G. Robinson. Durham, NC: Duke University Press, 1990. 22–45. Print.

Rogin, Michael. "Frances Galton and Mark Twain: The Natal Autograph in *Pudd'nhead Wilson*." *Mark Twain's Pudd'nhead Wilson: Race, Conflict, and Culture*. Ed. Susan K. Gillman and Forrest G. Robinson. Durham, NC: Duke University Press, 1990. 73–85. Print.

Roper, Moses. "A Narrative of the Adventures and Escape of Moses Roper, from American Slavery; with a Preface, by the Rev. T. Price, D.D." 1838. *African-American Slave Narratives: An Anthology*. Ed. Sterling Lecater Bland Jr. 3 vols. Westport, CT: Greenwood Press, 2001. 47–88. Print.

Rothman, Barbara Katz. *Genetic Maps and Human Imagination: The Limits of Science in Understanding Who We Are*. New York: Norton, 1998. Print.

Rountree, Helen. "The Indians of Virginia: A Third Race in a Biracial State." *Southeastern Indians Since the Removal Era*. Ed. Walter L. Williams. Athens: University of Georgia Press, 1979. 41–43. Print.

Rowe, Katherine. *Dead Hands: Fictions of Agency, Renaissance to Modern*. Stanford: Stanford University Press, 1999. Print.

Russell, Emily. *Reading Embodied Citizenship: Disability, Narrative, and the Body Politic*. New Brunswick, NJ: Rutgers University Press, 2011. Print.

Samuels, Ellen. "My Body, My Closet: Invisible Disability and the Limits of Coming-out Discourse." *GLQ: A Journal of Lesbian and Gay Studies* 9.1–2 (2003): 233–255. Print.

Sanchez-Eppler, Karen. *Touching Liberty: Abolition, Feminism, and the Politics of the Body*. Berkeley: University of California Press, 1993. Print.

Sandahl, Carrie. "Ahhhh Freak Out! Metaphors of Disability and Femaleness in Performance." *Theatre Topics* 9.1 (1999): 11–30. Print.

Saner, Emine. "The Gender Trap." *Guardian* 30 July 2008. Web.

Savitt, Todd. *Medicine and Slavery: The Diseases and Health Care of Blacks in Antebellum Virginia*. Urbana: University of Illinois Press, 1978. Print.

Schiebinger, Londa. *Nature's Body: Gender in the Making of Modern Science.* Boston: Beacon Press, 1993. Print.

Schweik, Susan M. "Disability and the Normal Body of the (Native) Citizen." *Social Research* 78.2 (2011): 417–442. Print.

——. *The Ugly Laws: Disability in Public.* New York: New York University Press, 2008. Print.

S'eiltin, Tania Maria. "Artist's Statement on *Resisting Acts of Distillation.*" Sacred Circle Gallery, Daybreak Star Arts Center. Seattle, May 3-23, 2002.

Shakespeare, Tom. *Disability Rights and Wrongs.* New York: Routledge, 2006. Print.

Siebers, Tobin. *Disability Theory.* Ann Arbor: University of Michigan Press, 2008. Print.

Smith, David. "Athlete Caster Semenya Returns Home to Rapturous Welcome." *Guardian* 25 Aug. 2009. Web.

——. "Caster Is a Cover Girl." *Guardian* 7 Sept. 2009. Web.

——. "Caster Semenya Row." *Guardian* 23 Aug. 2009. Web.

——. "Gender Row: Athlete Caster Semenya Wanted to Boycott Medal Ceremony." *Guardian* 21 Aug. 2009. Web.

Sorisio, Carolyn. *Fleshing Out America: Race, Gender, and the Politics of the Body in American Literature, 1833–1879.* Athens: University of Georgia Press, 2002.

Southworth, E. D. E. N. *The Hidden Hand.* 1859. New Brunswick, NJ: Rutgers UP, 1988. Print.

Spickard, Paul R. "The Illogic of American Racial Categories." *Racially Mixed People in America.* Ed. Maria P. P. Root. London: Sage, 1992. Print.

Spillers, Hortense. "Mama's Baby, Papa's Maybe: An American Grammar Book." *Diacritics* 17.2 (1987): 64–81. Print.

Spruhan, Paul. "A Legal History of Blood Quantum in Federal Indian Law to 1935." *South Dakota Law Review* 51 (2006): 1–50. Print.

——. "The Origins, Current Status, and Future Prospects of Blood Quantum as the Definition of Membership in the Navajo Nation." *Tribal Law Journal* 8 (2007): 1–17. Print.

Stacey, Jackie. *The Cinematic Life of the Gene.* Durham, NC: Duke University Press, 2010. Print.

Sterling, Dorothy. *Black Foremothers: Three Lives.* Old Westbury, NY: Feminist Press, 1979. Print.

Stiker, Henri-Jacques. *A History of Disability.* Trans. William Sayers. Ann Arbor: University of Michigan Press, 1999. Print.

The Sting. Dir. George Roy Hill, Universal, 1973. Film.

Stone, Deborah. *The Disabled State.* Philadelphia: Temple University Press, 1984. Print.

Stowe, Harriet Beecher. *Uncle Tom's Cabin: or, Life among the Lowly*. 1851. New York: Norton, 1994. Print.

Strong, Pauline Turner, and Barrik Van Winkle. "Indian Blood: Reflections on the Reckoning and Refiguring of Native North American Identity." *Cultural Anthropology* 11.4 (1996): 547–576. Print.

Sturm, Circe. *Blood Politics: Race, Culture, and Identity in the Cherokee Nation of Oklahoma*. Berkeley: University of California Press, 2002. Print.

Sullivan, Claire F. "Gender Verification and Gender Policies in Elite Sport: Eligibility and 'Fair Play.'" *Journal of Sport and Social Issues* 35.4 (2011): 400–419. Print.

Sully et al. v. United States et al. 195 F. 113. Circuit Court D. South Dakota, S.D. Feb. 28, 1912. Print.

Sundquist, Eric J. "Mark Twain and Homer Plessy." *Mark Twain's Pudd'nhead Wilson: Race, Conflict, and Culture*. Ed. Susan K. Gillman and Forrest G. Robinson. Durham, NC: Duke University Press, 1990. 46–72. Print.

———. *To Wake the Nations: Race in the Making of American Literature*. Cambridge, MA: Harvard University Press, 1993. Print.

TallBear, Kimberly. "DNA, Blood, and Racializing the Tribe." *Wicazo Sa Review* 18.1 (2003): 81–107. Print.

———. "Native-American-DNA.com: In Search of Native American Race and Tribe." *Revisiting Race in a Genomic Age*. Ed. Barbara A. Koenig, Sandra Soo-Jin Lee, and Sarah S. Richardson. New Brunswick, NJ: Rutgers University Press, 2008. 235–252. Print.

TallBear, Kimberly, and Deborah A. Bolnick. "Native American DNA Tests: What Are the Risks to Tribes?" *Native Voice* 3–17 Dec. 2004. Print.

Teuton, Sean Kicummah. *Red Land, Red Power: Grounding Knowledge in the American Indian Novel*. Durham, NC: Duke University Press, 2008. Print.

There's Something about Mary. Dir. Bobby Farrelly and Peter Farrelly. Twentieth Century Fox, 1998. Film.

Thomas, David Hurst. *Skull Wars: Kennewick Man, Archaeology, and the Battle for Native American Identity*. New York: Basic Books, 2000. Print.

Thomas, June. "Did Caster Semenya Lose the Women's 800 Meters on Purpose?" *Slate* 11 Aug. 2012. Web.

Thomas, Ronald R. "The Fingerprint of the Foreigner: Colonizing the Criminal Body in 1890s Detective Fiction and Criminal Anthropology." *ELH* 61.3 (1994): 655–683. Print.

Thornton, Russell. "Tribal Membership Requirements and the Demography of 'Old' and "New" Native Americans." *Population Research and Policy Review* 16.1–2 (1997): 33–42. Print.

Trading Places. Dir. John Landis. Paramount, 1983. Film.

Tremain, Shelley, ed. *Foucault and the Government of Disability*. Ann Arbor: University of Michigan Press, 2005. Print.

Trent, James W. *Inventing the Feeble Mind: A History of Mental Retardation in the United States*. Berkeley: University of California Press, 1995. Print.

Trimpi, Helen. *Melville's Confidence Men and American Politics in the 1850s*. Hamden, CT: Archon Books, 1987. Print.

Turner, Georgina. "'Think before You Say 'She's a Man.'" *Guardian* 20 Aug. 2009. Web.

Turner, Nat. "The Confessions of Nat Turner, the Leader of the Late Insurrection in Southampton, Va." 1831. *African-American Slave Narratives: An Anthology*. Ed. Sterling Lecater Bland Jr. 3 vols. Westport, CT: Greenwood Press, 2001. 23–45. Print.

Twain, Mark. "Personal Habits of the Siamese Twins." *Collected Tales, Sketches, Speeches, and Essays, 1852–1890*. New York: Library of America, 1992. Print.

———. *The Prince and the Pauper*. 1881. Ed. Victor Fischer and Michael B. Frank. Berkeley: University of California Press, 1983. Print.

———. *Pudd'nhead Wilson and Those Extraordinary Twins*. 1894. New York: Norton, 1980. Print.

———. "A Thumb-print and What Came of It." *Life on the Mississippi*. 1881. Oxford: Oxford University Press, 1990. Print.

U.S. Congress. 53rd Congress Rec. S2614. February 23, 1895.

United States v. First National Bank of Detroit, Minnesota; United States v. Nichols-Chisholm Lumber Company. 234 U.S. 245. Supreme Court of the United States. 1914. Print.

United States v. Kagama & Another, Indians. 118 U.S. 375. Supreme Court of the United States. 1886. Print.

The Usual Suspects. Dir. Bryan Singer. MGM, 1995. Film.

Van Cromphout, Gustaav. "*The Confidence-Man*: Melville and the Problem of Others." *Studies in American Fiction* 21.1 (1993). 37–50. Print.

van Dijck, José. *Imagenation: Popular Images of Genetics*. New York: New York University Press, 1998. Print.

Van Evrie, John. *Negroes and Negro "Slavery": The First an Inferior Race: The Latter Its Normal Condition*. Baltimore: J. D. Toy, 1854. Print.

Van Heesch, Margriet. "Do I Have XY Chromosomes?" *Critical Intersex*. Ed. Morgan Holmes. London: Ashgate, 2010. 123–145. Print.

Vital Signs: Crip Culture Talks Back. Dir. Sharon L. Snyder and David T. Mitchell. Brace Yourselves Productions, 1996. Film.

Vizenor, Gerald. *Earthdivers: Tribal Narratives on Mixed Descent*. Minneapolis: University of Minnesota Press, 1981. Print.

———. *The Heirs of Columbus*. Hanover, NH: Wesleyan University Press, 1991. Print.

Voss, Louis. "Sandy Mueller, the German Slave." *Louisiana Historical Quarterly* 12.3 (1929): 447–60. Print.

W. G. "Group One." *American Journal of the Medical Sciences* 62.123 (1871): 194–213. Print.

Wadlington, Warrick. *The Confidence Game in American Literature*. Princeton: Princeton University Press, 1975. Print.

"Website Makes Caster Boob." *Sport24* 16 Apr. 2011. Web. www.sport24.co.za.

Weinauer, Ellen M. "'A Most Respectable Looking Gentleman': Passing, Possession, and Transgression in *Running a Thousand Miles for Freedom*." *Passing and the Fictions of Identity*. Ed. Elaine K. Ginsberg. Durham, NC: Duke University Press, 1996. 37–56. Print.

Welburn, Ron. "A Most Secret Identity: Native American Assimilation and Identity Resistance in African America." *Confounding the Color Line: The Indian-Black Experience in North America*. Ed. James F. Brooks. Lincoln: University of Nebraska Press, 2002. 393–413. Print.

Welke, Barbara Young. *Law and the Borders of Belonging in the Long Nineteenth Century United States*. New York: Cambridge University Press, 2010. Print.

Wendell, Susan. *The Rejected Body: Feminist Philosophical Reflections on Disability*. New York: Routledge, 1996. Print.

When Billy Broke His Head and Other Tales of Wonder. Dir. Billy Golfus. Fanlight Productions, 1994. Film.

White, Deborah Gray. *Ar'n't I a Woman? Female Slaves in the Plantation South*. 1985. Rev. ed. New York: Norton, 1999. Print.

Whitley, John S. "*Pudd'nhead Wilson*: Mark Twain and the Limits of Detection." *Journal of American Studies* 21.1 (987): 55–70. Print.

Wiegman, Robyn. *American Anatomies: Theorizing Race and Gender*. Durham, NC: Duke University Press, 1995. Print.

Wigger, Ann P. "The Source of Fingerprint Material in Mark Twain's *Pudd'nhead Wilson*." *American Literature* 28.4 (1957): 517–520. Print.

Williams, Raymond. "Base and Superstructure in Marxist Cultural Theory." *Media and Cultural Studies*. Ed. Meenkashi Gigi Durham and Douglas M. Kellner. Malden, MA: Blackwell, 2001. 152–165. Print.

Williams, Richard. "Oscar Pistorius and Caster Semenya's Running Battle to Reach Starting Blocks." *Guardian* 26 Aug. 2011. Web.

Wilson, Philip K. "Eighteenth-Century Monsters and Nineteenth-Century Freaks: Reading the Maternally Marked Child." *Literature and Medicine* 21.1 (2002): 1–25. Print.

Wilson, Terry P. "Blood Quantum: Native American Mixed Bloods." *Racially Mixed People in America*. Ed. Maria P. P. Root. London: Sage, 1992. 108–125. Print.

Wonkam, Ambroise, Karen Fieggen, and Raj Ramesar. "Beyond the Caster Semenya Controversy: The Case of the Use of Genetics for Gender Testing in Sport." *Journal of Genetic Counseling* 19 (2010): 545–548. Print.

Woody, Elizabeth. "Translation of Blood Quantum." *Chicago Review* 39.3–4 (1993): 89–90. Print.

Wright, Luther, Jr. "Who's Black, Who's White, and Who Cares." *Critical White*

Studies: Looking behind the Mirror. Ed. Richard Delgado and Jean Stefanic. Philadelphia: Temple University Press, 1997. 164–169. Print.

Wu, Cynthia. "The Siamese Twins in Late Nineteenth-Century Narratives of Conflict and Reconciliation." *American Literature* 80.1 (2000): 29–55. Print.

Zackodnik, Teresa. "Fixing the Color Line: The Mulatto, Southern Courts, and Racial Identity." *American Quarterly* 53.3 (2001): 420–451. Print.

Index

Fausto-Sterling, Anne, 192–193, 196, 233n12
feeblemindedness. *See* mental disability
Fem cards. *See* femininity certificates
female masculinity, 206–207, 235n35
femininity certificates, 196–198, 234n21
Ferriman and Gallwey Hirsutism Scale, 207–208, 235n32
fingerprinting: disability and, 7, 98–99, 110–114, 226n10–11; Galton and, 6, 99, 111–113, 226n10–11, 232n2; race and, 6, 98–99, 111–113; science and, 6, 22, 186–187, 193, 224n14, 232n2, 233n12; Twain and, 7–8, 19, 97–101, 110–114, 117–118, 223n3; Will West and, 4–6, 8, 98, 100
Fjellman, Stephen M., 68–69
Foucault, Michel, 6–7, 102, 123, 141
Franklin, Sarah, 186
freak shows. *See* enfreakment
Fredricks, Nancy, 103

Galloway, Terry, 137
Galton, Francis, 6, 99, 111–113, 226n10–11, 232n2
Garber, Marjorie, 36, 218n2, 219n6, 220n21
Garland Thomson, Rosemarie, 18, 56, 102, 167, 220n23, 222n12, 222n16, 235n36
Garroute, Eva Marie, 150, 180
Gates, Henry Louis, Jr., 15, 36, 219n13
gender verification. *See* sex testing
General Allotment Act of 1887. *See* Dawes Act
genetic advantages in sports, 206
genetic essentialism, 186
genetic imaginary, 186, 188, 191–192, 214
genetic testing, 8, 20, 148, 186; Native identity and, 148, 187–190, 214, 228n5, 233n7–9; medical, 190–191; sex and, 11, 111, 191–198, 201, 203
genetic themes in American Indian literature, 158–159
Gercken-Hawkins, Becca, 183
Gillman, Susan K., 106–107, 226n5
Gross, Ariela J., 94, 171, 215n4, 216n16, 224n12–13
Guillaumin, Colette, 15, 85–86, 217n17
Guy, Abby, 92

Hagan, William T., 166
Halttunen, Karen, 78
Halualani, Rona Tamiko, 183, 228n13

Hamill, James, 141
Handicappedfraud.org, 133–140
Haney López, Ian F., 21, 92–93, 224n14, 232n27
Harmon, Alexandra, 157
Harris, Cheryl, 179
Hawaiian Homes Commission Act (HHCA), 170, 172–173, 175, 230n10
Hawthorne, Nathaniel, 1, 84, 87
Heggie, Vanessa, 206, 234n16–17, 234n21
Henderson, Carol E., 88, 224n8
Hensel, Abby and Brittany, 108
Herndl, Diane Price, 220n27
Hevey, David, 102
HHCA. *See* Hawaiian Homes Commission Act
Holmes, Morgan, 22, 218n28
Horkheimer, Max, 6
Hrdlicka, Ales, 177–178
Hudgins v. Wright, 92

IAAF. *See* International Amateur Athletic Federation
IACA. *See* Indian Arts and Crafts Act
Ignatieff, Michael, 1
IHS. *See* Indian Health Services
Indian Arts and Crafts Act (IACA), 145, 147, 151–153
Indian Health Services (IHS), 146–148, 229n16–19
International Amateur Athletic Federation (IAAF), 194–195, 199–205, 207–211, 234n21, 235n32
International Olympic Committee (IOC), 194–199, 203–205, 207, 209, 234n21, 235n33
intersex, 22, 193–194, 197, 201–203, 211
IOC. *See* International Olympic Committee

Jackson, Mark, 113
Jacobs, Harriet, 37
James, Jennifer C., 30
Jehlen, Myra, 103, 115
Jenks, Albert E., 177
Johnson, Georgia Douglas, 42, 43
Jones, Dale, 59–60, 64
Jones, Tom, 151–152, 229n15, 231n14

Kafer, Alison, 123, 217n22
Kauanui, J. Kēhaulani, 230n10, 231n15

About the Author

Ellen Samuels is an assistant professor of gender and women's studies and English at the University of Wisconsin at Madison.